HOLIDAY PROGRAMS
for
BOYS AND GIRLS

Holiday Programs
for
Boys and Girls

by

AILEEN FISHER

Publishers   PLAYS, INC.   Boston

Library of Congress Catalog Card Number: 52-11997

ISBN: 0-8238-0018-0

MANUFACTURED IN THE UNITED STATES OF AMERICA

Acknowledgments

Thanks are due to the following publications for permission to reprint some of the plays and verses: *Child Life*, *Children's Activities*, *Plays: The Drama Magazine for Young People*, *Story Parade*, and *Young America Magazines*.

Table of Contents

COLUMBUS DAY

PLAYS	The Weaver's Son.............	3
	Day of Destiny................	14
GROUP READINGS	Light in the Darkness..........	24
	Boy in Genoa.................	25
RECITATION	Across the Unknown...........	26

UNITED NATIONS WEEK

PLAYS	Three and the Dragon..........	27
	A Play Without a Name........	41
GROUP READING	United Nations Spell-Down.....	55
RECITATION	The Age of Walls Has Ended...	57

HALLOWEEN

PLAY	Ghosts on Guard..............	58
SKIT	On Halloween.................	69
GROUP READINGS	Jack-o'-Lantern...............	72
	Black and Orange.............	73
	Halloween Concert.............	74
RECITATION	Pumpkins.....................	76

ELECTION DAY

PLAY	The Voice of Liberty...........	77
GROUP READING	Voting Day...................	89

VETERANS DAY

GROUP READINGS	Veterans Day..................92	
	To an Unknown Soldier 93	
RECITATION	Prayer for Peace 94	

vii

CONTENTS

BOOK WEEK

PLAYS	Once Upon a Time.............	95
	Treasure Hunt.................	112
GROUP READING	Open Sesame!.................	123
RECITATION	Modern Magic................	125

THANKSGIVING

PLAYS	Mother of Thanksgiving........	126
	Unexpected Guests............	141
GROUP READINGS	Company Coming..............	148
	Thanksgiving Everywhere......	150
RECITATIONS	A Thankful Heart.............	152
	Thanksgiving.................	153

CHRISTMAS

PLAYS	Angel in the Looking-Glass.....	154
	The Merry Christmas Elf.......	165
	Time Out for Christmas........	177
	A Christmas Tree for Kitty.....	188
PLAYLETS	The Spirit of Christmas........	194
	The Christmas Cake...........	200
GROUP READINGS	Where Is Christmas?...........	204
	Christmas!	205
	The Christmas Mitten Lady.:..	206
RECITATIONS	With Christmas in the Air......	210
	At Last It Came.:.:..........	211

NEW YEAR'S DAY

GROUP READING	Benjy Makes a Resolution......	212
RECITATION	The Snowman's Resolution.:.:..	214

LINCOLN'S BIRTHDAY

PLAY	Abe's Winkin' Eye.............	215
GROUP READINGS	Abraham Lincoln Speaks:.:.....	232
	Young Abe Lincoln............	234
RECITATION	There Was a Lad Who Hungered	236

CONTENTS

VALENTINE'S DAY

PLAYS   New Hearts for Old............ 237

Hearts, Tarts, and Valentines... 250

GROUP READING   What's in a Name?............ 261

RECITATIONS   Valentines! 264

Valentine's Day.............. 265

WASHINGTON'S BIRTHDAY

PLAY   Washington Marches On........ 266

GROUP READINGS   That Spells Washington........ 288

George Washington, Farmer.... 290

Washington at Valley Forge 292

RECITATION   At Mount Vernon............. 294

ST. PATRICK'S DAY

GROUP READINGS   St. Patrick and the Serpent..... 295

Sure, Don't You Know?........ 298

RECITATION   Wearing of the Green.......... 299

EASTER

GROUP READINGS   Easter Morn.................. 300

Easter's All Dressed Up Today.. 302

RECITATION   Easter Tulip.................. 303

ARBOR DAY

PLAY   On Strike.................... 304

GROUP READING   Let's Plant a Tree............. 319

RECITATION   Planting a Pine............... 320

MOTHER'S DAY

PLAY   Mother's Day Off and On....... 321

GROUP READINGS   That's the Way Mothers Are.... 333

Who? 334

RECITATION   For Mother's Day............. 335

MEMORIAL DAY

GROUP READING — Memorial Day 336
RECITATIONS — Red, White, and Blue 338
The Soldiers Speak 339

GRADUATION

PLAY — Caves of the Earth 340
GROUP READING — The Mountain Trail 349

THE SEASONS

(Group Readings)

AUTUMN — School Again! 350
Autumn Leaves 352
A Gypsy Month 353
Leaf Boats 354
WINTER — Polar-Bear Pines 355
Wee Little Feb 357
To a Groundhog on February 2 . . 360
SPRING — Rain on the Roof 361
Early Crocus 362
Who Is It? 363
May Day 364

PRODUCTION NOTES 365

HOLIDAY PROGRAMS

for

BOYS AND GIRLS

COLUMBUS DAY

The Weaver's Son

Characters

CHRISTOPHER COLUMBUS, *14*
SUSANNA, *his mother*
DOMENICO, *his father*
BIANCHINETTA, *his sister, 7*
BARTHOLOMEW, *12*

TIME: *A spring day in 1465.*
SETTING: *The combination workroom-living room of the Colum-bus family in Genoa.*
AT RISE: BIANCHINETTA *is seated on a low stool near a basket of tangled wool yarn. She is trying to get order out of the tangles, winding the different colors on balls. In a few moments her mother,* SUSANNA, *comes in, wiping her hands on her apron.*

SUSANNA: There, I have done with the dyeing of the blue yarn. Always so much stirring and stirring! And to keep the big vats boiling, that is not easy. (*Looks at yarn basket*) Good, Bianchinetta. You are getting all the snarls out of the old yarn.
BIANCHINETTA: I have the black almost untangled.
SUSANNA: I am glad that my daughter, at least, is dependable in this house.

BIANCHINETTA: Bartholomew is busy, Mama. At the heap of new wool Papa bought.

SUSANNA: Bartholomew is carding it?

BIANCHINETTA: Yes, Mama. When I looked in the wool room he was combing so hard he did not see me.

SUSANNA: Or perhaps he was looking so hard out the window? (*Shakes her head*) No, I am afraid my sons are not weavers at heart. And Christopher is not back *yet*. Two hours he has been gone. Two hours! And on such a busy morning.

BIANCHINETTA: He had the woven cloth to deliver for Papa, you know.

SUSANNA: And how long does that take? Not two hours, I am sure. He promised to come home directly.

BIANCHINETTA: I saw him start out running.

SUSANNA: Then he should be back the sooner.

BIANCHINETTA: Mama, do you know why Christopher runs when he has errands to do? I know. It is to save time . . . so he can stop at the docks and watch the ships.

SUSANNA: Yes, or stand around at the map makers! As if there were nothing for him to do at home. (*Shakes head*) He is no weaver's son, with his head full of the sea. Yet we must live . . . and to live means to work. Especially when your father . . . Where is your father, by the way?

BIANCHINETTA: He said he had to meet a member of the guild at the wine dealer. On business.

SUSANNA: So? At the wine dealer? I do not see much business in that, except for the wine dealer.

BIANCHINETTA: Papa said he would not be long.

SUSANNA: Yet he has been gone all the time I was dyeing the yarn. Business, indeed! I must send Bartholomew to fetch him. Oh, Bianchinetta, a woman's lot is not an easy one. Work, work, work. And keep track of the menfolk besides. It is not easy, I tell you. (*Calls*) Bartholomew! (*Looks at work basket*) There, near the bottom, is more of the black. (*Calls*) Bartholomew! (BARTHOLOMEW, *a slight, dark-haired lad, enters.*)

BARTHOLOMEW: Yes, Mama.

SUSANNA: Is Christopher helping with the carding?

BARTHOLOMEW: He is not back yet from delivering the cloth.

SUSANNA: How do you explain that it takes him so long?

BARTHOLOMEW (*Shrugging*): It would take a long time to get way to the other side of the docks.

SUSANNA: Yes, when one keeps stubbing his toe from looking so hard at the ships. Go find him, Bartholomew, and bring him to me when you return. He was to have come home directly. That was a promise.

BARTHOLOMEW: Yes, Mama.

SUSANNA: And as you pass the wine dealer's shop, tell your father he is wanted at home immediately. It is important. Do you hear?

BARTHOLOMEW: Yes, Mama. Immediately. Important.

SUSANNA: Now, run. This is a busy morning. And my back aches from work already. (BARTHOLOMEW *runs out.* SUSANNA *and* BIANCHINETTA *work at the yarn.*)

BIANCHINETTA: Mama . . .

SUSANNA: Yes, daughter.

BIANCHINETTA: Is there to be a feast day soon?

SUSANNA: Not soon. Why do you ask?

BIANCHINETTA: Because of the cheeses.

SUSANNA: What cheeses?

BIANCHINETTA: The cheeses in the dark closet under the stairway.

SUSANNA: What are you talking of, Bianchinetta?

BIANCHINETTA: I was looking for my old doll this morning, and I saw them. Three big wonderful cheeses.

SUSANNA: Are you sure?

BIANCHINETTA: Yes, yes, Mama. Is it a surprise?

SUSANNA (*Sighing*): Yes . . . a surprise to me. Your father,

Bianchinetta, is full of surprises. Now he probably wishes to deal in cheeses instead of woolen cloth! Last month it was wine. He could see a fortune in dealing in wine, he said! To your father the far pasture is always the greenest.

BIANCHINETTA: Doesn't Papa like to be a weaver?

SUSANNA: I am afraid he likes most what he does not have to do. So now it is cheeses! Well. Is it any wonder his sons do not keep their minds on their work, seeing the example of their father? You and I cannot tend to everything, daughter . . . (DOMENICO *is heard singing offstage as he approaches.*)

BIANCHINETTA: I think that is Papa now.

SUSANNA: There is no doubt of it. Run out into the court-yard, Bianchinetta, while I speak to him. (BIANCHINETTA *exits.* DOMENICO *sings.* SUSANNA *works nervously at the yarn.*)

DOMENICO (*Still offstage*):

A jug of wine and a loaf of bread

And a lovely yellow cheese

And a jolly song in a fellow's head,

Oh, what is better than these?

Oh, what is better than these?

(DOMENICO *comes in.*)

My dear wife, here I am immediately. And what is so important?

SUSANNA: What is important is Christopher, Domenico.

DOMENICO: Christopher? Is anything the matter with Christopher?

SUSANNA: Yes. And I am afraid it is your fault.

DOMENICO: My fault? What has happened? Have I not been a good father? Have I not apprenticed my sons to a good trade?

SUSANNA: A good father! Is it a good father, Domenico, to make promise after promise that you do not keep? To set such an example to your sons? Time and again you tell me you will not go to the wine dealer's in the midst of a busy morning. Yet you go.

DOMENICO (*Weakly*): I have business with members of the guild of master clothiers, Susanna.

SUSANNA: At the shop of the wine dealer! Why must it always be at the wine dealer's? You come home without a coin in your pocket. (DOMENICO *feels in his pockets. They are empty.*) Time and again you promise to stick to the workshop as becomes a good weaver. But do you keep your mind on your weaving? No. Your head is full of cheeses!

DOMENICO (*Taken aback*): Cheeses?

SUSANNA: Yes, cheeses. What do you plan to do now, Domenico? Become a cheesemonger? And where did you get the money to buy three cheeses?

DOMENICO: Dear wife, I borrowed it. I have friends. I will pay it back. (*Catches himself*) What three cheeses, may I ask?

SUSANNA: The cheeses in the dark closet under the stairs. Oh, Domenico, do you not see what you are doing? How can we hope to raise our sons to be upright and dependable when their father . . .

DOMENICO: When their father is so undependable? (*He becomes very repentant.*) Dear little wife, flower of my heart, rose of my soul, I know what you say is true. I dream big dreams, and they keep me from tending to my business. Every morning, believe me, I wake up full of fire. "Today," I say, "I will work my fingers to the bone. Today I will weave the finest wool cloth in Genoa. Today I will show my dear Susanna what a man she married . . ."

SUSANNA (*Resignedly*): You show me, all right.

DOMENICO: Every morning this fire of ambition burns in my breast.

SUSANNA: And then the fire burns to ashes. (*She wipes her*

eyes) That itself is bad, but it is not the worst. Your sons suffer from your example! And I had such hopes for them, Domenico. A lad must learn discipline, or he will fail as a man. A lad must keep his promise. He must drive straight ahead and let nothing stand in his way. How long, Domenico, should it have taken Christopher to deliver the cloth this morning?

DOMENICO: Oh, an hour, perhaps. Maybe more.

SUSANNA: He has now been gone more than two hours, and he promised to return directly.

DOMENICO: That is bad. Indeed, dear wife, that is bad. But Christopher is a good lad. It does not happen often, you know.

SUSANNA: Too often. This is not the first time. For his own good, Domenico, you must punish him.

DOMENICO: Do you think so?

SUSANNA: I am sure of it. (*Looks at him pointedly*) It is so easy to get into bad habits.

DOMENICO (*Sighing*): Delightfully easy. (*Catches himself*) What punishment would you suggest, wife?

SUSANNA: Give him more to do; more responsibility, perhaps. Make him work harder, and longer. Then he will have less time for distractions. Promise me, Domenico. For his own good, promise me you will punish him. Then I will try to forget about the cheeses.

DOMENICO: Rest assured, little flower, I promise. Longer hours, you say? More to do? Responsibility? Yes, I will find a way. (BIANCHINETTA *runs in.*)

BIANCHINETTA: They are coming—Bartholomew and Christopher. And running, too.

DOMENICO (*Affectionately*): And you, little rose in the bud, have you not a kiss for Papa after all this time? (BIANCHINETTA *kisses him fondly and returns to unravelling the wool.*

BARTHOLOMEW *and* CHRISTOPHER *hurry in.* CHRISTOPHER
is a sturdy, fair-complexioned lad, with reddish hair.)

SUSANNA: So, Christopher. You are home at last. And what
has happened to your promise in the meantime?

CHRISTOPHER: But I *did* come home directly, Mama. Only
the wind was against me.

SUSANNA: The wind? And are you a bird, to be concerned
with the wind?

BARTHOLOMEW (*Grinning*): You should see his wings, Mama.
(*Makes shape of a square-rigged sail with gestures*) How they
fly in the wind!

DOMENICO: Come, what is all this talk in riddles? You send
a great confusion through my poor head.

SUSANNA (*Giving him a look*): I am afraid it is not only riddles
that make a confusion in your head, husband. (*To* CHRIS-
TOPHER) Well, what do you mean, Christopher, that you
came home directly, only the wind was against you?

CHRISTOPHER: I am sorry, Mama. But, you see, when the
wind on the bay is against you, *directly* may mean having
to sail in a zigzag fashion. Still it is as directly as possible.

SUSANNA: Sail? On the bay? What are you talking about,
Christopher? (CHRISTOPHER *is hesitant.* BARTHOLOMEW
speaks up.)

BARTHOLOMEW: Well . . . you see . . . whenever there is
a moment, Vittorio lets Christopher sail his little boat.

CHRISTOPHER: A beautiful little boat with square sails. And
Vittorio says I have the feel of sailing in my hands . . .
and in my heart.

SUSANNA: Oh, la. A weaver's son. Sailing a boat!

DOMENICO: And who is this Vittorio, may I ask?

BARTHOLOMEW: A fisherman. We have met him often at the
docks, Papa. He is a wonderful man.

SUSANNA (*Turning to* DOMENICO): So. You see what I mean,
Domenico. Something must be done, and immediately.

BIANCHINETTA: Oh, Christopher. That is why you are always running. So you can sail like a bird.

CHRISTOPHER: But for a sudden wind that came up, Mama, I could have come home much more directly. I am sorry. (*Brightens*) But Vittorio says I handled the sail like one born to it.

SUSANNA: What is the world coming to! (*Looks from* DOMENICO *to* CHRISTOPHER) A weaver with his head full of cheeses. And a weaver's son with his nostrils full of the sea. Oh, Bianchinetta, it seems the weight of this household is indeed on the shoulders of the womenfolk.

DOMENICO (*Soothingly*): We could not manage without our womenfolk, for a truth. On the rosebush of our home you are indeed the roses . . . and we, (*Looking at* CHRISTOPHER) the thorns. But how you bloom, Susanna and Bianchinetta!

SUSANNA: Always honey on your tongue, Domenico. You are like a bee who never misses his way to a flower. So be it. Now back to your carding, Bartholomew. And you, Christopher . . . your father has some words to say to you. Come, Bianchinetta. (*As she leaves, she turns back to* DOMENICO) You remember your promise?

DOMENICO: Indeed, I remember. How could I forget? (SU-SANNA *and* BIANCHINETTA *exit.* BARTHOLOMEW *lingers.*)

BARTHOLOMEW: Do not punish too hard, Papa. Can he help it if his heart is not with his hands in carding the wool? I know how he feels. I would rather draw maps than comb the oily wool . . .

DOMENICO (*Throwing up his hands*): What a weaver I must be, to have two such sons! Go along, Bartholomew. Christopher will not suffer too much, I promise you. (*Smiles*) Oh, la, today I am full of promises. (BARTHOLOMEW *exits.*) Well, Christopher, what have you to say?

CHRISTOPHER: I have said I was sorry. But (*He hesitates*) . . .

I must tell you the truth, Papa. Only part of me is sorry. It is the sea I love, not the workroom. The smell of salt, not of wool.

DOMENICO (*Sympathetically*): I know. As I love the smell of wine . . . and cheeses. (*Catches himself*) But I should not be agreeing with you. (*Sternly*) A lad must learn discipline, Christopher, or he will fail as a man. A lad must keep his promise. A lad must be dependable. Am I not right?

CHRISTOPHER: Yes, you are right.

DOMENICO: You have in this household a noble example to follow. I do not mean your father, Christopher. Unfortunately, your father is not an example to follow. But your mother! You see how she works, how she plans, how she drives ahead. Yet in her heart, I suppose, she does not like the oily smell of the wool or the bitter tang of the dye any more than you and I.

CHRISTOPHER: I had not thought of it, Papa.

DOMENICO: Then think of it from now on. (*There is silence as* DOMENICO *paces back and forth. Suddenly he gets an idea. His face beams.*) Your mother and I agreed you must be punished for not sticking to business. And I have thought of the way!

CHRISTOPHER: Yes, Papa?

DOMENICO: You are . . . how old? I keep forgetting.

CHRISTOPHER: I will be fifteen in September.

DOMENICO: Not a boy any more. How the time passes! But fifteen in the fall . . . that is good. Your mother and I have agreed that a lad of your age would take his work more seriously if he had more to do.

CHRISTOPHER: But there is so little time now for what pleases me most. Could you not give me a beating instead, and be done with it?

DOMENICO: Now wait. Not so fast. Your back is very tender —I am not in the habit of beating you.

CHRISTOPHER: But the day is mostly work already.

DOMENICO (*Mysteriously*): There is work . . . and work. This Vittorio, now. He says you are a good sailor?

CHRISTOPHER: He says I am born to it.

DOMENICO: And you can already handle a small boat?

CHRISTOPHER: Yes. Vittorio will tell you.

DOMENICO: Then here is how I keep my promise to your mother for extra work, longer hours! Listen, son. I am a weaver, yes. But my head is not only full of wool. Every morning I wake up with a fire in my breast. Today I will show Susanna what a man she married! I will gather in the liras! I will become a rich man! Now, at last, I see a way to do it.

CHRISTOPHER: By making me work doubly hard. Is that it, Papa?

DOMENICO: Come, come. I have said there is work and work. (*Confidentially*) This is a dream I have been fondling for a long time: I have been thinking if I were a wine dealer as well as a weaver, if I were a cheesemonger as well as a weaver, I could be a success. And now I see the way of weaving the many patterns with one shuttle, as it were.

CHRISTOPHER: How do you mean?

DOMENICO: I will buy a little boat. I have friends who will lend me the money, until I can repay. Your father has friends, Christopher. All right. I will buy a little boat with a square-rigged sail. You, Christopher, shall sail it. Oh, there will be long enough hours, sailing up and down the coast—you and I! We will buy raw wool from the peasants. And wine. And cheeses. In exchange we will sell them woolen cloth. What do you think, Christopher? Does it not sound like the way to riches and happiness?

CHRISTOPHER: It sounds like every dream come true, Papa. Sailing a boat! (*Hesitates*) But Bartholomew . . . ?

DOMENICO: When he is a little older, he shall come too.

(*Beaming*) "Domenico Columbus and Sons—Master Clothiers, Wine Dealers, Cheesemongers."

CHRISTOPHER: And sailors! Don't forget sailors.

DOMENICO: Of course. Does it not sound beautiful?

CHRISTOPHER: The most beautiful punishment in the world, Papa. But . . . what will Mama say?

DOMENICO: She has a good head for business, your mother. She will see the good business of it, I am sure, after I talk to her. I will bring her to our way of thinking. Did you not hear her say I am a bee who never misses the way to a flower? I shall fly to her as directly . . . as a boat in the wind, Christopher! I promise you.

CHRISTOPHER: And I promise you something too, Papa. I will become the best sailor on the Ligurian coast. And after that, the best sailor on the Tyrrhenian Sea. And after that, the best sailor on the Mediterranean. And after that . . . who knows? But I can dream of it.

DOMENICO: Ah, Christopher, I can see you are a weaver's son, after all. I can see you are a weaver . . . of dreams.

THE END

Day of Destiny

Characters

COLUMBUS
YOUNG PEDRO, *his page*
PEDRO DE TERREROS, *his steward*
FIVE SAILORS
DOMINGO, *able seaman and cooper*
SHIP'S BOY

TIME: *Late afternoon of October 10, 1492.*
SETTING: *On board the Santa Maria.*
AT RISE: COLUMBUS *and his* PAGE *are at one side of the stage, looking out as if over the sea.* PAGE *holds a book. A group of muttering* SAILORS *are on the other side. Their looks and gestures directed toward* COLUMBUS *suggest they are on the verge of mutiny.*

COLUMBUS: This weather is like April in Andalusia, Young Pedro. The only thing wanting is to hear nightingales!
PAGE: Yes, Captain. It would indeed be good to hear nightingales . . . in place of some of the sounds that come to our ears. (*He glances furtively at the* SAILORS).
COLUMBUS: The tenth of October, and such warm fragrance in the wind!
PAGE: More than fragrance in the wind, Master, (*Looks toward* SAILORS) I am sorry to say.

COLUMBUS: Boy, you could not know, but lately I had a birthday. I stood on deck many hours, looking out upon the sea, thinking. Let me tell you it is a rare thing to end one's fortieth year sailing, so close to the fulfillment of a dream.

PAGE: So close to the fulfillment? You still think . . .

COLUMBUS: For thirty years, lad, I have been waiting for these days. Waiting, waiting. When I was a boy of ten I used to sit on the docks in Genoa watching the ships come and go. Always the mast tops appeared first over the curving expanse of sea. Always the mast tops disappeared last. What, I wondered, lay out there leagues away, beyond the unknown? Japan? India?

PAGE: Still the unknown, my Captain.

COLUMBUS: I was a weaver's son, but I wove dreams instead of woolen cloth. And all these years I have waited for the pattern to come clear. You cannot believe how long the years of waiting were in Spain, Young Pedro. (*Sighs*) Six years . . . before the Sovereigns gave their consent. Yet I did not give up. Life is a river, lad. For some it twists and turns and doubles back upon itself. But my river flows straight ahead. Straight ahead.

PAGE: Yes, Sir, I know. And always to the west!

COLUMBUS (*Smiling*): You learn well. Now let me see the book you have brought. Today I have need of it, with doubts and fears lurking behind my back like tigers. (*Glances at* SAILORS *as he takes the book*) Seneca's *Medea*. The words are fourteen centuries old, Young Pedro, and now, at last, on the verge of proof. (*Finds place*) Listen, then. "An age will come after many years when the Ocean will loose the chains of things, and a huge land lie revealed . . ." (*With assurance*) The chains are loosening. The new land will soon lie revealed.

PAGE (*Straining eyes into distance*): Soon? Today, Sir, is the thirty-first day since we left the Canary Islands behind us. The thirty-first day we have been out of sight of land.

COLUMBUS: You have been listening to the grumblings of the crew! Confess it.

PAGE: Well, it is hard not to listen. Perhaps I should tell you, Master . . .

COLUMBUS (*Shrugging*): No need. (*Glancing at* SAILORS) I know without being told. One does not have to *listen* to know what a Spaniard thinks. I have smelled the vinegar on those Spanish breaths for many days. I have seen the sourness of their thoughts. But my river flows straight! Go, bring me a cup of fresh water, boy. (PAGE *exits*. COLUMBUS *looks at book*. SAILORS' *mutterings grow louder*.)

1ST SAILOR: First he takes us through the seaweed—days of seaweed, leagues of seaweed. Was ever a ship expected to sail through meadows of green and yellow, I ask you? Not an inch of open water! We might be there yet, but for a good wind at our backs. And how can we get home again with the wind in our faces?

SAILORS: Aye, that will be another matter. (*Angry muttering*)

1ST SAILOR: I say we will stick in the seaweed till we rot, if we don't starve first, or perish of thirst.

2ND SAILOR: The farther we go, the less sure we are of the way back. Don't forget the compass. (*Looks maliciously at* COLUMBUS) I tell you I do not trust his bearings. Why did the compass last month vary to the Northwest of the polestar by night, and vary to the Northeast by morning? Why? The compass is bewitched.

SAILORS (*Shaking fists at* COLUMBUS): Not only the compass.

3RD SAILOR: You notice how he keeps pointing out the birds. "Look at the birds," he says. "Land is near," he says. "With birds flying overhead land cannot be far away," he says. Ha! Have we not been seeing birds for weeks? And still no sight of land. Who knows these are not *sea* birds we have been seeing, with no need of land save at nesting time? (YOUNG PEDRO *returns with cup of water.* COLUMBUS *drinks, paying no attention to* SAILORS' *grumblings.* YOUNG PEDRO *exits.*)

2ND SAILOR: Have you noticed? He is varying his course to follow the birds that pass overhead. I do not trust his reckoning.

SAILORS: Foreigner! Genoese!

3RD SAILOR: "Land is near," he says. How many oceans away does he call near? For a month we have not seen land.

4TH SAILOR: And the soundings. Do we have a sounding line long enough to reach the bottom of this unknown sea? No. The sea here is bottomless. And endless. And that's a combination for you!

SAILORS: Aye, bottomless. Endless.

5TH SAILOR: How much longer must we put up with it then? Sailing into nowhere. He is only one. At the most a handful are with him. We are thirty, at the least. Why do we sail on? We must turn back at once, or the food will run out. And the water. Does it ever rain here in this bitter desert of sea? Have you seen a single drop of rain in the last week?

SAILORS: True, true. The sea is a desert here.

1ST SAILOR: This foreigner from Genoa is seeking to make himself a rich lord, a great Admiral . . . at our expense. King Ferdinand and Queen Isabella are *our* sovereigns, not his. Why should we take his orders? (PEDRO DE TER-REROS *comes in with a bird in his hand. He slows up as he passes* SAILORS, *though pretending not to listen.*)

SAILORS: Aye, why?

3RD SAILOR (*Slyly*): Who would know . . . I say . . . who

would know how it happened . . . if the Captain should fall overboard tonight while observing the stars? An accident, of course!

SAILORS: Of course. An accident.

3RD SAILOR: It would be dark. His foot would slip on the deck. Or he might lose his balance, you know.

4TH SAILOR: Ha—let him swim to land, then, if it is so close!

5TH SAILOR: Tonight, eh? An accident. Then assuredly we will have to sail back to Spain immediately to report the accident. (PEDRO DE TERREROS *has returned to* COLUMBUS *and holds the small bird out to him.*)

COLUMBUS (*Nodding to* PEDRO *briefly*): It is you, steward.

PEDRO: Captain . . .

COLUMBUS: Stand here quietly a moment and breathe this air. Is it not soft and fragrant as April in Seville?

PEDRO: Yes, Captain, but . . .

COLUMBUS (*Seeing the bird*): Ah, another bird. (*Takes it*)

PEDRO: One of several that alighted on the ship, Sir. Quite different from the others, it seems.

COLUMBUS: Yes, yes. Smaller. More frail. (*Glances at* SAILORS, *then confidentially*) You know, Pedro, I have concluded the others must be sea birds. They have been with us so many days. But this—it resembles a warbler, don't you think?

PEDRO: Yes, Captain. It seems somewhat like a warbler.

COLUMBUS: That means land, surely in a day or two.

PEDRO (*In low voice*): If meanwhile you should not accidentally slip tonight while observing the stars! If you should not accidentally lose your balance tonight in the dark!

COLUMBUS: Is that what they are talking now, Pedro? As bad as that?

PEDRO: I heard them as I passed just now. "Who would ever know how it happened?" they said.

COLUMBUS: Only a day or two more. That is all I ask—only a day or two. Now is not the time to turn back, when the ripe fruit is little more than arm's length away. I *know*, Pedro. Here, inside, I know it is not far now.

PEDRO: I believe it. But we who believe are few. *They* are many.

COLUMBUS: I have dampened their fears before, smothered their doubts, soothed their tempers. I must do it again.

PEDRO: This time it will take more than soft words, Captain, I am afraid.

COLUMBUS: Then, Pedro, that is what they shall have. Soft words. And more! (COLUMBUS *walks toward sullen* SAILORS, *carrying bird.* PEDRO *follows.*) Here is a song for your hearts, men, on a beautiful day. Here is a good omen. This bird has just alighted aboard the Santa Maria. You will see he is smaller than the others we have caught. (SAILORS *mumble.*) Like a warbler, would you not say? (SAILORS *mumble.*) Surely so small a bird cannot be far from land.

1ST SAILOR (*Gruffly*): We have seen your birds before. But we have seen no land since we left the Canaries on the 9th day of September. A month and a day ago!

COLUMBUS: I cannot think a bird this size, like a warbler, could be more than a day or two from land. Three days at the most. (SAILORS *mumble.*)

2ND SAILOR: Who knows the habits of birds in this uncharted desert? We must turn back at once. Otherwise we will starve. We will starve, or perish of thirst, if we do not turn back . . . today.

COLUMBUS: Starve, you say? Come, now. My steward here, Pedro de Terreros, will know about the food supplies. (*Turns to* PEDRO) Would you say, Pedro, that we are in danger of starvation?

PEDRO: As everyone knows, we left Palos, Spain, on the third day of August. That was two months and a week ago. And we were stocked for a twelvemonth, Sir . . . as everyone knows.

COLUMBUS: So you think you will starve, if we are gone a little over two months, on twelve months' supplies! And perish of thirst? Fetch me the cooper, Pedro. He will know the condition of the wine and water casks. (PEDRO *exits*. SAILORS *grumble menacingly*.)

3RD SAILOR: There is still the matter of the compass.

COLUMBUS: Still the matter of the compass! Did I not explain it to you, in great detail? Did I not tell you it was the Pole Star that varied in its rotation, not the compass needle? Besides, the variation is over now.

4TH SAILOR: The seaweed. How can we get back through the seaweed?

COLUMBUS: You saw how it was. The thin layer of weed parted easily before our ships. The worst fear was, as always, the unknown. But now you know, now you have seen the green and yellow meadow part neatly before us, what is the worry?

5TH SAILOR: The wind, that is the worry. The wind continually blows west, away from home. Not east, toward Spain.

COLUMBUS: A good sailor knows how to use the wind, man, however it blows. (PEDRO *returns with* DOMINGO) How now, Domingo Vizcaino, have you been seeing to the casks?

DOMINGO: Yes, Captain. Is anything wrong?

COLUMBUS: Tell us, are the casks leaky or tight?

DOMINGO: As tight as a cooper can make them.

COLUMBUS: And lashed so they can not roll?

DOMINGO: Aye, Sir. Safely lashed and stowed.

COLUMBUS: And the wine and water will last . . . how many months would you say?

DOMINGO: Oh, many months, Sir. Even without rain. We are well stocked with water and wine.

COLUMBUS: Good, Domingo. (*Nods to him in dismissal*) You will be rewarded one day. (DOMINGO *exits.* SAILORS *are still defiant.*)

5TH SAILOR: Rewarded? With what? The bottomless sea and the endless horizon?

COLUMBUS: Surely you have heard of the wealth of the Indies, of the great Khan . . .

5TH SAILOR: Aye, we have heard. But no one has ever reached the Indies by sailing west. We must return to Spain and sail south and east.

SAILORS: Tonight. We turn back tonight.

COLUMBUS: A little more time, men. I beg you. Land is so near now, would you throw to the winds all these days of sailing? Would you fail your King and Queen?

SAILORS: Tonight!

COLUMBUS: Come, I can understand your feelings. And do you think my heart is closed to your longings? Never have you been so long from land on uncharted seas. Of course, you are tormented by doubts. But have you suffered on the journey? Has not the wind been favorable and the sea well-behaved? Have not your tasks been light? To turn back now would be to let the riches of the Indies slip through your fingers.

1ST SAILOR: You have said that before.

2ND SAILOR: And still no sign of land.

SAILORS: Tonight.

COLUMBUS: Today is the tenth day of October. Give me until the thirteenth. Then, on my word, if we do not reach land, I will take you back to Spain. Safely. And without bitterness.

SAILORS: No. No.

COLUMBUS: Consider well what you are saying to your Captain, men. (SAILORS *withdraw a little, talking together.*)

PEDRO: As I said before, I am afraid it will take more than soft words, my Captain.

COLUMBUS: And as I said before, they shall have their soft words . . . and more.

SAILORS (*Turning back*): Three days is too long. We turn back tonight.

COLUMBUS (*Getting angry*): I have come on this journey of exploration under the flag of two great Sovereigns to find the Indies. I shall not turn back until I am satisfied that I have been mistaken. I am not yet satisfied! So far all is well. Land is near. I have no doubt of it in my heart. As long as I am Captain of the Santa Maria . . .

1ST SAILOR (*Mockingly*): Aye, as long as you are Captain!

2ND SAILOR: You are only one. At the most, you have a handful of men with you.

3RD SAILOR: We are thirty strong.

COLUMBUS: Enough. I know what thoughts you are thinking. The words are written on your faces for me to read, and in your gestures. You are thinking: "How easy it will be. How simple. The Captain's foot will slip accidentally while he is observing the stars tonight. The Captain will lose his balance tonight in the darkness and fall overboard." I know your thoughts. But let me tell you it is not so easy! It would do you no good to kill me. Do you hear what I am saying? It would do you no good to kill me! The Sovereigns have already been warned what might happen on such a voyage as this. (COLUMBUS *measures his words*) I tell you . . . if you return without your Captain, the King and Queen will have you hanged . . . the whole lot of you. It is already agreed. (SAILORS, *mumbling, huddle again for consultation.*)

PEDRO: That will give them something to chew on, Sir.

COLUMBUS: "He deserves not the sweet that will not take the

sour." (*After a few moments*, SAILORS *reach a decision, turn to* COLUMBUS)

4TH SAILOR: We are willing to sail on . . . for two more days.

5TH SAILOR: Only two.

SAILORS: Two days. If your land is so near, we should see it in two days.

COLUMBUS (*Looking at the bird*): A little bird like a warbler would not be far from land. (*To* SAILORS) Two more days? That is enough. It will be a compact, then, on both sides. And let us hear no more grumbling. Tell the others. Two more days, and no grumbling! (SAILORS *exit*.) As I told you before, Pedro, I need only a day or two more. It is the voice of destiny telling me.

PEDRO: Your faith is wondrous to behold, my Captain. (*There is silence for a moment as the two look out over the sea.* SHIP'S BOY *comes in with an unlit lantern, chanting.*)

SHIP'S BOY: "Amen and God give us a good night and good sailing; may the ship make a good passage, sir Captain and master and good company."

COLUMBUS: My faith burns in me like a fire, Pedro. Like an unquenchable white light. Two days are enough. Look, Pedro, the sun is setting in the western sea, toward the land of promise. And we sail toward it!

THE END

Light in the Darkness

(October 11, 1492)

BOYS: "I saw a light," Columbus said,
       straining his anxious eyes.
       "There in the darkness, straight ahead,
       seeming to fall and rise.
       The waxen gleam of a candle beam,
       seeming to fall and rise!"

GIRLS: Was it a light from far away?
        Was it a wind-blown star?
        Twelve leagues ahead the islands lay!
        Nothing could show so far.

BOYS: "I saw a light," Columbus cried,
       tense as a tightened wire.
       "There on the wave it seemed to ride,
       flashing its waxen fire.
       Yellow-bright as a taper's light,
       flashing its waxen fire!"

GIRLS: Was it a light the Captain saw?
        Was it but fancy's wraith?
        The only light that could show so far,
        bright as the brightest guiding star,
        was the light of the Captain's faith.

ALL: The light of the Captain's faith!

Boy in Genoa

GIRLS: What are you watching, lad,
shading your pale blue eyes?

BOYS: The mainmast tips
of the sailing ships
where the curving distance lies.

GIRLS: What are you thinking, lad—
Christopher is the name?

BOYS: That a ship at sea
is the place to be
and a weaver's life is tame.

GIRLS: What are you dreaming, lad,
smile on your freckled face?

BOYS: That the sea is wide
and the waves still hide
secrets for ships to trace.

GIRLS: What are you hoping, lad,
scanning the sweeping shore?

BOYS: That I'll sail away
in a ship some day
where nobody sailed before!

Across the Unknown

(1492)

Three little ships, well-built, well-manned,
set sail one day in search of land,
into a mystery of space . . .
and faith was in the Captain's face.

Three little ships sailed long and far,
checking the compass with the star,
till fearful sailors scorned the prize . . .
but faith was in the Captain's eyes.

Three little ships reached land at last,
after the anxious weeks crawled past.
Three little vessels found their goal—
for faith was in the Captain's soul.

Three and the Dragon

Characters

MR. GRABBEROFF
MRS. GRABBEROFF
BONNIE, *their daughter*
MR. STICKLER
MRS. STICKLER
TUCKER, *their son*
MR. DOOLITTLE
MRS. DOOLITTLE
SALLY, *their daughter*
A STRANGER
TWO DIFFERENT RADIO VOICES

SETTING: *A street in Anytown. Three signs, indicating the homes of the three families, are placed upstage, in front of the furniture of each living room.*

AT RISE: *The three families are at home. (When each family, in turn, has the action, the other two remain quiet.)* MR. GRABBEROFF *is sitting at the table, eagerly going over his account books.* MRS. GRABBEROFF *is fixing her nails and primping.* BONNIE *sits reading and listening at the same time.*

MR. GRABBEROFF (*Looking up proudly*):
Millions in the bank,

27

Millions underground,
Millions stored in hiding where they can't be found.
(*Rubs his hands, and looks at wife*)
Ah, my dear, it gratifies my feelings
To do so well in all my business dealings.

MRS. GRABBEROFF (*Pleased*):

Millions in the bank!
Millions underground!
No one has a bank account so sizable and sound.
Now I can be dressier,
And haughtier, and fickler
(If I really want to!) than that Mrs. Stickler.
(MRS. GRABBEROFF *makes a face out the "window" in the direction of the Sticklers' house.*)

MR. GRABBEROFF:

Doolittle says he may soon be needing money.
I'll charge interest till it won't be funny!
(*Rubs his hands again, then is confidential*)
We're more wealthy
Than our neighbors put together.
We're all fixed for any kind of weather.

BONNIE:

But we couldn't save our riches
With an auto or a wagon
If our country got invaded
By that wild Atomic Dragon!
We couldn't save our money
Or the goods that fill our shelves . . .
We maybe couldn't even save
The shoes that hold ourselves!

MR. GRABBEROFF:

Nonsense, daughter. If I'm an able judge,
That wild Atomic Dragon is so chained it cannot budge.

MRS. GRABBEROFF:

Cheer up, Bonnie. Your father's all prepared:
He's built a wall and tunnel,
So it's foolish to be scared.

MR. GRABBEROFF (*Pleased with himself*):

Moreover, all the gadgets
And the DDT
Designed for catching dragons,
I have bought, you see.
I've cornered all the market,
So we're safe, *we three*.
And why should we be worried about people like our
    neighbors?
You never get ahead these days by tenderness, bejabers.
You can't allow another's needs to handicap your labors!

BONNIE:

This Dragon, though, is different
From a dragon in the comics;
Traps and things are useless
In an era of atomics!

MR. GRABBEROFF:

Don't you worry.
I'll send some cash tonight
To pay for—a—er—something
That will hold the beast more tight.
(*He closes account books and consults watch.*)
Almost time to listen to the news. What station
Brings the news that's cheeriest in all the nation?
(MR. GRABBEROFF *looks at the radio. Then the* GRABBEROFFS
are quiet as things begin to happen in the Stickler house. MR.
STICKLER *sits reading the newspaper,* MRS. STICKLER *is writ-
ing a letter, and* TUCKER *works over a mechanical gadget.*)

MRS. STICKLER (*Looking up from her writing*):

I'm writing the Committee that they can't expect *me*, a
    member of the upper classes,

To rub elbows with people who make their living shining
shoes or polishing window glasses,

And, furthermore, that getting action through the Common
People is slower than January molasses.

MR. STICKLER (*Nodding*):

Especially when you consider all the shapes and colors of
humanity included in "the masses."

MRS. STICKLER (*Indignantly*):

Can you imagine! Mrs. Grabberoff is eager to join our Club,
and she's nothing but a social climber.

And that frumpy Mrs. Doolittle almost got in on the ground
that she's an historical old-timer . . .

But *I* put in a few well-chosen words, and they both were
blackballed as a sequel.

TUCKER:

Mother, didn't you know . . . haven't you heard . . . that
all men and women are created equal?

I don't think the Atomic Dragon, if he breaks loose, is
going to worry if

People have blue blood or new blood or shining-shoe blood
. . . because what's the dif?

MRS. STICKLER: Tucker! Haven't I warned you to be more
careful of your grammar and your speech?

MR. STICKLER: Besides, the Atomic Dragon, my son, is carefully chained and definitely out of reach.

MRS. STICKLER (*Smugly*):

And if he *did* escape, we'd just ascend our Family Tree
protected by our Coat of Arms,

And I'm certain that even an Atomic Dragon couldn't resist
our irresistible charms.

TUCKER:

But times have changed . . . and, Mother, I'm certain the
Dragon doesn't give a fig for

Things we want on a silver platter but are not willing to
stoop and dig for.

MRS. STICKLER:

Tucker! So *this* is what happens when you are permitted
to play with every old Tom, Dick and Harry!

Oh, for the good old days when having to be nice to your
neighbors wasn't necessary;

When boys with your background didn't soil their hands
tinkering with machinery so—so ordinary.

MR. STICKLER:

Not to change the subject, my dear, but isn't it almost time
for that commentator?

We can continue this conversation about our superiority to
the Common People a little later.

(MR. STICKLER *turns to fix radio. Then the* GRABBEROFFS
and STICKLERS *are quiet as things begin to happen in the
Doolittle house.* MR. DOOLITTLE *is tipped back in his chair,
half asleep.* MRS. DOOLITTLE *languidly darns socks.* SALLY
is at the table looking at a magazine.)

SALLY:

I'd like to join this Young Folks' Club
To make a better world.

MR. DOOLITTLE (*Singing, half asleep*):

Oh, when I was a sailor-boy
I wore my whiskers curled.

MRS. DOOLITTLE: Don't mind your father, Sally, dear.

SALLY: I'd like to join this Club . . .

MR. DOOLITTLE (*Singing*):

There's nothing *any*one can do
But sail off in a tub.
Hi ho, my hearties, what's the use?
We just get pushed around!
So close your eyes and dream of lands
Where paradise is found.

SALLY:

We'll never make a paradise
By sitting in a chair.

MRS. DOOLITTLE:

The things you youngsters think about
These days . . . why, I declare!

MR. DOOLITTLE (*Singing*):

She wore a yaller ribbon
Like a primrose in her hair.

SALLY:

Oh, Daddy . . . Mother, don't you see
We can't just hide our heads,
And pout, and pull the covers up,
And shiver in our beds?
We can't look jealously at what
Our neighbors do and wear,
And say *we* can't get anywhere
Because they don't act fair.
What if that awful Dragon
Breaks his chains and gets away . . .

MR. DOOLITTLE (*Sitting up straight*):

The Dragon! How can folks like us
Prevent it, would you say?
(*He begins to relax and sing again.*)
Oh, what's the use of worrying, lads?
Sit back and take your ease:
The Grabberoffs get all the fruit
And leave the empty trees,
The Sticklers run the show, while we
Hang flapping in the breeze.

SALLY (*Indicating magazine*):

But here it says that *everyone*
Can help, and do his part

Toward making this a better world.

I think it's time to start.

MR. DOOLITTLE: Time to start the singing, lads.

SALLY: But if the Dragon comes . . .

MRS. DOOLITTLE: It's chained, you know.

MR. DOOLITTLE (*Sarcastically*):

The Grabberoffs

Will hang it by the thumbs!

Say, isn't there a newscast soon?

I'd like to hear what's new.

(*He begins to dial radio, turning to* SALLY *as he does so.*)

Forget that better world, my dear.

There's nothing *we* can do.

(*As* MR. DOOLITTLE *turns on the radio,* MR. STICKLER *and* MR. GRABBEROFF *turn on theirs at the same time. An excited voice booms forth.*)

RADIO VOICE: . . . totally unexpected, and the world is completely unprepared. At the moment everyone is stunned, wondering what to do and where to turn. The entire globe is in a turmoil. London, New York, Paris, Berlin, Moscow, Tokyo . . . every large city is frantically trying to get more information. They will be wiped out first, when the Dragon really gets going. The ease and suddenness with which he broke his chains about ten minutes ago has shocked the whole civilized world . . .

All:

The Dragon!

Broke his chains!

The Atomic Dragon is loose! (*Shrieks, etc.*)

RADIO VOICE: Which direction the Dragon will take is anyone's guess. Our reporters, looking down on the scene from their stratosphere planes, say that as yet he seems to be undecided. Once he strikes, he will strike fast. The fire from his nostrils will burn a swath a hundred miles wide in front of him. The swish of his great tail will topple buildings over a five-hundred-mile radius. The peculiar texture of his skin, exuding cosmic rays, will pollute the earth down to the very core of our globe. Nothing . . . no one . . . will be safe in the path of the Dragon . . .

MR. GRABBEROFF (*Terrified*):

Millions in the bank . . .

Millions underground . . .

Walls and traps and tunnels—

Will they keep us safe and sound?

RADIO VOICE: Scientists say they have been unable to figure out any defense against the Dragon. No fence or wall will hold him. No tunnel will be deep enough. No trap can catch him. The rich man is as vulnerable as the poor! (MR. GRABBEROFF *and* MRS. GRABBEROFF *collapse in their chairs.* BONNIE *stands listening, not nearly as frightened as her parents.*) Family trees, and silver spoons, and special privileges, and coats of arms will save no one . . . (MR. *and* MRS. STICKLER *collapse completely.* TUCKER *stands listening.*) And those who have looked jealously at their neighbors and coveted their goods, or buried their heads in the sands, (MR. DOOLITTLE, *terrified, pulls a pillowcase over his head.*) saying over and over again, "What can one person do?" will find that it may now be too late to try . . . (MRS. DOOLITTLE *sits with head in hands.* SALLY *listens intently.*) Just a moment, ladies and gentlemen. A reporter has just rushed in from the teletypes with the latest news. . . .

NEW RADIO VOICE (*Breaking in*): A strange thing has happened. Perhaps there is a shred of hope, after all. Our stratosphere reporters looking down at the Dragon through their telescopes, have spotted a solitary human figure standing near the Dragon. His presence seems to drain the power of the beast. The stranger stands perilously close to the

Dragon's head, yet the flames do not scorch him. The cosmic rays do not affect him. He seems to cast a magic spell over the Dragon. So far, our scientists have been unable to figure it out, but whatever it is, the Atomic Dragon lies quietly waiting, his mighty tail as still as the bated breath of the world.

BONNIE:

A stranger . . . not afraid,
Who has some magic power!
(MR. *and* MRS. GRABBEROFF *sit slumped in their chairs, their heads in their hands.* BONNIE *tiptoes out of the house.*)

TUCKER: A stranger whom the Dragon is unable to devour!
(MR. *and* MRS. STICKLER *sit with their heads in their hands.* TUCKER *tiptoes out of the house.*)

SALLY:

A stranger who can stand against
The Dragon like a tower!
(MRS. DOOLITTLE *has thrown her apron over her head.* MR. DOOLITTLE *is still buried in the pillowcase.* SALLY *tiptoes out of the house and the three children meet in the front of the stage.*)

BONNIE: You've heard.

SALLY: The Dragon's loose.

TUCKER: No one is safe now.

BONNIE: My father thought his walls and tunnels would protect us.

TUCKER: My mother thought we could hide behind our family tree and the Dragon would never detect us.

SALLY: My father thought he could cover up his fears by singing, and the Dragon would neglect us.

BONNIE: But the Dragon has broken his chains.

TUCKER: He can strike in any direction.

SALLY: What can we do?

BONNIE: Did you hear about the stranger?

SALLY *and* TUCKER: Yes.

BONNIE: He seems to have some magic power against the Dragon.

TUCKER: Scientists say there is no defense . . . but this stranger has a defense! He has more strength than the Dragon. If only we . . .

BONNIE: If only we could find him and ask him, before it's too late. If he would tell us the secret of his magic power, we could tell others, and help hold off the Dragon.

TUCKER: Or destroy him altogether.

SALLY: But where *is* the stranger? Where can we find him? According to the radio he seemed to be a long way off. Where shall we look?

BONNIE: Everywhere. We shall have to look everywhere until we find him.

TUCKER: We shall have to look forwards and backwards and sidewards and upwards and behind him. (*They all look.*)

SALLY: We shall have to ask what charm he has so the flames of the Atomic Dragon cannot blind him. (*The three children look around, walking back and forth. Then, silently, a* STRANGER *enters. When the children see him they are momentarily startled; then they go to him eagerly.*)

CHILDREN: Are you the stranger?

STRANGER: I am a stranger, but not the one you are looking for. I am one of his brothers.

BONNIE: If you are one of his brothers, do you know . . .

STRANGER: Yes, I know, Bonnie. All his brothers know.

TUCKER: You mean you know how he can stand in front of the Atomic Dragon and not be burned by the fire from its nostrils, and how he can wait so close and not be touched by the cosmic rays?

STRANGER: Yes, I know, Tucker.

SALLY: And you know how he can keep the Dragon's tail from swishing and knocking down towns and cities?

STRANGER: Yes, I know, Sally.

BONNIE: Do you think, if we could find him, he would tell us the secret, so *we* could help keep the Dragon away?

STRANGER: He told me there would be three children asking for him. He told me I would find you here.

CHILDREN (*Amazed*): He did!

STRANGER: Yes. He said children are the hope of the world, holding all the tomorrows of history in their hands. They can choose either of two patterns. They can work to fashion a better world. Or they can let the Dragon run loose over the globe, breathing fire, sending out deadly rays, destroying everything and everyone in his path.

CHILDREN: Not that. Not the Dragon!

STRANGER: He said you would say that: "Not the Dragon!" You see, he has faith in you. He is sure, if you try, you will be able to starve the Atomic Dragon to death.

TUCKER: Oh. Starve him to death! That's a good idea.

STRANGER: Yes. It's the only way. No one can defeat the Dragon in battle. We must starve him to death.

TUCKER: But what does the Dragon eat, Sir?

BONNIE: Does he like a certain kind of grass or clover?

SALLY: Does he like a dumpling with the top turned over?

TUCKER: Does he like potatoes, or tomatoes, or some cheese?

BONNIE: Or, maybe, squares of carrots cooked with little rounded peas?

SALLY: Or berries off of bushes or bananas off of trees?

STRANGER (*Amused*): My dear children, this Dragon is different from the dragons you read about in fairy tales. There has never been an *Atomic* Dragon before in the history of the world. Story-book dragons may eat things like leaves and clover. But the Atomic Dragon feeds on thoughts and actions.

CHILDREN: Thoughts and actions!

STRANGER: Yes. The Atomic Dragon feeds on all the evil thoughts and deeds in the world. He licks his chops over greed, and grabbing, and selfishness. He grows fat on hate, and intolerance, and suspicion, and the idea some people have that they are better than others. He laps up fear, and jealousy, and ignorance, and indifference . . . until he becomes more powerful than any chains or traps or defenses our scientists can invent.

BONNIE: He turned our wrongs to bone and muscle
Till he broke his chains without a tussle.

TUCKER: And he'll break *us* . . . if we don't hustle.

SALLY:
Sir, can you tell us, if you will,
How the Stranger holds the Dragon still?
Did he give him a certain kind of pill?

STRANGER: How can the Stranger ward off the flames and rays and terrible strength of the Dragon? Because, my friends, he stands in front of the Dragon with love in his heart in place of hate, with charity and kindness in place of selfishness and greed, with good will and brotherhood in place of intolerance and suspicion, and with hope and understanding in place of ignorance and indifference. For a short time, for today alone, he will be able, single-handed, to hold off the Dragon. At this moment none of the world's evil can pass the Stranger to nourish the Dragon's strength, because the power of good is greater than the power of evil. But tomorrow . . .

TUCKER: Yes . . . you said "for today alone." What will happen tomorrow?

BONNIE: Will the Dragon trample the earth and leave only tears and sorrow?

SALLY: Hasn't the Stranger some help we could beg from him or borrow?

STRANGER: For this brief today, you are safe. Tomorrow is up to you! All the tomorrows of history are up to you. But the Stranger has given me a guide for you, that will help.

You must pass it along to everyone you know, and they to everyone they know . . . until the words spread over the world like the color of sunrise. Then good will supplant evil, and the Atomic Dragon will perish, and there will be to-morrows and tomorrows of sunlight shining around the globe.

TUCKER: But will there be time, by tomorrow?

STRANGER: Yes, if you start now. Today. Here is the message he sent for you. (*Takes out three papers and gives one to each of the children*) Read it. Read it out loud.

CHILDREN (*Reading slowly from First Corinthians 13, Goodspeed translation*):

"If I can speak the languages of men and even of angels,
But have no love,
I am only a noisy gong or a clashing cymbal."

(*The children's parents begin to raise their heads.* MR. DOOLITTLE *slowly takes off the pillowcase and* MRS. DOO-LITTLE *puts down her apron. As the children read the next stanza, their parents rise hopefully from their chairs.*)

"If I am inspired to preach and know all the secret truths and possess all knowledge,
And if I have such perfect faith that I can move mountains,
But have no love,
I am nothing."

(*The parents now go out of their houses toward the children, slowly.*)

"Even if I give away everything I own,
And give myself up,
But do it in pride, not love,
It does me no good."

(*Now the parents are behind the children. They join hands, and all recite together as in a choral reading.*)

ALL:

"Love is patient and kind.

Love is not envious or boastful.

It does not put on airs.

It is not rude.

It does not insist on its rights.

It does not become angry.

It is not resentful.

It is not happy over injustice, it is only happy with truth.

It will bear anything, believe anything, hope for anything, endure anything.

So faith, hope, and love endure.

These are the great three,

And the greatest of them is love."

STRANGER:

The great three

That will defeat the Dragon!

THE END

A Play Without a Name

Characters

STAGE MANAGER
DRAMA CRITIC
SARAH, *of today*
ELIZABETH, *of today*
SARAH, *of 1787*
ELIZABETH, *of 1787*
U. S. SENATOR
REPORTER
THOMAS PAINE
LONDON REPORTER
FOUR CONGRESSMEN
FIVE DELEGATES
HIGH SCHOOL GIRL
HIGH SCHOOL BOY

SETTING: *A bare stage.*
AT RISE: STAGE MANAGER *comes out to address the audience.*

STAGE MANAGER: Ladies and gentlemen, you are about to
see a play without a name . . .
DRAMA CRITIC (*Interrupting from audience, standing up*): Just
a moment. May I ask a question?
STAGE MANAGER: Why, yes . . .

DRAMA CRITIC: I'm the drama critic from the *Daily Bugle*. My paper has sent me here to cover this program, but it's going to be rather difficult to write a review of a play that hasn't a name. Why hasn't it a name? That's what I want to know—why hasn't it a name?

STAGE MANAGER: A very logical question. And I'll try to give you a logical answer. You see, a name—a good name— is a label that stresses the point of a play. Take Ibsen's "A Doll's House," for example. The title points up the husband's treatment of his wife. He reduced her to a doll living in a doll's house. It is her revolt against the doll's house that makes the plot. And who can deny that through- out the play the sympathies of the audience are influenced by the title? They see the wife trapped in her doll's house.

DRAMA CRITIC: I follow you, all right, but what's that got to do with this play we are about to see?

STAGE MANAGER: We who are responsible for this program today do not want to be accused of influencing our audience. We don't want to propagandize by supplying a ready-made label. We hope the facts will speak for themselves. That is why we have purposely avoided giving the play a name.

DRAMA CRITIC: I see. You want the audience to draw its own conclusions?

STAGE MANAGER: Precisely.

DRAMA CRITIC: Then, sir, may I ask a favor of the audience?

STAGE MANAGER: It's all right with me.

DRAMA CRITIC (*To audience*): Ladies and gentlemen, it would be very helpful to me in reviewing this play if it had a name. Would you be so kind as to keep the question of a name in the back of your minds while watching the performance? Then, after the curtain falls, we can choose a label of our own. What do you say? (*Murmurs of approval from the audience*) Is that agreeable to you, Mr. Stage Manager?

STAGE MANAGER: Fair enough.

DRAMA CRITIC: All right, then. The play without a name will have a name when we get through with it.

STAGE MANAGER: That suits me fine. And then I'll know how well we've played the piece. How well the point has been put across. (*Nods to* DRAMA CRITIC, *who sits down again in audience*) The stage directions, friends, are few and brief. (*Takes a piece of chalk and draws a line down the middle of the stage, dividing it into two halves*) This chalk line separates the present from the past. This side of the stage is "Now." That side is "1787." (*Goes to wings and brings in two signs, setting the "Now" sign on one side and the "1787" sign on the other.*) That's all you need to know. (*Brings in two chairs for each sign*) Some of the actors may prefer to sit. (*Looks at "1787" sign*) There's one more point. We're not concerned with costumes in this play—with powdered wigs and silver-buckled shoes. So if you yearn for costumes, just imagine them. What matters here is not how people look, but what they say. (*Looks around, remembers something, goes to wings for another sign which reads "Any Town, U.S.A." He places it near the "Now" sign*) All right, the play is on, beginning here . . . in Any Town. (*As* STAGE MANAGER *exits,* SARAH *and* ELIZABETH *come on to the "Now" half of the stage.*)

SARAH: Can you make head or tail out of what those husbands of ours are arguing about, Elizabeth? They and their politics!

ELIZABETH: This is something that goes beyond politics, Sarah.

SARAH: All I know is that John says it's impossible. Can't be done! Out of the question! (*She sits down and takes out knitting.*)

ELIZABETH: I don't agree with you. (*Sits and takes out knitting too*) We've gone into it pretty thoroughly in our Study Club. There's certainly another side to it.

SARAH: But how can we *possibly* get all the countries of the world to agree on one government? All those different races, languages, cultures, religions! It's impossible.

ELIZABETH: Difficult, as Dr. Einstein says, but not impossible.

SARAH: John says all you have to do is look at the countries of Europe. They can't get along together, and never could . . . and they're just a little part of the globe. When little parts can't agree, how can you expect the whole world to? Be realistic, Elizabeth.

ELIZABETH: But "one world" is our only hope. People have always said things can't be done. And if we don't do something soon, Sarah, we'll all be blown up in another war.

SARAH: We just haven't enough in common . . . with the Chinese and the Africans . . . and people like that. And how could we possibly cooperate with Russia in a world government? We can't understand the Russians. You know that as well as I do.

ELIZABETH: We didn't have trouble working with them during the War.

SARAH: That's because we were fighting a common enemy—Hitler. It's impossible without something in common.

ELIZABETH: We'll have plenty in common, once we belong to the same world government. If the Russians don't come in at first, they will later on. They can't afford to be the only nation on the outside.

SARAH (*With a shrug*): Oh, I leave politics to John. He keeps up on things. (*Knits in silence for a moment*) I almost forgot —there's something else John said. He said the League of Nations failed, and the United Nations isn't much better, so what makes people think a world union can succeed? People just aren't made that way. And besides, you wouldn't want other countries meddling in our affairs, would you? You wouldn't want Russia interfering in our business. No, thanks! John says the whole idea of world government is unworkable. He simply can't imagine us giving up our sovereign power as a nation.

ELIZABETH: Certainly the present world of separate selfish nations doesn't work very well.

SARAH: N . . . no. But a world union . . . oh, Elizabeth, it's *impossible.* (*She gets up, puts away knitting.* ELIZABETH *follows suit.*)

ELIZABETH: I faintly remember that word was used before. Impossible! Back in 1787, when our own Union was being formed. Impossible, indeed! (*They exit.*)

STAGE MANAGER (*Coming in with a sign "Boston," which he puts near the "1787" sign*): Now we'll see what was happening in 1787. (*As he exits,* SARAH *and* ELIZABETH *of 1787 enter with sewing.*)

SARAH: Oh, I'm so glad to see you, Elizabeth. Have you been well? And the children? And have you heard from your husband? How are things going in Philadelphia? Of course, the paper is always *days* late by the time we get it, but I see there have been heated debates at the Convention. (*She sits and sews.*)

ELIZABETH: Heated in more ways than one, Sarah. (*She sits, sews.*) Philadelphia has been very hot this summer! Unusually hot. Oh, Sarah, do you know about the wonderful plan that has been proposed for a new government? A federal government of all the thirteen states, under one head. It goes *far* beyond strengthening the Articles of Confederation, which is all the Convention was called for.

SARAH: I've heard John talking to grandfather about it. Of course, John realizes that something must be done . . . all those quarrels among the states over trade, and boundaries, and worthless money! But he's quite upset over this new plan.

ELIZABETH: He *is?*

SARAH: He is sure a federal union is unworkable and impractical. He says the states won't ever give up enough of their sovereign power to make it work. They want states' rights and won't stand for interference.

ELIZABETH: My husband is sure it will work. A real union of the states has to come, Sarah. It's our only hope for a strong America.

SARAH: Oh dear, and your husband's a delegate. (*Quickly*) Personally, I don't know anything about it. Of course, the whole countryside is aroused, and wherever you go people are taking sides. But I leave politics to John. And he feels . . . he feels very strongly, Elizabeth . . . that the notion of having a United States of America is ridiculous. It can't possibly work. Oh dear, such things seem so far away and so difficult, don't they. Come, tell me, Elizabeth, how are the children? And does baby Frederick still have his curls? (U. S. SENATOR, *with* REPORTER *at his heels, comes in from "Now" side of stage and walks toward "Any Town" sign which is still in place.* SARAH *and* ELIZABETH *quietly exit from "1787" side.*)

REPORTER: Senator, I'd like to speak to you for a moment. I know you're on vacation, but the *Evening News* would like a statement from you. Do you have time to answer a question?

SENATOR: A Senator always has time, don't you know that? (*He smiles wryly.*)

REPORTER: It's about what scientists are saying, now we're making the hydrogen bomb. A good many of them insist that the only salvation for the world lies in federation . . . in a United States of the World. What do you think, Senator. Won't you give me a statement? (*Poises pencil on pad expectantly*)

SENATOR: Yes, I'll give you a statement. (*Smiles mischiev-*

ously) I . . . I don't say about world government what Thomas Paine said about union of the states in 1787. I take the opposite view. And I think history will prove me to be right.

REPORTER (*Baffled*): Thomas Paine? The famous pamphleteer of the Revolution? What did he say about union, sir?

SENATOR: Why, I thought you reporters knew everything.

REPORTER (*Scratching his head*): Thomas Paine. Let's see . . . he was a powerful force behind the Declaration of Independence. How would he feel about union . . . ?

SENATOR: Not the way I do, I can tell you that. That'll be all for today. (*Hurries out*)

REPORTER (*Leaving more slowly*): Now where under the sun am I going to find out what Thomas Paine thought! (*Sighs heavily and exits.* STAGE MANAGER *comes in with a sign reading "London," which he puts near the "1787" placard. He exits. In a moment on the "1787" side of the stage* THOMAS PAINE *enters, with a* REPORTER, *a rather dignified Englishman.*)

LONDON REPORTER: Mr. Paine? Mr. Thomas Paine? Now that you are in London, sir, the English press is eager for an expression of opinion from you.

THOMAS PAINE: Yes?

LONDON REPORTER: About the debates that are now going on at the Convention in Philadelphia. About the proposed union of the thirteen separate American states.

THOMAS PAINE: Philadelphia seems very far away at the moment.

LONDON REPORTER: But surely you have an opinion, sir. (*Smiles*) You used to have rather strong opinions, did you not, sir? Do you favor this proposal for a United States of America?

THOMAS PAINE: Hmmmmm. (*Takes out paper and pencil*) I've

thought about it, of course. Let's see . . . I'll formulate a statement. (*Hesitates, then writes. Hands paper to* REPORTER *when finished*) Can you read my writing?

LONDON REPORTER (*Reading*): "Made up as it is of people of different nations, accustomed to different forms and habits of government, speaking different languages, and more different in their modes of worship, it would appear that the union of such a people is impracticable." (*Looks up*) Impracticable! Thank you, sir. I am inclined to agree with you. (*As* PAINE *and* REPORTER *exit,* STAGE MANAGER *enters on "Now" side of stage with a sign "Washington, D. C.", which he puts in place of "Any Town" sign.*)

STAGE MANAGER: Washington, D. C., is a pretty busy place these days. (*He slips out as a group of* CONGRESSMEN *enter.* FIRST CONGRESSMAN *carries a folded newspaper with which he gesticulates.*)

FIRST CONGRESSMAN: The heat of Washington is insufferable this summer. This committee ought to adjourn like the rest of Congress. Instead of that, we have to hang around debating an impractical plan for world union. I tell you the difficulties are insurmountable! The idea may be all right in theory, but in practice it's insane.

SECOND CONGRESSMAN: Why insane? Why even impractical? A lot of spadework has already been done by the United Nations.

THIRD CONGRESSMAN: Let the United Nations alone, then. Give it a chance. Don't shove it overboard for a wild scheme like world union that never would work.

FOURTH CONGRESSMAN: Why wouldn't a union work? It's worked pretty well with us, ever since 1787.

FIRST CONGRESSMAN: A union of struggling states was one thing, but a union of *nations* . . . that's something else again. (*Holds head*) I get dizzy to think of it. The committees, the sub-committees, the sub-sub-sub. . . . Just the mere matter of *detail* of running a world government! How to choose a president? Would representatives be by country or according to population? What about all the differences in language, races, money, religions . . . (*Throws up his hands*) Bah! It's like trying to visualize a billion dollars.

SECOND CONGRESSMAN: We have to put an end to world anarchy somehow. We can't go on this way . . . nation against nation, race against race, man against man. There's only one outcome to that, and it's destruction. Don't forget atomic bombs and hydrogen bombs.

FOURTH CONGRESSMAN: Yes, how can we ever get real international control of such bombs without a world government? You simply can't fit atomic force into a world split up into separate nations, all trying to get the best of each other.

THIRD CONGRESSMAN: But look what we'd have to give up to join a world union. We can't do it, I say. It's too radical. Too revolutionary. Why, we'd be in a minority. A minority, think of it. We, the United States of America submitting our welfare to a world government where we'd be in the minority!

FOURTH CONGRESSMAN: Rather a minority in a peaceful world than a great power in a doomed one. The last war was enough to bankrupt us. You heard the War Department's testimony as well as I did . . . World War II cost us more than a trillion dollars. Think of it! We can't go through that again.

FIRST CONGRESSMAN: But, I tell you, gentlemen, the difficulties are insurmountable. (*To emphasize his point he bangs his newspaper down on the chair. The* CONGRESSMEN *exit amid a jumble of disagreements. The* STAGE MANAGER *appears on the other side of the stage. He brings a sign reading "Philadelphia" and removes "London." Turns to audience*)

STAGE MANAGER: Perhaps we need something more than just a sign to set this stage. (*Gestures to "1787" half of stage*)

This is Philadelphia, under a sweltering July sun, in the momentous year of 1787. The Constitutional Convention is hard at work, and no one knows just what will come of it. (*Looks towards wings*) I see some of the delegates are coming out of the Hall now. . . . (*He exits, as* DELEGATE FROM NEW JERSEY *and* DELEGATE FROM PENNSYLVANIA *enter*.)

NEW JERSEY: Such heat. The Convention ought to adjourn. The good Lord knows we've been on the point of disbanding often enough. We are getting nowhere.

PENNSYLVANIA: And why aren't we? Because men like you can see only the state you come from. You can't rise to the idea of a national union of all the states.

NEW JERSEY: I want to protect the interests of New Jersey, first, last, and always. Do you think I will ever submit the welfare of my state to any union government where Virginia would have sixteen votes and New Jersey only five?

PENNSYLVANIA: And yet you complain about New York taxing vegetables hauled in from your state of New Jersey, don't you? (*Two other* DELEGATES *enter,* HAMILTON OF NEW YORK, *and the* DELEGATE FROM SOUTH CAROLINA.) How about it, Hamilton? Will your state stop taxing vegetables from New Jersey of its own free will?

HAMILTON: No. Not as long as it is a sovereign state. But wait till we get a strong federal union. A union of states would have the power to regulate trade, and that's one of the reasons I'm for it . . . as opposed to anarchy. The name of Alexander Hamilton will always be connected with a strong central government!

NEW JERSEY: I'll never live long enough to see New York carrying out a law it doesn't want!

HAMILTON: Of course you won't, as long as there are no federal courts to enforce the laws of the union. That's why I favor a system of federal courts.

SOUTH CAROLINA: Come, come, Hamilton. A system of federal

courts—that's going too far. Our own state courts should have the say. I'll never consent to South Carolina giving up its sovereignty.

HAMILTON: Sovereignty! It's time we stopped using imposing words and looked facts in the face. I say it is still true that if we don't hang together, we'll hang separately.

NEW JERSEY: Trust you to quote whatever suits your purpose, Hamilton. It was one thing to stick together during the Revolution. But that's over and done with. We're at peace now. (*A* FIFTH DELEGATE *appears, listens. He carries a folded newspaper.*)

HAMILTON: True, we're at peace. But how long will it last? None of the thirteen states is strong enough to withstand the attack of a foreign power. Would your little state of New Jersey be able to defend itself in a war with New York? And that is just where the present anarchy is leading . . . to war. Mark my words, gentlemen, unless we get a union to keep the states in line, their rivalries will end in war.

FIFTH DELEGATE: I agree, Hamilton. But where do we get with these bull-headed delegates at the Convention? (*Slams his paper down on chair with emphasis*) We might as well go home. The Convention is split wide open! (*He stalks out, with* HAMILTON *hurrying after him. The other delegates exit, arguing.* STAGE MANAGER *removes "Washington" and "Philadelphia" signs. For a moment the stage is empty. Then a* HIGH SCHOOL BOY *and* HIGH SCHOOL GIRL *come in at the back of the stage. Hand in hand, they walk slowly forward, one on each side of the chalk line.*)

BOY: Oh, what a beautiful morning!

GIRL: Yes, if we think only of ourselves. But there's a shadow . . . .

BOY: I know . . . over the sun of the world. But let's forget about it. We have a right to our happiness. (*They swing hands and smile at each other.*)

GIRL: If only we could face the future without that shadow.

BOY: Let's try. (*Starts to hum "Oh, What a Beautiful Morning." GIRL joins in.*)

GIRL (*Suddenly seeing the chalk line on the stage, separating the two halves. Stops singing abruptly*): Look! I wonder what this means. This white line.

BOY: I wonder. Maybe just some kid having fun. Remember how we used to chalk up the sidewalks?

GIRL: This doesn't look like play to me.

BOY (*Seeing the signs*): Maybe the signs will give us some idea of what it's all about. You look on your side.

GIRL (*Skipping to "1787" sign*): Why, that's funny. "1787." That's all it says. Do you think it stands for the number of miles to somewhere?

BOY (*Looking at sign on his side*): This one says "Now." Just . . . "Now."

GIRL: There must be some explanation. (*Sees newspaper on "1787" chair. Picks it up curiously*) Why, look. Here is a Philadelphia paper . . . an old one . . . way back in July, 1787. (*Turns to sign*) So that's what it means. It stands for a date.

BOY (*Picking up paper from chair on his side*): Here's a paper too. Yesterday's *Washington Post*. I wonder . . . (*Scans the front page*)

GIRL (*Reading from 1787 paper*): "Deadlock continues. The Constitutional Convention in session at the State House came dangerously close to disbanding today."

BOY (*Reading from his paper*): "Deadlock continues. The Joint Congressional Committee on World Federation came dangerously close to disbanding this afternoon."

GIRL: Isn't this strange? Doesn't it make you feel queer? As if there were no time at all between 1787 and now! (*Turns back to paper and reads*) "Without union, Governor Randolph of Virginia insists there will be anarchy among the states. There will be bitterness and warfare."

BOY (*Reading*): "Without world federation, the sub-committee reports, there will be anarchy among the nations. There will be bitterness and warfare." (*Looks up*) Why, practically the same words! 1787 and now. The same thing!

GIRL (*Reading*): "Many delegates still hold that the problems are insurmountable."

BOY (*Reading*): "Many Congressmen still insist that the problems are insurmountable." (*Looks up*) What do you make of it?

GIRL: What do I make of it? Just this. (*Slowly, as she looks around*) We have been here before. But in spite of the dire prophecies, in spite of the difficulties, in spite of the unsurmountable problems . . . (STAGE MANAGER *rushes in.*)

STAGE MANAGER: Don't say it! Don't say it! I assured the audience at the beginning that there would be no propagandizing in this play. It is for them to draw the moral if there is one.

GIRL: I'm sorry. I guess I was carried away, beyond my lines in the script. But it seems so *obvious* that . . .

STAGE MANAGER: Don't say it. If there is any obvious inference, let the audience make it. And the drama critic . . . where is the drama critic?

DRAMA CRITIC (*Standing up in audience*): Here I am.

STAGE MANAGER: You wanted a name for this play without a name.

DRAMA CRITIC: Yes. I wanted a name. But I don't want one any more. I have it . . . if the audience is willing.

STAGE MANAGER: You've thought of a name already?

DRAMA CRITIC: Not I. But the young lady. (*Nods to* GIRL *on stage*) If the audience approves. . . .

GIRL: I? I thought of a name? When?

DRAMA CRITIC: You said, "We have been here before." That's what you said. We have been here before! What better label could there be for this play? (*Looks around at audience*) What do you think, folks? We *have* been here before, haven't we? (*Murmurs of approval from the audience, increasing into shouts of* "*Yes*," "*Yes*," *and* "*We have been here before*.") It's settled then. Read all about it in the *Daily Bugle* tomorrow morning, friends. Read all about it . . . and don't forget WE HAVE BEEN HERE BEFORE.

THE END

Spell-Down

*Boys and Girls stand towards back of stage holding large cards
with letters spelling* UNITED NATIONS. *As each one speaks he
takes a step forward.*

U   for understanding
      other people's ways.

N   for all the nations
      with a forward gaze.

I   for individuals
      pledged to work for peace.

T   for tireless teamwork,
      making warfare cease.

E   for everybody
      equal on the earth.

D   for deep devotion
      to ideals of worth.

N   for new-found neighbors
      from across the sea.

A   for firm allegiance
      to all liberty.

T   for trying together:
      trying and trying again.

I   for insight into
     lives of other men.

O   for oath to honor
     one-world point of view.

N   for need of courage
     to put the program through.

S   for willing sharing
     with you, and you, and you.

ALL: Nations united,
      nations big and small,
      all-for-one united,
      united one-for-all!

The Age of Walls Has Ended

We thought the sea a sturdy wall around us:
"Let others fight it out—we're safe enough,"
we said. "Why let their trials and troubles hound us?
Hands off. Sit tight. It may be just a bluff."
We whistled, with our hands inside our pockets,
but learned (before the mortar even dried)
that walls are tissue in the face of rockets.
We fought. And split up atoms on the side.

That's over, and the age of walls has ended.
It's not a question now of cold expense:
we can't rely on walls and be defended.
"There is no secret. There is no defense!"
Now only pulling up the roots of war
can save our planet's unprotected shore.

HALLOWEEN

Ghosts on Guard

Characters

MRS. BRIGGS, *who doesn't want her windows soaped*
MR. BRIGGS, *her long-suffering husband*
TOM
PEGGY
DONNA
DICK
} *out for Halloween fun*
HARRY, *younger brother of Donna and Dick*

SCENE 1

TIME: *Early evening, Halloween.*
SETTING: *The living room of the Briggs's home*
AT RISE: MRS. BRIGGS *is dressing her husband in an old white shirt and sheets, making him into a ghost.* MR. BRIGGS *is very unhappy about it.*

MRS. BRIGGS (*Pinning and fixing*):
    To dress a ghost requires some skill.
    Clarence Briggs, will you stand still?
MR. BRIGGS (*Giving a jump*):
    Ouch!
MRS. BRIGGS: Well, *now* perhaps you will!
MR. BRIGGS: What a wife—to prick her spouse.

MRS. BRIGGS:
  Stand as quiet as a mouse.
  Tonight you must protect our house.
  Tonight the children will be mean,
  And *you* must keep our windows clean.
  Who ever thought of Halloween! (*Sighs*)
MR. BRIGGS (*Looking at costume*):
  I feel silly.
MRS. BRIGGS:
  Don't you mope.
  You'll scare the children off, I hope.
  For every windowpane they soap
  I'll hide your pipe for one whole day.
MR. BRIGGS (*Horrified*): Hide my precious pipe away?
MRS. BRIGGS:
  That's the price you'll have to pay
  If you permit the Toms and Dicks
  To play their silly stunts and tricks.
MR. BRIGGS: Ouch! That safety pin . . . it pricks.
MRS. BRIGGS (*Standing off to survey him*):
  You make a lovely ghost, my man.
  These sheets are old, but spick and span.
MR. BRIGGS:
  Oh, Maggie, if the truth were told,
  I'd rather *play* with kids than scold.
MRS. BRIGGS:
  You'd think you were a 10-year-old!
  (*She takes an extra sheet and drapes it around his shoulders.*)
  Now, keep this sheet on for a shawl
  To shut away the cold and all.
MR. BRIGGS (*Trying to walk*):
  These skirts will surely make me fall.
  Let the youngsters have their fun!

MRS. BRIGGS:

My windows shan't be soaped—not one!

You go and make the hoodlums run.

MR. BRIGGS:

I'd rather give them little treats . . .

You know, an apple or some sweets.

MRS. BRIGGS:

Give away our hard-earned eats?

Well, I guess not. And now, be gone:

Go slink around the yard and lawn,

And don't you dare to nod and yawn.

MR. BRIGGS: No youngsters will appear, I hope.

MRS. BRIGGS:

Better take this piece of rope

To tie the hands that hold the soap.

(*She hands him a piece of clothesline.*)

MR. BRIGGS (*Sighing*): I think this being a ghost is silly.

MRS. BRIGGS: Well, go and be one, willy-nilly. (*She leads her husband out.*)

CURTAIN

* * *

SCENE 2

SETTING: *In front of the Briggs's home.*

AT RISE: TOM *and* PEGGY *come in dressed in old clothes and masks. They carry paper bags for their treats. They also carry laundry soap for windows, if they don't get treats.* TOM *has a tick-tack and* PEGGY *a noisemaker which she shakes every now and then.*

PEGGY: I wonder if we'll get some treats.

TOM: If not, we'll do some tricks.

PEGGY:

    Mrs. Briggs won't give us sweets—
    Her heart is hard as bricks.

TOM:

    We'll have to soap her windows, then.
    We promised Mom and Dad
    We'd never do *mean* tricks again . . .
    And soaping isn't bad.

PEGGY:

    It's worse than making doorbells go,
    Or making tick-tacks rattle.

TOM:

    Mrs. Briggs deserves it, though:
    She's always set for battle.

PEGGY: *Mr.* Briggs seems nice and kind.

TOM:

    If we could know him better
    I think we'd like his type of mind.

PEGGY:

    His wife is such a fretter. (*Appeals to* TOM)
    Could you make my mask hold tight—
    It wiggles on my nose.

    (TOM *adjusts* PEGGY'S *mask, then looks up and down the street.*)

TOM: Dick and Donna aren't in sight.

PEGGY:

    They had to change their clothes
    And find the masks they wore last year.
    I only hope their mother
    Will let them come and meet us here
    Without their little brother.

TOM:

    Harry? Oh, he's much too small.
    He'd make our plans go wrong:

He'd fall, and slow us up, and all!

We can't have *him* along.

PEGGY: We can't? (*Points*)

Well, look, they're coming now—

Donna, Dick, and Harry.

Tom, you mustn't make a row . . .

TOM (*Obviously displeased*):

I hope my mask is scary,

Enough to send him home, and quick!

DICK (*Calling*): Hello. I'm sorry, Tom . . . (DONNA *and* DICK, *dressed in Halloween costumes and wearing eye-masks, come in.* HARRY, *a rather pathetic little fellow, tags behind.*)

DONNA (*Indicating* HARRY):

I think it is a mean old trick.

They *made* us, Dad and Mom.

(*As the children talk,* MR. BRIGGS, *the ghost, tiptoes in behind them, cocks his ear, hides behind a bush and listens. The children, of course, do not see him.*)

DICK:

They said that they were going out.

They said we had to take him.

TOM:

Perhaps if we should run about

We'd . . . accidentally . . . shake him.

DICK:

Let's leave him here at Briggs's gate

While we go up the street. (*To* HARRY)

Now you be good and sit and wait,

And we may bring a treat.

HARRY: It's dark.

DONNA: Perhaps I ought to stay.

DICK (*To* HARRY): If you get scared, just yell.

TOM:

Or, if you'd rather run away,

Start home . . . you might as well.
But if you're here when we get back,
We'll let you watch the fun.
(*Boastfully points to Briggs's house*)
We'll cross that hedge, and then attack
Those windows, one by one.
(*Gestures as if soaping windows*)

PEGGY:
Just make a face and you will scare
A ghost, if any comes!

HARRY: I'd rather go along . . .

TOM: No fair.
You sit and twirl your thumbs.
(*The children run off and leave poor HARRY alone. He is forlorn and a bit frightened. At first he starts after the children, then turns back slowly.*)

HARRY (*Almost crying*): Donna! Dick!
(MR. BRIGGS *pops up from behind the bush.*)

MR. BRIGGS: Sh! Listen here,
Cross my heart, I'm not a ghost.
There's not a thing for you to fear.

HARRY: I'm not . . . a bit afraid . . . almost. . . .

MR. BRIGGS: I'm only Mr. Briggs, you see.

HARRY: Are you dressed up for Halloween?

MR. BRIGGS: My wife rigged up these sheets on me.
It wasn't *my* idea, I mean.

HARRY: I'd like to be a ghost.

MR. BRIGGS: You would?

HARRY: I'd love to be a ghost.

MR. BRIGGS: Why not?
Between us we might do some good,
We might accomplish quite a lot.

HARRY: They wouldn't let me go along . . .

MR. BRIGGS:

    I know. I hid and heard it all.

    When they come back, if I'm not wrong,

    They'll find *two* ghosts, one big, one small.

    Stand up and see how this will fit . . .

    (MR. BRIGGS *takes off his extra sheet and begins to drape it over* HARRY.)

HARRY: They're going to soap your windowpanes.

MR. BRIGGS:

    They *think* they are. I question it.

    We ghosts are noted for our brains.

    (*Works over costume*)

    I'll have to make two slits for eyes—

    It's good these sheets are old and thin. (*Fixes hood*)

    There! As a ghost you'd take a prize . . .

    You even give *me* prickly skin. (*He shivers, and* HARRY *giggles*. MR. BRIGGS *looks over the situation*.)

HARRY:

    They said they'd cross the hedge right there . . .

    And soap your windows, one by one.

MR. BRIGGS:

    They made you stay. It wasn't fair!

    If they could see you now, they'd run.

HARRY: They'll run a mile when we say, "Boo."

MR. BRIGGS:

    But what about those treats they've got?

    We wouldn't want to lose them too.

HARRY: Oh, no.

MR. BRIGGS: I have a plan. Here's what:

    You hide behind that little tree,

    I'll hide behind the bigger one,

    We'll stretch this rope between us, see?

    And trip them gently, just for fun,

    And then we . . . listen! here they come.

Careful. Hide yourself. Keep mum.

(MR. BRIGGS *and* HARRY *hurry and hide behind the "trees," holding the rope between them. In a moment the four children come in, looking at each other's treats.*)

TOM: I got a doughnut.

DONNA: I got *two.*

DICK: Some apples and some candy.

PEGGY: And see these peanuts—quite a few.

TOM: They'll surely come in handy!

DONNA (*Looking around for* HARRY):

Harry must have got a fright—

He isn't at the gate!

TOM:

Don't worry—he will be all right.

He didn't want to wait.

Let's soap the Briggs's windows first,

Then hustle home and eat.

DICK:

I bet that Mrs. Briggs will burst

When we have left the street:

Her precious windows full of soap!

PEGGY: She'll fuss to all the neighbors.

DICK:

When we go by tomorrow, I hope

We'll see her at her labors.

DONNA:

Her husband must have quite a time—

No fun at all, I bet.

TOM:

His wife thinks having fun a crime.

Well, here we are. All set?

(*The children approach the hedge and jump over. As they begin to move stealthily toward the house, they trip over the rope* MR. BRIGGS *and* HARRY *hold. They fall, clutching their*

treats. The ghosts begin to make weird noises. Quickly MR.
BRIGGS *loops the rope around the captives.*)

MR. BRIGGS (*In a quavering, ghostly voice*):
  Villians . . . rascals . . . mischief-makers . . .
  Scoundrels . . . bullies . . . child-forsakers . . .
  Give a treat, or stand a trick
  For every evil deed. Be quick.

TOM: W-w-we didn't d-d-do a thing unlawful.

PEGGY: Eek! I think that ghosts are awful.

MR. BRIGGS (*Threateningly*):
  For every piece of wickedness
  We'll play a trick on you, unless
  You give a treat, as you confess!

DICK:
  B-b-but, Sir, wh-what damage did we do?
  Wh-what evil d-d-deeds did we pursue?

MR. BRIGGS:
  First. You planned on playing some jokes
  On innocent, hard-working folks:
  Soaping windows, for example.
  (*Picks up soap*)
  See, this bar is just a sample.

DICK (*Nodding in the direction of Briggs's house*):
  With *her* there wasn't any use
  To ask for treats . . .

MR. BRIGGS: That's no excuse.
  You planned to give those panes a soaping.

DICK (*Pushing his bag of treats toward* MR. BRIGGS): This
  treat will help us out, I'm hoping. (MR. BRIGGS *picks up
  the bag and peeks in, nodding happily.*)

MR. BRIGGS:
  Next. You left a child alone
  This night when ghosts and witches groan.

You left a child . . . that takes explaining!
There's just a *ghost* of him remaining.

DONNA (*Thoroughly frightened, feeling guilty*):
Just a ghost! The little dear . . .
We never should have left him here.
Just a . . . oh, I can't repeat it!
Take this treat . . . I couldn't eat it.
(*She pushes her bag toward* MR. BRIGGS, *who takes it with pleasure*.)

MR. BRIGGS:
Third. You boasted—shame on you—
How smart you were, and what you'd do.
Boasting is an evil habit.

TOM: Guilty! There's a doughnut—grab it. (*He shoves his bag toward* MR. BRIGGS.)

MR. BRIGGS:
Fourth. You know it's very wrong
To trespass where you don't belong.
You did a thing that's bad and vicious.

PEGGY: Yes. (*Guiltily gives up her treat*)
            These peanuts are delicious!
Now you have our treats, please say
That we can run a mile away!

DICK: We promise to be nice to Harry.

DONNA (*Tearfully*): If we find him. Oh, how scary.

PEGGY: We'll never soap those panes, or boast. (*Nods at house*)

TOM: Or jump the hedge again, Sir Ghost.

ALL:
So, please, just let us go—untie us.
We promise to be good. Just try us.

MR. BRIGGS:
I'll have to ask my pal. (*To* HARRY) What say?
Do they deserve to get away?

HARRY: Yes. They all sound sorry—very.

DICK: Hear that voice?

DONNA (*Excitedly*): It sounds like Harry!
   Harry! Harry! Is it you?
   (HARRY, *laughing, takes off his ghost hood. So does* MR. BRIGGS.)

MR. BRIGGS: I guess our little game is through.

TOM: Mr. Briggs!

MR. BRIGGS: I thought you'd guess it.
   Now, my friends, I must confess it:
   My wife insisted I must be
   This frightful ghostly ghost you see,
   And though I seriously objected,
   I've had more fun than I expected—
   More fun than I have had for years.

TOM: I'm glad of that. I say, "Three cheers."

MR. BRIGGS:
   And, thanks to you, it now appears
   That we are going to have a party.
   (*He holds up the bags of treats.*)

DICK: Our appetites are pretty hearty.

MR. BRIGGS:
   It's been an age since I have seen
   Such special treats for Halloween.
   Let's sit around and all be merry.
   (*He passes the bags around, and everyone joins in the fun.*)
   I know some stories that are scary.

CHILDREN:
   Tell them! That will be just right
   For such a scary sort of night.

MR. BRIGGS: I'll tell you all you want to hear . . .
   If you will come again *next year!*

THE END

On Halloween

(A skit for many boys and girls)

AT RISE: TWO GIRLS *in Halloween costumes enter and look around timidly.*

1ST GIRL: This is the night
that is dark and scary.

2ND GIRL: *Much* more scary
than ordinary.

1ST GIRL: Witches loom
through the eerie gloom
as they zip and zoom
on a magic broom.

2ND GIRL: Their voices boom
with the sound of doom.

BOTH: And oh, but we must be wary. (*They shrink back as they see* WITCHES *approach on broomsticks.* WITCHES *chant and dance around weirdly.*)

WITCHES: Swish . . . swish . . . swish,
Tonight is so spooky-ish,
We feel right at home wherever we roam.
Swish . . . swish . . . swish.

(*The* GIRLS *watch the dancing for a few minutes, then begin to clap.* WITCHES, *startled, swish to sides of stage and crouch there.*)

1ST GIRL: This is the night
           that is dark and scary.

2ND GIRL: Much more scary than ordinary.
           But don't you feel merry?

1ST GIRL: Very! (*They sit down with* WITCHES)

(TWO BOYS *in Halloween costumes enter and look around nervously.*)

1ST BOY: This is the night
           when ghosts are stary.

2ND BOY: Much more stary
           than *necessary.*

1ST BOY: They glide in view
           on the avenue,
           and clutch at you
           with a wailing "Woooo."

2ND BOY: Or pierce you through
           with a fearful, "Boo!"

BOTH: And oh, but we must be wary. (*They shrink back as they see* GHOSTS *glide in.* GHOSTS *dance in slow motion as they wail.*)

GHOSTS: Wooooo . . . wooooo . . . woooo,
           Tonight we have things to do:
           We'll make folks shake and quiver and quake.
           Wooooo . . . woooooo . . . woooo.

(*The* BOYS *watch the dancing a few minutes, then begin to clap.* GHOSTS, *startled, glide behind the* WITCHES.)

1ST BOY: This is the night
        when ghosts are stary.

2ND BOY: Much more stary
        than necessary.
        But don't you feel merry?

1ST BOY: Very! (*They sit down with* GIRLS, WITCHES *and*
    GHOSTS. *A* BOY *and a* GIRL *come in with jack-o'-lanterns.*)

BOY: This is the night
        that is legendary.
        Pumpkin-lanterns
        are gay and glary.

GIRL: Cats are seen
        with their eyes of green.

(BLACK CATS *come in meowing and meowing. They stalk
around, then take places with the others.*)

BOY: Spooks convene
        on the ghostly scene.

(*Various* SPOOKS, GOBLINS, SCARECROWS *and other Halloween
characters come in trying to frighten each other. Then they
take their places with the others.*)

BOTH: But pleasure is keen
        for it's . . .

ALL (*Shouting gaily*): H A L L O W E E N !
        And everyone's merry.
        Very!

THE END

Jack-o'-Lantern

BOY: Who wears a grin
      from ear to chin?

ALL: Jack-o'-lantern.

GIRL: Whose teeth are few
      and jagged, too?

ALL: Jack-o'-lantern.

BOY: Who shows a light
      all orange-bright
      that makes his face a jolly sight?

ALL: Jack-o'-lantern.

GIRL: Who has a pair
      of eyes that stare?

ALL: Jack-o'-lantern.

BOY: Whose nose is flat—
      no doubt of that?

ALL: Jack-o'-lantern.

GIRL: Who sports a smile
      that shows a mile,
      and once a year is all in style?

ALL: JACK-O'-LANTERN.

Black and Orange

BOYS: Black for cats
and black for bats
and black for witches' cloaks and hats.

GIRLS: Orange for the harvest moon
rising like a bright balloon.

BOYS: Black for shadows,
black for shades,
black for masks at masquerades.

GIRLS: Orange for a pumpkin—bright
with orange eyes or orange light.

ALL: Black and orange, side by side,
on the night that witches ride—
black and orange always mean
heaps of fun on Halloween,
heaps of fun on Halloween!

Halloween Concert

BOYS: "It's cold," said the cricket,
"my fingers are numb.
I scarcely can fiddle,
I scarcely can strum.
And oh, I'm sleepy,
now summer has gone."

ALL: He dropped his fiddle
to stifle a yawn.

GIRLS: "Don't," said the field mouse, "act so sober.
You can't stop *yet*, when it's still October."

BOYS: "I've played," said the cricket,
"for weeks and weeks.
My fiddle needs fixing—
it's full of squeaks.
My fingers need resting . . ."
He yawned. "Ho, hum,
I'm quite . . . (*Yawn*) . . . ready
for winter to come.
I've found me the coziest,
doziest house . . ."

GIRLS: "You can't stop *now*," said his friend the mouse.

BOYS: "No?" yawned the cricket,
and closed his eyes.
"I've played so much
for a chap my size.
It's time (*He yawns*)
for my winter snooze:
I hear the creak
of November's shoes."

GIRLS: "You *can't* . . ." said the mouse in a voice of sorrow,
"you can't desert us until tomorrow.
Tune up your fiddle for one last scene . . .
don't you remember it's HALLOWEEN?"

BOYS: "What!" cried the cricket.
He yawned no more.
"You should have mentioned
the fact before!
Is everyone ready?
And where's the score?
What in the world
are we waiting for?"

ALL: The cricket fiddled,
the field mouse squeaked,
the dry weeds twiddled,
the bare twigs tweaked,
the hoot-owl hooted,
the cornstalks strummed,
the westwind tooted,
the fence wires hummed:

Oh, what a concert all night long!
The fiddle was shrill, and the wind was strong.
"Halloween, Halloween, crick, crack, creak.
Halloween, Halloween, scritch, scratch, squeak."

Pumpkins

Cinderella's pumpkin
is not the only one
that turned to something magic—
when all is said and done.

Our October pumpkin
felt a magic knife,
turned into a smiling face
with teeth as big as life.

And its orange insides
under Mother's eye
turned into a luscious,
        squishious,
            spicy pumpkin pie!

ELECTION DAY

The Voice of Liberty

Characters

Mr. Dawson
Mrs. Dawson
Gram
Joel
Isaac
William
Stephen
A Young Woman
A Man
An Old Woman

Time: *The present, with flashbacks to the past.*
Setting: *The Dawson living room.*
At Rise: Mr. *and* Mrs. Dawson *and* Gram *are seated in the living room.*

Mr. Dawson: There's not much use to vote. Such candidates!
    Why bother to go down to vote at all?
    Why make the effort?
Mrs. Dawson: That's the way I feel. What good is it?
    Besides, it breaks my morning work time up,
    Having to stand in line for half an hour.
    The men we like the most don't have a chance!

GRAM: If folks like you stay home,
　The peoples' candidates are sure to lose.
　I think you ought to go.

MRS. DAWSON: Now, Gram, you know *you* plan to stay at
　　home
　And lose your vote again!
　Why don't you vote yourself?

GRAM: With all this rheumatism in my bones?
　Besides, I'm not much hand at politics,
　And I'm too old.
　Ten years from now I won't be here to care
　Who's President or Senator or Judge
　But you'll be here, and so you ought to vote
　And let your voice be heard.

MRS. DAWSON: The weather's so uncertain.
　Why did they pick this month as election time?
　The chances are there'll be a blizzard on.

MR. DAWSON: As like as not.
　Besides, there's not much chance that folks like us
　Can do a bit of good, filling a ballot in.

JOEL (*Entering excitedly*): I've just been reading of a resident
　Of Philadelphia since way back when,
　Who hasn't said a word for—let me see—
　More than a hundred years,
　And yet whose voice is heard from coast to coast,
　From North to South, across the U.S.A. . . .

MR. DAWSON: What's that you say?

MRS. DAWSON: Don't talk such nonsense, son.
　How can a voice be heard when it is still?

JOEL: Well, here's a hint:
　If you should go to Independence Hall, in Philadelphia,
　You'd see it for yourselves—
　A great American, still holding open house
　And drawing quite a crowd year after year!

GRAM: A great American?

JOEL (*Laughing*): Yes. Three feet high. A good big ton in
  weight.

  And slightly cracked!

MRS. DAWSON: You sound that way yourself.

JOEL: There's something masculine about the size,
  The crudeness of the finish, and the strength.
  The shape is classic, though—quite feminine . . .

MR. DAWSON (*Impatiently*): Come, come, my boy.

JOEL: It's really quite a bell!

MRS. DAWSON: What's that?

GRAM: A bell!

JOEL: The story is a thriller any day
  But now *especially*—around election time.
  I wish that I could vote!
  Well, want to hear?
  It's all about a bell called Liberty . . .

MRS. DAWSON: Of course, we want to hear.

JOEL: You have to start way back to set the scene.
  You start with Philadelphia, the town
  That William Penn laid out on a peninsula
  Between the Schuylkill and the Delaware.
  The colonists put up a State House there—
  Began the year Ben Franklin started publishing
  His old Gazette. 1729, to be exact.
  Well, they had quite a time, those colonists,
  Getting the State House up
  With all their ties to Britain's apron strings.
  The British wanted trade:
  They forced their products on the colonies.
  They made them pay.
  Some colonists approved—the tie was strong
  Between them and the mother-country still.
  But others fumed,

And even children had their dander up.

(*Flashback to* ISAAC *and* WILLIAM, *two colonial boys*)

ISAAC: My father calls them blasted British nails!

Why can't we make our own?

When I grow up, I'm never going to pound a British nail!

WILLIAM: They *had* to use them in the State House here.

It makes my father mad.

That building should have been American

From start to finish—that's what Father said.

When I grow up, I'm going to make some nails!

ISAAC: Let's both make nails when we grow up, what say?

I'd like to work with iron.

Let's hang around at Pass and Stow's and watch,

So we'll know how to handle it.

WILLIAM: They used good native lumber though, at least,

To build the State House of,

And Uncle Edward says we kilned our bricks.

He helped to lay them up.

BOTH: But British nails! (STEPHEN *enters*)

STEPHEN: Say, wait—

I bet you haven't heard the latest news

Or you'd have something sharper than a British nail

To bother you!

I've hung around the State House, and I know . . .

ISAAC: Know what?

STEPHEN: The Superintendents plan to buy a bell . . .

ISAAC: That's good. It's time the State House had a bell.

WILLIAM: I hope it's big and loud.

ISAAC: My father says we need a good strong bell

That can be heard across the countryside,

Way out past Germantown.

Who'll make it? Pass and Stow?

They're good at iron. We've watched them lots of times.

STEPHEN: Huh! Pass and Stow!

The Superintendents never even thought of them.
They've ordered us a *British* bell, my lads!
If you've been fussing over British nails,
What do you say about a bell, I ask?

ISAAC: You're sure that's right?
I bet my father hasn't heard it yet . . .
He'd say a bell like that would never ring!

STEPHEN: Of course it will.
The British know their bells . . .
That's why a firm in London got the job.

WILLIAM: But if it doesn't ring . . .

STEPHEN: No chance at all.
They've made a lot of bells, the British have.

ISAAC (*Belligerently*): There must be someone in the colonies
Who'd know the way to cast a metal bell.

WILLIAM: A British bell will never ring, I say.
We'll bet on that!

STEPHEN: I'll bet a shilling's worth of British nails
The bell will ring.

ISAAC: We'll take you up.
You'll buy the shilling's worth, because we'll win!

STEPHEN: What difference does it make who casts the bell?
Just so it's good.
Just so it rings, I say. (*Shrugs and goes out*)

WILLIAM· When we grow up
Let's learn to turn out bells as well as nails. (*They go out.*)

GRAM: And how did it turn out, about the bell?

MR. DAWSON: They got an English one?

MRS. DAWSON: And did it ring?

JOEL: The bell was cast by Englishmen all right,
And at a bargain, too.
It came in August of the following year—1752,
Across the sea from London, up the Delaware,
Suspended from the hardwood beam that still supports

Our bell in Independence Hall.
It had these words around the top of it,
According to the order that went in:
"Proclaim Liberty throughout all the land and unto all
   the inhabitants thereof."
Folks didn't rush it to the belfry though.
They swung it on a temporary frame
Inside the State House yard, to try it out.
A crowd turned out to watch . . .
A few were certain that the bell would fail,
Being British made;
But, by and large, the crowd was confident.
Of course, the bell would ring.
Why shouldn't it?
That's what a bell was for.

MRS. DAWSON: Of course. Of course.

JOEL: But when the rope was pulled . . .
   (*There is an abrupt clang offstage, stopping almost as soon as
   it starts. In a minute* ISAAC *and* WILLIAM *come in excitedly.*)

ISAAC: We heard it start to ring, and then it stopped!
   The woman next to me
   Was sure the sound would carry miles and miles.
   But, say, it didn't even ring one round!

WILLIAM: It cracked . . . it broke!
   The bell split up the side. We won our bet.

ISAAC: I never thought we'd get some British nails
   And feel so glad about it.
   British nails!
   Let's throw them in the river, one by one.

WILLIAM: I wonder if they'll throw the bell in too.
   It's not much good like that, with such a crack.

ISAAC: The first clap of the knocker and it split.
   My father said it would.
   Now will they let us make one in the colonies?

WILLIAM: I heard John Pass and Charley Stow suggest
  They'd like a try.
  They'd make a bell that wouldn't crack, I bet.
ISAAC: They never made a bell but they can try.
  They know their iron.
  We'll have to watch them every chance we get. (*They
  go out.*)
JOEL: Pass and Stow, two eager colonists,
  Turned out a bell.
MR. DAWSON: What happened to the English one that
  cracked?
JOEL: They broke it up, and then they melted it
  With native copper ore, to make it strong.
  They tried a formula:
  For each ten pounds of broken British bell,
  Not quite one pound of copper.
MR. DAWSON: Did it work?
JOEL: They tried it out on little bells at first,
  To test the strength and sound,
  And then they made a mould and cast the bell!
  It looked quite good when taken from the mould.
  The size and shape were pleasing . . .
GRAM: And the words? The words around the top?
JOEL: The lettering was better than the British,
  People said.
  The words were still the same:
  "Proclaim Liberty throughout all the land and unto all the
  inhabitants thereof."
MRS. DAWSON: And did it ring?
JOEL: Just wait!
  It's spring in Philadelphia this time, 1753.
  The trees aren't yet in leaf, but swelling at the tips;
  And farmlands greening off beyond the town.
  Another day for hanging up a bell,

For crowds to gather in the State House yard . . .
(ISAAC *and* WILLIAM *come in.*)

ISAAC: It's *got* to ring. It musn't fail to ring.

WILLIAM: There's Stephen coming. Shall we make a bet?

ISAAC: We'll bet *this* time the bell will ring, not fail. (*Calls*)
Say, Stephen, wait. You think the bell will ring?

STEPHEN (*Coming in*): Well, even if it does, it won't be good.
You can't make music in a blacksmith shop!

WILLIAM: You'll bet on that?

STEPHEN (*Hurrying off*): There isn't time. I want to find a
place. (WILLIAM *and* ISAAC *exit.*)

JOEL: The crowd is waiting, and the moment tense.
The rope is pulled amidst a mighty cheer.
The second bell is swung . . .
(*There is a discordant crash offstage, like a crash of kitchen
pots and pans.*)

A YOUNG WOMAN (*Offstage*): You call that thing a bell?
A noise like that?
We'd be a town of deaf mutes in a year
If we were forced to listen to that din!

A MAN (*Offstage*): Let's Pass it up and Stow the bell away.
Aye, Pass and Stow!
They deal in iron, not bells. We might have known.

AN OLD WOMAN (*Offstage*): You'd think they caught a thou-
sand cawing crows
And made a bell of them.
We'd hear it, heaven knows. But what a sound!
(*Colonists' voices trail off, as* WILLIAM *and* ISAAC *come on.*)

WILLIAM (*Trying to be cheerful*): It didn't crack at least. It
made a noise.

ISAAC (*Sorrowfully*): A noise is right . . . but not the noise
of bells.
It's just as well we didn't make that bet.

WILLIAM: There's something wrong . . .

They put in too much copper, someone said;
They melted too much copper with the iron.
They'll know next time.

ISAAC: You think they'll break it up and try again?

WILLIAM: Of course they will.

ISAAC: But people made some pretty mean remarks
About poor Pass and Stow.
You heard them, standing near us in the crowd.

WILLIAM: I wouldn't care. I'd want to try again.
And so would you.
And so will Pass and Stow. (*They go out.*)

MR. DAWSON: And did they try?

GRAM: Of course they did! They couldn't wait to try.

JOEL: They broke the bell and changed the formula:
They cut the copper down, and made a mould,
And cast another bell.
It didn't take so long—a couple of months—
And it was ready to be swung again.
Summer. 1753.
Three times and out, you know!
The crowd is sober now, and questioning,
Not jubilant, expectant as before.
This time the crowd is on the anxious seat:
Two bells have failed, is this a blunder too?
(ISAAC *and* WILLIAM *appear.*)

WILLIAM: My father still is full of confidence.
Three times and out, he says.
This time it works!

ISAAC: We'd better climb the fence so we can see. (*They
go out.*)

JOEL: A little ritual, and the rope is grasped.
The bell begins to swing . . .
And then it sounds . . .
(*Sounds of a clear bell ringing offstage.*)

MRS. DAWSON: I'm glad of that! The trouble those folks had.

JOEL: The bell rang strong and clear—
Over the town, over the fields, it rang,
Into the hills along the Delaware,
All up and down the rich green countryside.

MR. DAWSON: At last, at last.
Those fellows made a fight, by Jove, and won.
They didn't just sit back . . .

JOEL: For years the big bell rang:
For meetings, celebrations, deaths,
For summoning the Philadelphians to hear
(July the fourth, 1776)
The Declaration from the State House yard.

GRAM (*Remembering, slowly*): "We hold these truths to be self-evident—that all men are created equal; that they are endowed by their Creator with certain inalienable rights; that among these are life, liberty, and the pursuit of happiness . . ."

MRS. DAWSON: Why, Gram, how you remember! Every word.

MR. DAWSON: I learned it, too, but not as well as that.

JOEL: And then it rang of war.
The colonists against the Britishers!
It rang of Washington—the day he took command,
And early victories.
And then the British marched on Philadelphia!

GRAM: They didn't get the bell—don't say they did!

MRS. DAWSON: They couldn't have . . .

MR. DAWSON: Their fingers itched to melt it down, I bet,
For cannon balls, to shoot the rebels with!
And was it safe?

JOEL: The Continental soldiers saw to that.
They moved the bell away,
Just put it in a wagon, one of those
For hauling troop supplies.

And carted it away to Allentown—
A creaky, bumpy ride of fifty miles—
To hide it safely there inside a church.

GRAM: I'm glad of that.

JOEL: Next year the bell was back,
Rehung, and going strong in Independence Hall.

MRS. DAWSON: In Independence Hall? The State House, then,
Was harmed perhaps?

JOEL: Oh no, it's standing yet, it's still the same.
You see, with victory, they changed the name . . .
To Independence Hall.

MR. DAWSON: And what about the bell?

JOEL: It rang for more than eighty years. Then cracked.
It's in the Hall on exhibition now.

MRS. DAWSON: Too bad it had to crack.

JOEL: Well, strange to say, that crack has made the bell
More famous than it ever was before:
It's down where folks can look at it these days,
And looking makes them think,
It makes them pause . . .

MR. DAWSON: It makes me pause, myself.
They fought for things I take for granted now,
Those colonists.
My liberty has come the easy way.
They took a stand. They saw a problem through—
By Jove, they did.
I must confess the story makes me blush . . .
I wasn't going to vote!
Oh, what's the use? I said. What good is it?
We'd still be pounding British nails, I guess,
If *they'd* said things like that, and just sat back.

MRS. DAWSON: They had to *work* for liberty, and I
Felt taking time to vote would be a chore.

GRAM: I'm guilty too.

Perhaps I will be gone in ten more years—
But that's no reason for being silent now!
I ought to care what kind of world there'll be
For you folks left behind.
My rheumatism—fiddlesticks! I'll vote.
Why, even with the crack, the clapper dead,
That bell still speaks to me
I still can hear it with my inner ear.

JOEL: The voice of liberty is more than just a weight
Of iron and copper in a cracked old bell:
It's still alive,
It still has things to say . . .

MR. DAWSON: I know. We can't stop now.
We can't stop here.
If I lived where I wasn't free to vote,
Where liberty and voting were a farce,
I'd realize then, by Jove . . .
I'd prize these free elections we have here!
The only way to keep democracy
Is taking part in it. No other way!
There still is work to do, for all of us.

JOEL: Those words around the bell . . .
We've got to keep on hearing what they say.

ALL: "Proclaim Liberty throughout all the land and unto all
the inhabitants thereof."

THE END

Voting Day

A group of boys and girls are looking at a large sign (tacked to a screen or desk) which says VOTING DAY. *Behind the screen hide three girls and three boys, each holding a placard with a letter of the word* VOTING.

1st Girl (*Looking at sign*): Today, they say, is Voting Day,
with posters everywhere.
But all the fuss is not for *us*—
we're much too young to care.

1st Boy: We cannot vote, it's sad to note,
until we're twenty-one,
so why should we care one-two-three
what voting-things are done?

2nd Girl: Today, they say, is Voting Day-
for grownups. Some are keen,
but some stay home and sigh and groan:
"Huh, what does voting mean?"

2nd Boy: The posters shout, "Turn out, turn out
and vote! It's up to you
what laws get passed." But, first and last,
I wonder if that's true.

ALL: Today, today, is Voting Day.
                Before the day is spent,
                we wish we'd hear, as clear as clear,
                exactly what is meant!

(*Boys and girls behind the sign run out in order, so the letters
   they hold spell* VOTING.)

ALL SIX: You wish to know what's thus and so
                in VOTING? Listen well,
                and we will try to clarify
                just what our letters spell.

BOY WITH V: V for vision of the kind
                of life that's worth foreseeing.
                Voting is the way to bring
                that vision into being.

GIRL WITH O: O for obligation
                on the part of you, and me,
                to keep Old Glory waving
                in a land of liberty.

BOY WITH T: T for thought and teamwork
                in choosing right from wrong.
                And no one is too young or old
                to help that cause along!

GIRL WITH I: I for international—
                applied to point of view,
                for insight into others' needs,
                ideas of what to do.

BOY WITH N: N for nation that we love;
                and need of serving, giving.
                If we cannot vote, we still
                can serve by friendly living.

GIRL WITH G: G for government in gear
to serve the greatest good,
government not based on force,
but faith and brotherhood.

ALL SIX: That spells VOTING. You'll agree
that a simple word can be
mighty big, although it's small—
full of meaning for us all.

(*Boys and girls of first group summarize the meaning of* VOTING, *as each member of the letter-group steps forward in turn and holds his letter high.*)

1ST GIRL: *V*ision!

1ST BOY: *O*bligation
to keep our country free.

2ND GIRL: *T*eamwork!

2ND BOY: *I*nsight!

1ST GIRL: *N*ation
in need of you and me.

1ST BOY: *G*overnment in gear to serve
the greatest good . . .

ALL: It's clear
all of us have parts to play,
today . . . and all the year!

Veterans Day

BOYS: Eleventh month. Eleventh day.

GIRLS: Eleven in the morning.

BOYS: A solemn bell begins to sway
and ring its solemn warning:

ALL (*Softly*): "Silence . . . silence . . . face the east.
Silence . . . think upon the men
who supposed, when fighting ceased,
war would never come again."

GIRLS: Eleventh month. Eleventh day.

BOYS: Eleven, on the hour.

GIRLS: The silent soldiers seem to say
that faith is still a tower:

ALL (*Softly*): "Listen . . . listen . . . can you hear?
We who battled and were killed
know the dream that we held dear
some bright day will be fulfilled."

BOYS: Eleventh month. Eleventh day.

GIRLS: Eleventh hour. A prayer
sent by voices far away
is hanging in the air:

ALL (*Softly*): "Onward . . . onward . . . do not flinch,
now the task is up to you,
push the vision, inch by inch,
make our dream of peace come true."

To an Unknown Soldier

1ST BOY:	We do not know your age, or name,
2ND BOY:	or how you looked, or what you thought,
3RD BOY:	or from what town or farm you came—
ALL THREE:	we only know how well you fought.
1ST GIRL:	We do not know what books you read,
2ND GIRL:	what gave you pleasure and release,
3RD GIRL:	what poems you thought but never said—
ALL THREE:	we only know you died for peace.
ENTIRE GROUP:	We do not know so many things,
	but you must know (somehow, somewhere)
	your dream of peace still spreads its wings
	above our heads and hovers there.

Prayer for Peace

Swing out, oh bells,
sing out, oh bells,
our prayer that strife be ended,
that guns be still
on plain and hill
and all our discords mended.
Let weapons turn to plowshares now
and fighting planes be grounded
as through the air of Everywhere
the words of peace are sounded.

Ring out, oh bells,
swing out, oh bells,
sing out from every steeple
the burning hope
the yearning hope
for peace by weary people.
Let understanding be our aim,
the goal for which we're heading,
as through the earth a strong rebirth
of brotherhood starts spreading.

Once Upon a Time

Characters

READER
OLD WOMAN
HER CHILDREN
BAKER'S MAN
WHIZZER, *a young magician*
GEORGIE
PETER RABBIT
THE HARE
THE WHITE RABBIT
THE MARCH HARE
ALICE
PINOCCHIO
HEIDI
MR. POPPER
CHRISTOPHER ROBIN
MARY POPPINS
ROBIN HOOD
CINDERELLA

SETTING: *Inside the Old Woman's shoe.*

AT RISE: *The* READER, *with nose in book, comes on stage and begins to read aloud. The* READER *soon curls up in easy chair and remains there throughout play. Throughout the play,*

while the READER *reads, the* OLD WOMAN *and the* CHILDREN
should pantomime as much as possible.

READER: Once upon a time . . . there was an old woman
   who lived in a shoe. She had so many children she didn't
 • know what to do. (*The* OLD WOMAN *comes in shaking her
   head. Her* CHILDREN *swarm around her, hopping, skipping,
   dancing, turning cartwheels, etc.*)
   She had fat children, and lean children,
   And frumpy children, and clean children,
   And sort-of-in-between children,
   And big children, and small children,
   And short children, and tall children,
   And nothing-to-do-at-all children.
   And since it is often upsetting to have even one child in a
      family, or two . . . (*A* CHILD *almost upsets the* OLD
      WOMAN.*)
   No wonder the poor Old Woman didn't know what to do!
OLD WOMAN (*Holding her head*):
   They get underfoot
   Wherever I stand.
   They never stay put,
   They get out of hand,
   They occupy all the available inches.
   Oh dear, when you live in a shoe, how it pinches!
   (*She sits down on a stool, her head in her hands.*)
   I must think of something before it's too late . . .
   The day is approaching . . . the King will not wait.
   I wish I could gather my thoughts in a cup
   Like berries or cherries. The time's almost up.
READER:
   But, unfortunately, before the Old Woman could gather a
     single thought,

Her children began asking many more questions than they
    ought,

Or else they came up with an adventure to tell, or two,

So . . . no wonder the poor Old Woman didn't know what
    to do!

A GIRL: Mama, when I asked the little red hen for a kernel of
corn, she gave me a *peck*.

A BOY: Mama, what is the difference in size between a bird
and a beast? (*He waits a moment, then shouts.*) *Two feet.*

A GIRL: First I was in a jam, then I was in a pickle, then I
was in a stew, and now I'm in the soup.

A BOY: Mama, who has four eyes but cannot see? (*Calls
over his shoulder as he hops away*) *Mississippi.*

A GIRL: Mama, when I went to the orchard, they told me to
sleep on an apri*cot*, but I'd much rather lie on a rose-bed.

A BOY: Mama, if you want to pick a flower that's good to
eat, what do you do?

SEVERAL CHILDREN: Picc-a-lilli!

READER:

    And so it went from morning till night,

    Until the Old Woman who lives in a shoe

    With so many children so lively and bright

    Simply didn't know what to do!

    And all the time it was becoming very important for the
        Old Woman to determine

    How she was going to entertain the King, in his robe trimmed
        with ermine,

    For, you see, everyone had to take turns entertaining the
        King for one whole day,

    And the Old Woman's turn was only a few (*three*, to be
        exact) days away.

    But how could she think—with so many children crammed
        into the shoe?

No wonder she couldn't decide what to do, what to do,
	what to do.
OLD WOMAN (*To the tune of "Three Blind Mice"*):
	Three more days. Three more days.
	Oh, how they race. Oh, how they race.
	If I don't think of a plan at once,
	The King will call me a frightful dunce—
ALL: Three more days!
OLD WOMAN:
	Oh, hum. Hum, ho,
	What's to come, I don't know.
	All my thoughts have taken wing—
	I cannot think of *any*thing
	To entertain his Nibs, the King.
A BOY: Mama, you could throw a party, if you didn't throw
	it too far.
A GIRL: Mama, you could *spring* a surprise . . . if it weren't
	fall.
READER:
	And so the *first* day came, and went,
	Till every single hour was spent,
	And still the Woman in the shoe
	Had not a thought of what to do
	To entertain the King.
OLD WOMAN: Boo, hoo!
	If I could think . . . if I were wise . . .
	I might receive a royal prize:
	A ten-cent pearl, or even ruby.
	But, as it is, I'll get a *booby*.
READER:
	Now, a booby, as you know, is a dumb and witless bird
		from tropical isles,
	And everybody getting a booby is the object of lifted eye-
		brows and smiles,

Especially since people receiving a booby from the King
are ordered to tie it

Right out in the front yard where everybody passing by
can spy it.

So . . . is it any wonder the poor Old Woman who lived
in a shoe

Wanted her children to be quiet so she could figure out
what to do?

OLD WOMAN:

Ho, hum. What's to come?

Hum, ho. I don't know.

READER:

There she sat, leaning her head on her hand and using her
arm for a bracket,

Not knowing what she could do in the midst of the muddle
and racket.

A BOY: What can we do?

A GIRL: What can we play?

A BOY: Give us a clue, and we'll go away.

READER:

But their mother wasn't able to think of a single pastime,
or a single clue,

Because she had come to the end of her shoelace, and didn't
know what to do.

Then the Eldest Boy, who was always hungry because he
was always growing,

Thought of a plan that set all the other children to ah-ing
and oh-ing.

ELDEST BOY: Mama, why don't you get in touch with the
Baker's Man? Have him cook up a great big special kind
of pie. Then when we are all busy eating, with our mouths
full of pie, we will be so quiet you will be able to think.
Then you can figure out how to entertain the King.

READER:

That seemed like a wonderful plan indeed.

If only . . . if only it would succeed!

So the Old Woman called up the bakery and put in a hurry-up order

For a special kind of pie with goodies in the middle and a crusty border,

And that very evening the Baker's Man set foot in the shoe before dinner

With a pie that was certainly a great deal *thicker* than it was thinner.

BAKER'S MAN (*Coming in with big platter*):

I've baked them big, and I've baked them little,

I've baked them soft, and I've baked them brittle,

I've baked for many a man and miss,

But I *never* have baked such a pie as this.

A BOY: Can you put in your thumb and pull out a plum?

(BAKER'S MAN *sets the pie down on the table, smiles and bows, then hurries out.* CHILDREN *rush to the table in great excitement.* OLD WOMAN *makes believe she is cutting the pie and passing it around.*)

READER:

My, but it was a wonderful pie—

Big and broad, and deep and high!

Every son and every daughter

Felt his mouth begin to water.

Oh, the filling! Oh, the batter!

One thing only was the matter:

The pie, unfortunately, was so *very* special, and so very nice,

So unusually full of raisins and cocoanut and spice

That the children, instead of keeping quiet, kept repeating "Yummy, yummy, yummy," *all* the time they were eating.

CHILDREN: Yummy, yummy, yummy.

READER:

And so the poor Old Woman saw all of her hopes take wing,

Because she hadn't time to think about the King, the King.

OLD WOMAN: Boo, hoo, hoo. What shall I do?

READER:

And thus the *second* day slipped past—

The time was going very fast!

The poor Old Woman wiped her eyes—

She'd lost all hope of any prize

(A trinket or a red-glass ruby)

But still she *didn't* want a booby.

And then the Youngest Girl, who liked to look out of the window and dream,

Thought of—at least, so it seemed to the Old Woman— a wonderful scheme.

YOUNGEST GIRL: Mama, if only you knew someone who could make *magic*, instead of a pie! Then maybe you would be able to figure out what to do.

OLD WOMAN:

Magic! My dumpling, that's just what we need.

I'll hire the Wizard of Oz. Yes, indeed. (*She goes to the phone.*)

READER:

But, unfortunately, when the Old Woman called up the Employment Agency in the city,

She learned that the Wizard of Oz was booked for a good long time. What a pity!

And when she asked if the Agency could supply some other magician,

The man-at-the-other-end said they had only one person for the position.

OLD WOMAN (*Holding hand over phone to talk to the children*):

It seems that the best they can do after dinner

Is send a magician who's just a *beginner*. (*Speaking into phone*)

Well, send him on over. I'm in such a fix

Perhaps a beginner can pull enough tricks.

READER:

So Whizzer, who was just learning to be a magician, whizzed into the shoe. (WHIZZER *swoops in to the sound of a slide whistle*.)

With his wand and his stiff black hat and great big how-do-you-do.

WHIZZER: How do you do! Hocus . . . pocus . . . dominocus.

CHILDREN (*Excited*): Play your tricks, but do not joke us.

OLD WOMAN:

Do you know the clever magician's habit

Of reaching into your hat and pulling out a rabbit?

WHIZZER (*Consulting a little book of instructions, which he has tied around his neck on a string for easy reference*):

Rabbit? Rabbit? Why, yes, I can bring you so many

You may, in the end, be sorry you asked for any.

(*He moves to the door, waves his wand over his hat, and chants*)

Abra . . ca . . dabra . . . and other such words as that!

Come, little magical rabbits, jump out of my hat!

(*He sweeps his hat near the door, and a boy hops into the room like a rabbit.*)

GEORGIE: New folks coming, oh my! (*Hops toward other exit*)

Hi, Uncle Analdas, new folks coming! Hi, Phewie Skunk, new folks coming! (*He goes out.*)

CHILDREN: Who in the world was that?

WHIZZER:

Why, that was Georgie from *Rabbit Hill*.

Abra . . ca . . dabra . . . look your fill!

(*He goes through the motions again and another small boy hops in like a rabbit. He seems very excited.*)

PETER RABBIT: I lost one of my shoes among the cabbages in Mr. McGregor's garden, and the other shoe among the potatoes. And my little blue jacket with brass buttons got caught on a gooseberry net. What will Mama say! (*Exits*)

A GIRL:
Who was that, and how did he lose
His little blue jacket and both his shoes?

WHIZZER:
That was Peter Rabbit, and he didn't mind his mother.
Presto . . . jesto! Here come another!
(*He goes through his gestures again, and another boy hops in quickly. He seems very sure of himself.*)

THE HARE: Imagine that slow old Tortoise thinking he can beat me. I can run like the wind . . . I can run like the wind! I can beat him all to pieces in a race. (*He hurries out.*)

A BOY: Of course, he can.

WHIZZER: Oh, no—you'll find
That boastful Hare gets left behind!
(*He goes through his motions and another rabbit hops in, this time with a pair of white gloves and a fan. He is in a hurry.*)

WHIZZER:
Here's a rabbit in a hurry,
Wrinkling up his nose with worry.

WHITE RABBIT: Oh, the Duchess, the Duchess. Oh, won't she be savage if I've kept her waiting! Oh, my fur and whiskers. (*Exits*)

A GIRL: What's the matter? And who was that?

WHIZZER:
I pulled the White Rabbit out of my hat.
And, while I'm at it, the March Hare, too,
To show what Wonderland rabbits do. (*Gestures. The MARCH HARE, yawning, hops slowly across the stage. Stops in the middle and yawns.*)

MARCH HARE: Suppose we change the subject. (*Yawns again*)
   I'm getting tired of this. (*Exits slowly, mumbling under his breath.*)

WHIZZER (*Consulting his little book*):
   Had enough rabbits? I see there are more.
   In fact, it appears there are rabbits galore.

A BOY: Are they all wild ones or are they all tame?

A GIRL: How do you happen to know each one's name?

A BOY:
   Can you, instead, pull a dog or a cat
   Or maybe an *elephant* out of your hat?

WHIZZER:
   Goodness, the questions! Be patient a minute.
   My hat, as you noticed, has magic within it,
   But since I am not yet a full-grown magician,
   The things I pull out must fulfill *one condition:*
   I can't pull out someone by hook or by crook
   Unless he is written about *in a book!*

READER:
   Well, you can imagine how the Old Woman and her children
      gasped at that information,
   Because they hardly ever got around to read books—not
      even in vacation,
   And so they knew very little about books and all the magic
      that hovers
   On black and white sheets under yellow, and red, and green
      covers.
   That is the reason their eyebrows went up, and their chins
      went under
   And they stared and stared with their mouths wide open in
      wonder.
   And it was in that moment of quiet, when the air was as
      still as a feather

That the Old Woman was able to gather a few of her
thoughts together.

OLD WOMAN:

Wait, I think I have a plan!

May I speak to you, my man? (*She beckons to* WHIZZER.)

READER:

Then the Old Woman whispered something into the magician's right-hand ear,

Something to the effect that—if he could make all those
magical rabbits appear—

Why couldn't he pull some magical *people* out of his hat
as well?

Some who would entertain the children by the stories
they had to tell?

Then they would be quiet, and there would be peace in the
Shoe,

And then the Old Woman could think what to do, what
to do.

WHIZZER (*To* OLD WOMAN):

As long as folks are *in a book*

My magic works on them, but look,

(*Shows his little book*)

There are so *many* I can use

It will be hard to pick and choose.

I guess I'll close my eyes, and go

"Eeny, meeny, miney, mo."

(*He closes his eyes and finds a place in his book. Then he
moves over near the door and waves his wand over his hat.*)

Twinkle, twinkle, little hat—

Who's a girl to wonder at? (ALICE IN WONDERLAND *comes
running in, with something small in her hand. When
she sees the* OLD WOMAN, *she curtsies.*)

ALICE: My name is Alice, so please your Majesty. (*Looks at
what is in her hand.*) This little cake says EAT ME. Well,

I'll eat it, and if it makes me grow larger, I can reach the key; and if it makes me grow smaller, I can creep under the door; so either way I'll get into the garden.

A GIRL: Will you let me go along?

ALICE: Of course. Come on! (*Starts to exit and* GIRL *follows*) Dear, dear! How queer everything is today. And yesterday things went on just as usual. (*They exit.* NOTE: *If more than eight boys and girls have been used for the* OLD WOMAN'S CHILDREN, *more than one should exit with each book character, so that by the time the eight book characters have left the stage, all the* CHILDREN *are gone.*)

WHIZZER (*Making more magic, after finding another name in his book*):
Twinkle, twinkle, my chapeau—
Where's that scamp Pinocchio?
(PINOCCHIO *walks in stiffly, because he is made of wood.*)

PINOCCHIO: I may be made of wood, but I hope I'm not a blockhead. Jacket of wall paper, shoes of wood, hat of bread crumbs—that's me, Pinocchio. Oh, I'm a very unusual fellow. (*Looks at* CHILDREN) Who'd like to sit in the front row with me at the marionette show? You'll be surprised at what will happen—me, coming out with five gold pieces as a reward for valor!

A BOY: Let's go, Pinocchio. (*Exits with* PINOCCHIO)

WHIZZER (*Finding another name in his book and making magic*):
Twinkle, twinkle, who is this?
Hmmm . . . she looks a little Swiss.
(HEIDI *comes in.*)

HEIDI: Oh dear, I mustn't stay away from grandfather so long. I must go back to the fir trees and the goats. I must climb up to the rocks where the sun paints the mountains with his most beautiful colors before he goes to bed . . . so they won't forget him before morning.

A GIRL: Who are you?

HEIDI: I'm Heidi. Would you like to go to the mountains with me?

GIRL: Oh, yes. (*Goes out with* HEIDI)

WHIZZER (*Finding another name and going through his gestures*):
Twinkle, twinkle, little topper—
Where's that funny Mr. Popper?
(MR. POPPER *comes in.*)

MR. POPPER: Who'd like to take a look at the penguins? Popper's Performing Penguins! Seems a long time since I got those holes drilled in the refrigerator so Captain Cook . . . that was my first penguin . . . could live there. Now you ought to see them. You just ought to see them!

A BOY: *I'd* like to see them, Mr. Popper.

MR. POPPER: Come along, then. (*Exits with* BOY)

WHIZZER (*Going through the motions again*):
Twinkle, twinkle, hat to wear,
Halfway isn't *any*where—
Not the bottom, not the top . . .
Who's that coming hop, hop, hop?
(CHRISTOPHER ROBIN *hops in.*)

CHRISTOPHER ROBIN: Christopher Robin goes hoppity, hoppity. (*Stops hopping and begins to remember*) Silly old Bear, getting his head stuck in a honey jar so Piglet thought he was a Heffalump! Silly old Winnie-the-Pooh. Remember the time he went down the hole to call on Rabbit? He couldn't get out again—at least, not all of him could. Only his head and shoulders. Remember what happened?

A BOY: No. What?

CHRISTOPHER ROBIN: Come with me and I'll show you. (*Starts to hop out, followed by* BOY.) Nice, silly old Bear!

WHIZZER (*Making his magic again*):
Twinkle, twinkle, little bonnet,
With a wizard's magic on it,
Bring us from the windy sky

Mary Poppins—on the fly.

(MARY POPPINS *comes in hanging on to an open umbrella and a carpet bag.*)

MARY POPPINS (*Tossing her head*): Know there is a Red Cow out in the yard, looking for something? I think it was a mistake for the King to tell the Red Cow how to get that fallen star off her horn. Now she can't dance any more. (*Sniffs the air*) Humph, wind's right for adventures. Anybody want to come along and have tea on the ceiling with my uncle, Mr. Wigg?

A GIRL: I do! (*She hurries out after* MARY POPPINS.)

WHIZZER (*Making more magic*):

Twinkle, twinkle, little hat,

Now who's there to marvel at?

(ROBIN HOOD, *with bow and arrow, comes in with great gusto.*)

ROBIN HOOD: Who would like to speed a gray goose shaft from a longbow? Who would like to fool the Sheriff of Nottingham by going to the archery contest in disguise . . . and winning the golden arrow? Come along, then, to Sherwood Forest where my merry men are waiting. Come along with Robin Hood.

A BOY: I'm coming! (*Runs after* ROBIN HOOD *as he exits*)

WHIZZER (*Going through his gestures again*):

Twinkle, little hat, once more.

One more magic visitor!

(CINDERELLA *comes in.*)

CINDERELLA: My stepsisters used to make me sleep in the ashes on the hearth. That is why they called me Cinderella. Then, one night everyone went to the ball and left me home alone. Oh, how I wanted to go to the ball! But I had only an ugly old dress and heavy shoes. Then something happened—and I went to the ball in a gown of gold-colored cloth.

A GIRL: What happened?

CINDERELLA: Come with me and I'll tell you all about it. (GIRL *exits with* CINDERELLA. *All the* CHILDREN *have now left the stage, and the* OLD WOMAN *is alone with* WHIZZER. *The Shoe seems very quiet.*)

OLD WOMAN:

Well! I never knew such peace
Inside the Shoe, in every crease.
Now I'll think from A to Izzard.
Thank you, Whizzer. You're a wizard.
I only hope it's not too late
To keep that booby from my gate!

READER:

And so the Old Woman collected her thoughts in a hurry,
For now that the shoe had stopped pinching, she lost every worry.
And before you could say "Tra-la-la" like the birdies in spring,
She thought of a way to entertain the King, the King, the King!

OLD WOMAN:

With such a life as the King is leading
He can't have very much time for reading—
For every day is filled to the brim
With teas and parties to honor him.
So how can he meet, in his marble palace,
Georgie, and Winnie-the-Pooh, and Alice,
And Mary Poppins, and folks like that?

WHIZZER: He couldn't, Madam, I bet my hat. (*Taps his hat*)

OLD WOMAN:

So I have decided when my turn comes,
The King shan't sit and twiddle his thumbs,
Because my children and I will bring
Our book-friends over to visit the King,

And with their magical gifts and powers

They'll entertain all of the Court for *hours*.

WHIZZER:

That's an excellent thing to do.

Madam, I take off my hat to you.

(*He bows with a sweep of his hat, then exits.*)

READER:

And so the Old Woman began to dance and to sing "Toodle-oo, toodle-oo,"

Because she was no longer a woman who didn't know what to do.

OLD WOMAN (*Dancing*): Toodle-oo, toodle-oo.

READER (*As* CHILDREN *start coming in*):

And now, as we come to the end of this tale, it is fitting and proper

To say that the King was *so* pleased with the penguins and Mr. Popper,

And Christopher Robin, and Winnie, and Alice, and Heidi,

He wanted them all to remain—at least till next Thursday or Friday!

In fact, he thought *every* new book-friend worth more than a ruby,

Which means that the Old Woman *didn't* get given a booby.

Instead, as a special reward . . . for the red-letter day of the year,

The King had the high-uppy-ups of the Shoemakers' Union appear,

And told them to make the Old Woman a much bigger Shoe,

And to line the old one with bookshelves . . . so there would be *two*.

CHILDREN: Goody *two* shoes! Goody *two* shoes!

READER:

And so, with more room underfoot (without hanging from ceiling or rafter),

And with shelves full of magical books, and with hearts
   full of laughter,
The Old Woman lived with her children . . . happily . . .
   ever after!

THE END

Treasure Hunt

Characters

ALICE ⎱
DODO ⎬ *from "Alice in Wonderland"*
MOUSE ⎰

TOM SAWYER ⎱
HUCKLEBERRY FINN ⎰ *from "Tom Sawyer"*

MEG ⎫
JO ⎬
BETH ⎬ *from "Little Women"*
AMY ⎭

MICHAEL BANKS, *from "Mary Poppins"*
HEIDI
ROBIN HOOD
CHRISTOPHER ROBIN
FERDINAND
MISS BROOKS, *the teacher*
FIVE BOYS
FOUR GIRLS

SCENE 1

SETTING: *A sidewalk in front of the school, or a corridor where children pass back and forth.*
AT RISE: *The girls come in talking excitedly.*

1ST GIRL:

She says there's a treasure—a treasure to find.

2ND GIRL:

She says it is priceless, and more than one kind.

3RD GIRL:

Where is it, I wonder?

4TH GIRL:

Look up, and look under,

Look sideways, and frontwards, ahead and behind!

(*They all look around, baffled.*)

1ST GIRL:

I can't think what treasure Miss Brooks has in mind.

(*A group of boys, talking, come in from the other direction.*)

1ST BOY:

She says if we guess it, we all can take part

In a play for the school . . .

2ND BOY:

Let's hurry. Let's start.

3RD BOY:

She says it's a treasure

Too mighty to measure.

4TH BOY:

Can't *somebody* guess it? (*He notices one of the girls and nods at her.*)

　　　　　　　　　　　　Alberta, you're smart,

You surely must know all the treasures by heart.

ALBERTA (*One of the girls*):

Well, money's a treasure—like silver and gold,

And emeralds and rubies and pearls you can hold,

And bracelets and lockets,

And coins in your pockets,

And all kinds of valuable things that are sold,

And bonds are a treasure—or so I've been told.

1ST BOY:

Miss Brooks says this treasure is found everywhere.

1ST GIRL:

She says it is riches all people may share.

BOYS:

Look hither and thither. (*They look.*)

GIRLS:

We're all in a dither. (*They look.*)

2ND BOY:

I can't see a treasure, wherever I stare.

2ND GIRL:

And, goodness, there isn't a moment to spare!

(*Another boy,* NATHANIEL, *comes in hurriedly and eagerly. He calls to the others.*)

NATHANIEL:

Listen, I've thought what the treasure might be!

I've just had a hunch, and I hope you'll agree . . .

BOYS: Tell us, and hurry.

GIRLS: We're wasted with worry.

NATHANIEL: It seems like a pretty good treasure to me.

(*The children go into a huddle around* NATHANIEL. *There is much whispering and giggling.*)

ALL: Let's bring some to Teacher tomorrow, and see!

1ST GIRL: I'll bring her some slippers.

1ST BOY: I'll bring a dead cat.

2ND GIRL: I'll bring her some rolls that are crusty and fat.

2ND BOY: A bow and an arrow.

3RD BOY: A tail—long and narrow.

3RD GIRL: A thimble.

4TH BOY: A compass.

NATHANIEL: Some flowers for her hat.

ALL (*Merrily*): We'll make her guess *what* kind of treasure is that! (*Laughing and excited, the children exit.*)

*   *   *

SCENE 2

SETTING: *A classroom.*

AT RISE: *The children, dressed in costumes, are sitting in the classroom showing each other their "treasures."* MISS BROOKS *enters and the children are suddenly quiet and angelic.*

MISS BROOKS:
Good morning, my children.
CHILDREN:
Good morning, Miss Brooks.
MISS BROOKS:
You must have a secret . . .
I know by your looks.
CHILDREN:
We thought of the treasure!
MISS BROOKS:
You did? You don't say.
Well, if you are right
You may put on a play
And ask all the children
In school to attend.
CHILDREN:
And dress up in costume?
MISS BROOKS:
That all will depend.
Now, come, what's the treasure
Too mighty to measure
That gives us all pleasure?
(*A girl dressed like Alice in Wonderland gets up and goes to* MISS BROOKS. *Holds out a thimble*)
ALICE:
I brought you a thimble.
It's only a symbol

Of all kinds of treasure
That give people pleasure.

MISS BROOKS (*Baffled*):

A thimble? That's grand . . .
But I don't understand.
I may appear green,
But *what* does it mean?

(*Two boys representing* TOM SAWYER *and* HUCKLEBERRY
FINN *hurry up with the stuffed cat.*)

TOM:

We've brought a dead cat.

MISS BROOKS (*Horrified*):

W-w-what treasure is th-that?
Oh, take it away
This moment, I say!

(*The* BOYS *quickly hold the cat behind them. Four* GIRLS,
representing MEG, JO, AMY, *and* BETH *of "Little Women"*
come up and hold out a pair of slippers.)

JO:

A new pair of slippers.

MEG:

They haven't got zippers.

AMY:

They may not be stylish.

BETH:

But oh, they're worthwhilish.

MISS BROOKS:

Look, children, I'm baffled.
What treasures are these?
I fear you're in error.
Explain yourselves, please:
This isn't a matter
About which to tease.

MICHAEL BANKS (*Running up*):
　I've brought a fine compass.
HEIDI (*Coming up*):
　Some rolls for your lunch.
ROBIN HOOD:
　A long bow and arrow.
CHRISTOPHER ROBIN:
　A tail that is narrow.
FERDINAND:
　Some flowers in a bunch.
CHILDREN:
　The treasure is endless!
MISS BROOKS:
　But . . . what do you mean?
CHILDREN:
　We'll never be friendless.
MISS BROOKS (*Softly*):
　It's most unforeseen.
　(*Louder*)
　Now, children, I warn you,
　You've gone far enough.
　Just what is the meaning
　Of . . . all of this stuff?
ALICE (*Turning toward class for help*):
　Dodo, Mouse . . . be quick, be nimble.
　Help explain this treasured thimble.
　(DODO *and* MOUSE *stand up from among children in seats.
　The following scene is adapted from "Alice in Wonderland."*)
DODO:
　*Every*body has won, and all must have prizes.
CHILDREN:
　But who is to give the prizes?
DODO (*Pointing to* ALICE):
　Why, *she*, of course.

CHILDREN:

Prizes! Prizes!

(ALICE *searches in her pockets and pulls out a box of candies. She passes them around for prizes. There is just exactly one apiece, but none for* ALICE.)

MOUSE:

But she must have a prize herself, you know.

DODO: Of course. (*To* ALICE) What else have you got in your pocket?

ALICE:

Only a thimble.

DODO:

Hand it over here.

(ALICE *gives* DODO *the thimble, and* DODO *solemnly hands it back.*)

We beg your acceptance of this elegant thimble.

(ALICE *bows, and hands the thimble to* MISS BROOKS.)

MISS BROOKS (*Merrily*):

I think you have guessed, I think you have found
The key to the treasure that lies all around!
This thimble is part of the wealth we collect
From "Alice in Wonderland." Am I correct?

CHILDREN:

That is the answer.

MISS BROOKS (*Looking at the cat, drawing back*):

And now for the cat . . .

TOM:

Wait just a minute, we'll help you with that.

(*The following scene is taken from* "*Tom Sawyer.*")

Hello, Huckleberry.

HUCK: Hello yourself, and see how you like it.

TOM: What's that you got?

HUCK: Dead cat.

Tom: Lemme see him, Huck. My, he's pretty stiff. Where'd you get him?

Huck: Bought him off'n a boy.

Tom: What did you give?

Huck: I give a blue ticket and a bladder that I got at the slaughter-house.

Tom: Say—what is dead cats good for, Huck?

Huck: Good for? Cure warts with.

Miss Brooks:
Splendid. Splendid. That is treasure
From "Tom Sawyer." (*She eyes the cat.*) Doubtful pleasure!
Let me make just one more test
To be sure you've really guessed:
What about this pair of slippers
That, you say, do not have zippers?
(*The following scene is adapted from "Little Women."*)

Jo: Christmas won't be Christmas without presents.

Amy: It's dreadful to be so poor!

Meg: You know the reason Marmee proposed not having any presents this Christmas was because it's going to be a hard winter for everyone; she thinks we ought not to spend money for pleasure, when our men are suffering so in the army.

Jo: But I don't think the little we could spend would do any good. We've each got a dollar, and the army couldn't be much helped by our giving that . . . but I do want to buy a book for myself.

Beth: I planned to spend mine on new music.

Amy: I shall get a nice box of Faber's drawing pencils; I really need them.

Jo: Let's each buy what we want, and have a little fun; I'm sure we grub hard enough to earn it.

Beth: Marmee will be home soon. I've brought her slippers to warm.

Jo (*Looking sadly at the slippers*): Marmee must have a new pair.

BETH: I thought I'd get her some with my dollar.

AMY: No, I shall!

MEG: I'm the oldest . . .

Jo: I'm the man of the family now Papa is away, and I shall provide the slippers.

BETH: I'll tell you what we'll do. Let's each get her something for Christmas, and not get anything for ourselves.

MISS BROOKS:

That is treasure of the ages
Out of "Little Women's" pages!
(*She looks at the other "treasures."*)
Now, these other things . . . let's see . . .
Heidi saved these rolls for me.
(HEIDI *nods and smiles.*)
And this must be Eeyore's tail—
(CHRISTOPHER ROBIN *nods.*)
Let's return it without fail.

Can this compass be the one
That gave Michael so much fun
When Mary Poppins made it run?
(MICHAEL *nods.*)

And this long bow must belong
To Robin Hood . . . or am I wrong?

CHILDREN:

Right! You're right. And now the flowers.

MISS BROOKS (*Sniffing at them*):

Hmmmm. They have bewitching powers.
Let me take them in my hand.
Were they sniffed by . . . Ferdinand?

CHILDREN:

Yes! You guessed!

MISS BROOKS: And you guessed too.

You guessed the treasure, that is true,

But, tell me, children, how you *knew?*

1ST BOY:

We thought and thought and thought, Miss Brooks.

1ST GIRL:

We looked in all the cracks and nooks,

2ND BOY:

In chests, and drawers, and pocketbooks,

2ND GIRL:

And then, Nathaniel thought of *books!*

He said in books there is a treasure

More than anyone can measure,

Giving everybody pleasure.

MISS BROOKS:

Good! And now what do you say

To putting on a Book Week play

That's based upon some special stunt

Like . . . acting out a treasure hunt,

So boys and girls will ever after

Know the wealth of friends and laughter,

Fun, and joy, and daring deeds

In books that everybody reads.

CHILDREN:

Let's rehearse this very day.

Oh, hooray, hooray, hooray!

(*Children begin to march around the room singing gaily to the tune of "Oh, My Darling Clementine."*)

Cinderella, Toby Tyler,

Little Women, Ferdinand,

Rip Van Winkle, Thimbelina—

Treasure lies on every hand.

Refrain:
Who can measure all our pleasure
From the treasure that is found
In the pages—wealth of ages—
Of the books we have around!

Mary Poppins, Peter Rabbit,
Mr. Popper, Little Pear,
Polly Pepper, and Aladdin . . .
Treasured friends are everywhere.
(*Repeat refrain*)

Georgie, Winnie, Heidi, Bambi,
And the Cheshire Cat himself,
Uncle Remus, Long John Silver—
Treasure waits on every shelf.
(*Repeat refrain*)

THE END

Open Sesame!

BOY: You needn't buy a ticket
        on a bus-line or a train,
GIRL: You needn't ride a rocket
        or a steamer or a plane,
BOY: To go to famous highlands
        and peninsulas and islands
        and to jungle-lands and drylands
        or a cannibal's domain.
GIRL: You needn't pay a penny
        for a long and careful look,
GROUP: You only need,
            you only need,
                you only need A BOOK.

GIRL: You needn't own a panda
        and you needn't buy a gnu,
BOY: Or an elephant or monkey
        or a jumping kangaroo,
GIRL: To learn about a creature—
        every tooth and claw and feature
        and the tricks that you can teach her
        (or can teach *him*) how to do.
BOY: You needn't peek from bushes
        for a scientific look,

GROUP: You only need,
      you only need,
         you only need A BOOK.

BOY: And so it is with wonders
    in a test-tube and a vat,

GIRL: And astonishing adventures
    of a cowboy or a cat,

GIRL: And the customs and the rations
    of the folks of other nations,
    and their games and occupations,
    and their thoughts, and such as that.

GROUP: You needn't spend a lifetime
    trying to peer in every nook,
    you only need,
      you only need,
         you only need A BOOK!

Modern Magic

Aladdin had a magic ring
and magic lamp, indeed,
a little rub on each would bring
whatever he might need.
  But *I* have something just as grand
  to bring me wealth from every land:
  a card for books to read!

There have been magic bottles too,
which (when the corks are freed)
have sprites inside to make come true
each wish, with magic speed.
  But *I* have something just as fine:
  a card with space on every line
  for magic books to read!

And once there was a magic rug
much faster than a steed
which whisked its rider, nice and snug,
to any place agreed.
  But *I* have something that can swish
  me all the places that I wish:
  a card for books to read!

THANKSGIVING

Mother of Thanksgiving

(A play in radio style)

Note: Since all parts may be read before a mock microphone, lines need not be learned, and this play may be produced with few rehearsals.

Characters

NARRATOR
SOUND EFFECTS BOY
SARAH JOSEPHA HALE
DAVID HALE, *12*
HORATIO HALE, *10*
FRANCES ANN HALE, *8*
JOSEPHA HALE, *7*
WILLIAM HALE, *5*
AUNT HANNAH HALE
A WOMAN
LOUIS GODEY
MRS. LEWIS B. HUNTER, *Frances Ann grown up*
A SOUTHERN LADY
HER HUSBAND
CHARLES HUNTER
ABRAHAM LINCOLN

SETTING: *Since parts are read before a mock microphone, no settings are necessary. Characters should be near the microphone, stepping up when their turns come. At one side is a sound-effects table.*

NARRATOR: This is the story of the mother of Thanksgiving, a woman with vision, fighting a lone battle over the years. She fought with patience and persistence, and she won. And we give thanks to her.

This is the story of a woman who, in a way, became a link between two great presidents: George Washington and Honest Abe.

You've heard it asked a dozen times, no doubt: "But what can one man do to change the world, or even make a pinprick in its skin? One woman even less! The country's much too big for anyone, working alone, to make a dent in it."

You'd be surprised.

This is the tale of what one woman did over a stretch of years. And we give thanks to her.

Where shall we start?

Well, 1827 seems as good as any time. Our heroine was thirty-nine that year, five years a widow, with five children to support . . . three boys, two girls. They ranged in age from twelve down to five. It wasn't easy in those early days for mothers to support a family. There wasn't much a "lady" found to do, to earn a living. But our Mrs. Hale—Sarah Josepha Hale, that was her name—succeeded somehow. Heaven knows just how.

She tried to sew at first, after her lawyer husband passed away. She wasn't good at it. But all the while her fingers stitched, her mind wove thoughts. She put them down. Some poems she wrote were published in a book. And then she did a long, two-volume tale called *Northwood*. It wasn't published when this play begins . . . but will be soon.

So here we are, in 1827. Mid-November. Days are getting cold, with a New Hampshire wind. The town is Newport, inland from the sea. The time, late afternoon. (SOUND EFFECTS BOY *strikes gong five times*.) Thanksgiving's in the air. And all the Hales are home.

DAVID: Read us what you wrote in your book again, Mother —about the food.

HORATIO: The savory stuffing! The flavory stuffing!

FRANCES ANN: The pumpkin pie. (SOUND EFFECTS BOY *rustles pages of manuscript*.)

MRS. HALE: Again? (*As if reading*) "The roasted turkey took precedence . . . sending forth the rich odor of its savory stuffing . . .

HORATIO: Flavory, savory stuffing!

MRS. HALE: ". . . and pumpkin pie was an indispensable part of a good and true Yankee Thanksgiving."

JOSEPHA *and* WILLIAM: Thanksgiving, Thanksgiving!

DAVID: Will we be having a good and true Yankee Thanksgiving, mother?

MRS. HALE: Not this year, I am afraid, David. But the publishers plan to bring out my book next month, and if *Northwood* sells well . . . if it sells even half as well as they hope, we shall be eating roast turkey and pumpkin pie next November.

HORATIO: And don't forget the stuffing!
    I never get enough-ing
    of savory, flavory stuffing,
    and I am not a-bluffing.

MRS. HALE (*Laughing*): What a poet we have in the family, Horatio.

DAVID: When I grow up I'll always have a good and true Yankee Thanksgiving dinner and invite everybody!

MRS. HALE: Everybody, David?

DAVID: Well, everybody in Newport, New Hampshire. (*Hesitates*) At least, everybody on our street. (*Hesitates*) All the family, anyway. What was it like when father was alive, mother? Was our Thanksgiving good and true and Yankee?

MRS. HALE: Don't you remember? You were six years old, David, that last Thanksgiving we had together.

HORATIO: Then I must have been four.

MRS. HALE: Yes, and Frances Ann was two.

JOSEPHA: How old was I?

MRS. HALE: So little you couldn't even walk. And William wasn't born until months later. Oh, it seems a long time ago—such a long time ago. I remember how your father and I wished that *everyone* could be sitting down to such a festive dinner on the same day, all over the country. What a wonderful thing it would be, having Thanksgiving on the same day, in all the States.

DAVID: It would make a lot of noise, if everyone gave thanks at the same time, out loud!

HORATIO: But doesn't everyone give thanks on Thanksgiving, mother?

MRS. HALE: Yes, of course, Horatio. Only Thanksgiving comes at different times in different places. Just once in all these years has it come on the same day for everyone in the United States. Do you know when that was, David?

DAVID: Yes. In 1789. When President Washington proclaimed the last Thursday in November as Thanksgiving. I know part of his speech—shall I recite it?

HORATIO: If you do I'll make up some more poetry, and I can talk louder than you can.

MRS. HALE: Come, come.

FRANCES ANN: Why *isn't* Thanksgiving on the same day? Isn't it always on Thanksgiving Day?

MRS. HALE: David?

DAVID: It's always on Thanksgiving Day, but Thanksgiving Day is different in some places . . . because of the cows.

FRANCES ANN: What cows?

DAVID: Well, some of the towns want to keep Thanksgiving on the first Thursday . . . is it after, or before, mother?

MRS. HALE: After.

DAVID: On the first Thursday after they drive the cows home from summer pasture. And if it's an early winter that's sooner, and if it's a late winter, it's later.

MRS. HALE: And no one knows just when it will be, late or soon. Your father and I used to wish there could be the same Thanksgiving for everyone. I wrote about it in *Northwood*. (SOUND EFFECTS BOY *turns pages*.) Yes, here it is. (*As if reading*) "We have too few holidays. Thanksgiving like the Fourth of July should be considered a national festival and observed by all our people."

HORATIO: I think so, too. We don't have nearly enough holidays. Holidays . . . loll-idays . . . always capital-idays!

JOSEPHA *and* WILLIAM: Holidays, holidays.

MRS. HALE (*Slowly*): I think . . . I think it would be a good thing to work for. A national Thanksgiving. Everyone giving thanks on the same day. A union of hearts and minds . . . as well as a union of States.

NARRATOR: Two months go by. It's January now, of 1828. A Boston firm brought out the book last month—*Northwood*, by Sarah Josepha Hale. It's selling well. There's even talk of printing it abroad.

This bitter afternoon Aunt Hannah Hale, the author's sister-in-law, has come to call. That's Frances Ann who's skipping to the door. (SOUND EFFECTS BOY *makes sound of skipping*.)

FRANCES ANN: Aunt Hannah, oh, Aunt Hannah. Have you come to see?

AUNT HANNAH: See what, child? (SOUND EFFECTS BOY

makes sound of door closing.) Mercy, but it's cold. When the snow creaks and cracks underfoot so early in the afternoon, you may be sure it's cold. The sun's like a little green persimmon, I do declare. Have I come to see what, Frances Ann?

FRANCES ANN: The letters mother's getting. About the book.

AUNT HANNAH: Already? Oh, I'm glad. Then it's a success, a real success. And a first novel, too. Where is your mother, child?

FRANCES ANN: She's working, at her desk. But I'll tell her you're here. She's expecting you. Oh, Aunt Hannah, there's one letter 'specially . . . that came yesterday.

AUNT HANNAH: 'Specially? What do you mean, Frances Ann?

FRANCES ANN: It's a secret. I heard mother telling David he mustn't breathe a word about it until everything was decided.

AUNT HANNAH: Then I must see your mother at once. I love secrets!

MRS. HALE (*Calling*): Is that you, Hannah?

AUNT HANNAH: Yes, Sarah. I'm coming. Hang up my wraps, will you, Frances Ann? That's a good girl. (SOUND EFFECTS BOY *makes sound of steps, door opening and closing.*)

MRS. HALE: I'm so glad you could come. Did David tell you it was important? Were you able to find someone to tend the shop?

AUNT SARAH: Mrs. Philton could come in for the afternoon. Now, tell me, Sarah, what is it?

MRS. HALE: This letter. From a publishing firm in Boston. Read it.

AUNT HANNAH (*Between pauses*): Hmmmm. Proposing to establish a magazine for *ladies*. Hmmmm. Offering you the editorship. But, Sarah, you don't know anything about being an editor.

MRS. HALE: Not a thing. Only I'm sure I'd be better at it

than I was at millinery. I couldn't be worse! You were very patient with me at the shop, Hannah.

AUNT HANNAH: A lady editor. It's unheard of. And a lady's magazine!

MRS. HALE: There has to be a first for everything, you know. I find the proposal a little frightening, Hannah, but very, *very* appealing. I . . . I think I shall accept, if you are not too strongly opposed. I treasure your good judgment.

AUNT HANNAH: It would mean leaving Newport? Leaving your friends and relatives? Moving to Boston?

MRS. HALE: Yes.

AUNT HANNAH: It would mean being definitely on your own, in a strange place, in a strange new position, with your family to care for?

MRS. HALE: Yes.

AUNT HANNAH: Dear Sarah, I shall miss you and the children. More than I can tell, I shall miss you. But Boston is not too far away . . .

MRS. HALE: Oh, Hannah, then you think I should? A lady editor . . . doesn't it sound exciting! Thank you, thank you. Be assured, Hannah, I shall go to the task with much more confidence and hope of success than . . . than if I were helping you trim hats. (*They laugh.*)

NARRATOR: So Sarah Hale became an editor. *The Ladies' Magazine* was soon in press, was soon a black and white reality. The introduction said:

A WOMAN (*As if reading*): "The work will be national . . . American . . . a miscellany which, although devoted to general literature, is more expressly designed to mark the progress of female improvement . . ."

NARRATOR: For nine successful years the Lady Editor held forth, making *The Ladies' Magazine* a living thing, part of America. She liked her Boston home. But then a better opening came her way from Philadelphia, from Louis Godey, "prince of publishers," proprietor of *Godey's Lady's Book*. He wanted Mrs. Hale as editor. Triumphantly in 1836 he achieved this. These are his words:

LOUIS GODEY: "The present number of the *Lady's Book* closes our career as sole editor. The increasing patronage of the work requires more of our attention to the business department. We are confident our readers will not regret this change, when they learn that Mrs. Sarah Josepha Hale, now editor of the American *Ladies' Magazine*, will superintend the Literary Department of the Book. Mrs. Hale is too well known to the public to need eulogy from us . . ."

NARRATOR: So *Godey's Lady's Book* it was, for Mrs. Hale.

Let's jump ahead across the busy years, to 1845, in Philadelphia, the home of *Godey's Lady's Book* and Mrs. Hale. Thanksgiving time again, on Locust Street—where Frances Ann resides. She's Mrs. Lewis B. Hunter now, a doctor's wife, and married just a year.

Our editor is 57 years—not old, but *young*. She's done a lot for women and their rights, and still has much to do. Thanksgiving, now. That still is on her mind. She must begin in earnest on her plan to make Thanksgiving national. Yes, soon . . . Her daughter Frances interrupts her thoughts:

MRS. HUNTER: I wish the rest of them could be here for Thanksgiving, mother.

MRS. HALE: I wish it too. Some day we may all be together again . . . (*She chokes a little.*) . . . all except David.

MRS. HUNTER: Dear David. I still shudder to think of him being sick so far away from home, and alone. He had so much ahead to live for.

MRS. HALE: My world has been dark and desolate without him.

MRS. HUNTER: I know. But, mother, you have the rest of us . . . such as we are. I wish Josepha could be here today.

Why, oh why, did she have to go way off to Georgia to teach?

MRS. HALE: Because she loves it. Josepha is a born teacher. (*Brightening*) Do you know she writes that she wants to start a school of her own some day, here in Philadelphia?

MRS. HUNTER: Yes. She even has a name for it: Boarding and Day School for Young Ladies. She'll do it, too. (*Pause*) I tried to get Horatio to come for Thanksgiving, mother. But he's so far away, and so engrossed in his Indians.

MRS. HALE: What he is doing is very important, and I'm proud of him. Too little has been recorded about the languages and dialects of our North American Indians.

MRS. HUNTER: Well, for so young a man Horatio has certainly made himself a reputation.

MRS. HALE: He has a natural gift for languages. And I used to think he might be a poet!

MRS. HUNTER: Remember the rhymes he used to make up? That one about the stuffing . . .

MRS. HALE (*Laughing*): "I never get enough-ing

　　　　　　　　of flavory, savory stuffing." (*Sobering*)

Thanksgiving! It's still my hope to see it a national holiday, Frances Ann—one day, the same day, for everyone in the United States. In fact, I am seriously starting a great campaign next year . . . and I shan't give up until I win, no matter how many years it takes.

MRS. HUNTER: What kind of campaign, mother?

MRS. HALE: A campaign of letters. And editorials in *Godey's*. But mostly letters . . . to influential men, to governors, to Presidents. I shall write them myself. Never will there be such a campaign of letters!

MRS. HUNTER: Oh, mother, as if you haven't your hands full already. But don't think about it today! I have a surprise, a Thanksgiving surprise for you. Guess what.

MRS. HALE: I never have been good at guessing.

MRS. HUNTER: William's coming! I couldn't wait another minute to tell you.

MRS. HALE: William? From Virginia . . . just for Thanksgiving?

MRS. HUNTER: It's a sort of celebration for him . . . for passing the bar examination.

MRS. HALE: Oh, I'll be glad to see him. Especially since he talks of going farther south next year. To Texas, of all places! I am afraid when William gets as far away as Texas, we shan't see him again for many Thanksgivings.

MRS. HUNTER: Isn't it good, mother dear, we have such an enthusiastic letter-writer in the family!

NARRATOR: The campaign of letters began, in 1846.

Year after year the editor of *Godey's Lady's Book* wrote to the powers-that-be to make Thanksgiving national. A great crusade! One woman all alone!

MRS. HALE (*Slowly, as if writing*): "Let us join in establishing Washington's choice, the last Thursday in November, as a universal holiday." (SOUND EFFECTS BOY *makes sound of sealing and stamping letters.*)

MRS. HALE (*As if writing*): "Thanksgiving Day has a value beyond all expression. It reunites families and friends. It awakens kindly and generous sentiments. It promotes peace and good will among our mixed population. . . . Thanksgiving like the Fourth of July should be considered a national festival."

NARRATOR: Letters, letters, letters. Stacks of them. All neatly penned and sealed. Year after year, year after year again. Letters to congressmen and governors. Letters to presidents—Polk . . . Taylor . . . Fillmore . . . Pierce . . . Buchanan. And finally to Lincoln.

And editorials, too, in *Godey's Lady's Book*. In 1852 she wrote this news:

MRS. HALE: "Last year twenty-nine states and all territories united in the festival. This year we trust that Virginia and Vermont will come into this arrangement and that the Governors of each and all the states will appoint Thursday, the 25th of November, as the Day of Thanksgiving. Twenty-three millions of people sitting down, as it were, together to a feast of joy and thankfulness . . ."

NARRATOR: Year after year, tireless, confident, and firm, she sent the letters out.

In 1859 with war clouds gathering, threatening to crash and break from North to South, she wrote an editorial full of hope. How many women read it (yes, and husbands, too) it's hard to say. A couple of hundred thousand, probably. The words were stirring ones, the editorial's name—"Our Thanksgiving Union."

Wait, here's a southern lady with it now:

SOUTHERN LADY: Tell me what you think of this, George. In *Godey's*, dear. You always know so much about such things, and your poor wife simply never, never can make up her mind without you. Read it, George.

HER HUSBAND: What? Oh, that. "Our Thanksgiving Union." (*Begins to mumble as he reads*) "Seventy years ago . . ." (*Mumble, mumble, mumble.*)

SOUTHERN LADY: Out loud, George. So I can hear . . .

HER HUSBAND (*Clearing his throat, getting oratorical*): "The flag of our country now numbers thirty-two stars on its crown of blue—God save the United States! He has saved, enlarged, blessed and prospered us beyond any people on this globe. If every state would join in Union Thanksgiving on the 24th of this month, would it not be a renewed pledge of love and loyalty to the Constitution of the United States which guarantees peace, prosperity, progress and perpetuity to our great Republic?"

SOUTHERN LADY: Would it not, George?

HER HUSBAND: What?

SOUTHERN LADY: Would it not be as Mrs. Hale says?

HER HUSBAND: Er . . . how's that?

SOUTHERN LADY: Would not Union Thanksgiving be a renewed pledge of love and loyalty to the Constitution of the United States?

HER HUSBAND: Oh, that. Not at all. Not at all! Union Thanksgiving, indeed. What's Thanksgiving got to do with the slavery issue?

SOUTHERN LADY: Quite a great deal, I should think, George.

HER HUSBAND: You should think! Have you not agreed, Millicent, to leave all the thinking to me?

NARRATOR: Letters, letters, letters. Editorials. Pleas. And then came civil war. In 1861 our Lady Editor was urging a Thanksgiving Day of Peace. Lincoln was President. Her Peace Day failed.

She tried again in 1862. A national Thanksgiving! Still no luck. In 1863 she tried again.

Success . . . yet not success!

How's that, you ask?

Let's stop and see. It's summer, 1863, in Philadelphia. A warm July. Our Mrs. Hale is just about three quarters of a century old, but going strong. Still editor of *Godey's*, still alert, still full of eager plans. She's living with her daughter Frances Ann on Locust Street, and there are grandchildren—admiring ones.

After a busy working day, her grandson, Charles, waylays her in the drawing room:

CHARLES (*Eagerly*): You've seen the paper, grandmother?

MRS. HALE: No, not yet. What is it, Charles?

CHARLES: You've probably been expecting it.

MRS. HALE: Expecting what? Come, Charles, don't tease.

CHARLES: Get ready to give us a song and dance, grandmother. Look! And on the front page, too. Only there ought to be a credit line somewhere . . . to Sarah Josepha Hale. (SOUND EFFECTS BOY *rattles newspaper*.)

MRS. HALE: What *are* you talking about, Charles?

CHARLES: Listen to this: "Proclamation for Thanksgiving, July 15, 1863, by the President of the United States of America."

MRS. HALE: At last! And by the President. I've waited years for this, Charles. Ever since 1827, when *Northwood* was published, you know. That's . . . goodness me, 36 years ago! At last—a Presidential proclamation for a national Thanksgiving. It hasn't happened since 1789. Washington to Lincoln—a long gap, Charles. I only hope the gap is closed now, forever. What does the proclamation say?

CHARLES: "It has pleased Almighty God to hearken to the supplications and prayers of an afflicted people . . ." Well, it goes on like that for quite a while.

MRS. HALE (*Eagerly*): Skip down to the "Now, therefore," and we'll go back later.

CHARLES (*After some mumbling*): "Now, therefore, be it known that I do set apart Thursday, the 6th day of August next, to be observed as a day for national thanksgiving . . ."

MRS. HALE Wait. Did I hear you correctly? The sixth day of *August?*

CHARLES: That's what it says.

MRS. HALE: Thanksgiving in August! Who ever heard of such a thing? Oh, Charles, after all my work for a national Thanksgiving . . . to have it proclaimed for August. August! It should be November—the last Thursday in November President Washington's choice.

CHARLES: Why, you're right, grandmother. You're not through crusading yet, are you?

MRS. HALE: I shall call on President Lincoln myself. I shall bring a copy of President Washington's proclamation. I shall plead the case for a national Thanksgiving on the last Thursday in November.

CHARLES: And you'll win. I'll bet my last penny on that. You'll win!

NARRATOR: And win she did. The very next year, too.

In 1864, when civil war was like a dripping knife cutting the States apart, Lincoln, the President, proclaimed Thanksgiving Day. He pointed out that though the war was cruel within the States, full peace with other nations was preserved, order maintained, and federal laws obeyed. And for these gifts the President gave thanks.

LINCOLN: "They are the gracious gifts of the Most High God. . . . It has seemed to me fit and proper that they should be solemnly, reverently, and gratefully acknowledged as with one heart and one voice by the whole American people. I do, therefore, invite my fellow citizens . . . to observe the last Thursday of November next as a day of Thanksgiving and praise."

NARRATOR: The gap was bridged, between two Presidents. Washington's Thanksgiving was proclaimed again—by Lincoln, now. And every year since then it has been national, a holiday in all the many states.

Sarah Josepha Hale, mother of Thanksgiving, could sit back at last. All those letters, and those worn-out pens! (SOUND EFFECTS BOY *scratches pens on paper*.)

NARRATOR: All those stamps, and seals of colored wax! (SOUND EFFECTS BOY *makes sound of stamping letters and seals*.)

NARRATOR· All those words, those earnest paragraphs!

She could sit back . . . but did she? Not at all. She still was much too young to stop and rest. She checked Thanksgiving off, but there was still a list, a bulging list, of things to do. And, after all, she wasn't 80 yet!

For many years—she died at 91—she had her good and true

Thanksgiving holiday. She smiled to think that everyone in every single State, on that same day, was giving thanks as well. Thanksgiving in November—everywhere!

ALL: All hail to Mrs. Hale, mother of Thanksgiving.

She fought the long hard fight all by herself, and won.

Who'll say it now, "But what can one man do? One woman even less!"

One vision and one spirit can achieve a miracle.

Mother of Thanksgiving, we lay thanks like oak leaves at your feet . . . like acorns, bittersweet, and purple grapes . . . pumpkins, sheaves of grain, and yellow corn . . . all the symbols of the harvest time. For you have harvested a national Thanksgiving. We give thanks!

THE END

Unexpected Guests

Characters

GOVERNOR BRADFORD
MILES STANDISH
MISTRESS BREWSTER
MISTRESS WINSLOW
PRISCILLA
REMEMBER
MARY
DESIRE
WILLIAM
THREE OTHER BOYS

PROLOGUE

TIME: *Morning of the first Thanksgiving, late fall, 1621.*
SETTING: *In front of the curtain.*
AT RISE: GOVERNOR BRADFORD *and* MILES STANDISH *walk in, talking to each other. They cross slowly in front of the curtain.*

GOV. BRADFORD: We have had our trials in this new land, Captain Standish. Our hardships. Our sorrows. But how much we have to be thankful for!
MILES STANDISH: Aye, Governor Bradford.

GOV. BRADFORD: Nowhere in England could we have grown such a crop of corn on twenty acres.

MILES STANDISH: That is true. And such barley! (*Sniffs the air*) I smell barley loaves baking this very minute. Ah, and pigeon pasty, too, I do believe.

GOV. BRADFORD: 'Tis a busy day today in Plymouth town. Think you Chief Massasoit and some of his braves will heed our invitation to join in the feast of thanksgiving?

MILES STANDISH: Aye, a few will come, I believe, Governor. The Indians have been very friendly.

GOV. BRADFORD: Another thing to be thankful for. Our cup is indeed full. (*As they exit*) Shall we see if the tables are properly set up under the trees, and the meat-spits ready?

* * *

SCENE 1

SETTING: *Kitchen-living room of one of the Pilgrim houses.*

AT RISE: MISTRESS BREWSTER *is working at one of the tables where food for the feast is being prepared. In a moment MISTRESS WINSLOW hurries in, takes off cape, adjusts apron.*

MISTRESS WINSLOW: Good day, Mistress Brewster.

MISTRESS BREWSTER: Good morning to you.
   And, oh, Mistress Winslow,
   There's *still* much to do.
   As sure as I'm living
   This feast of Thanksgiving
   Takes planning and hustling
   And labor . . .

MISTRESS WINSLOW: How true! (*She consults list on wall.*)
   Let's see what is finished.
   The pies are all made,
   Both pumpkin and berry.

The tables are laid? (*Glances out window to see*)
The loaves are a-baking
Next door, no mistaking. (*Sniffs, turns back to list*)
The turkeys need stuffing,
And soon, I'm afraid.
(PRISCILLA, REMEMBER, MARY, *and* DESIRE *hurry in to help.*)
GIRLS: Good morning, good morning.
  Thanksgiving is here!
MISTRESS BREWSTER: The busiest morning,
  For us, of the year.
  Remember and Mary,
  Grind corn and don't tarry.
  Priscilla, shell beechnuts
  For stuffing, my dear.
PRISCILLA: The boys were to help us.
  They're always so slow! (*Looks around*)
  The woodpile has vanished.
  The water is low.
  That William—where is he?
  (WILLIAM *and three other boys hurry in.*)
BOYS (*Cheerfully*): Good morning.
PRISCILLA: Get busy,
  There's company coming
  For dinner, you know.
  (MISTRESS BREWSTER *gives empty buckets to one boy, indicates the other two should get wood. She puts* WILLIAM *to work helping* PRISCILLA *husk beechnuts.*)
MISTRESS BREWSTER: Desire, start taking
  The platters outside—
  The fruits we have gathered
  And carefully dried,
  The grapes and the cherries,
  The nuts and the berries . . . (DESIRE *goes in and out.*)

WILLIAM (*Hungrily*): I'm thankful the platters
Are big ones and wide!

MISTRESS WINSLOW: We all can be thankful
This bright autumn morn—

PRISCILLA: For Squanto—who taught us
The way to plant corn.

REMEMBER: For rain and for weather
And crops . . .

MARY: Being together!

MISTRESS BREWSTER: For finding a homeland
Where faith is reborn.
(*They all work busily. Suddenly* WILLIAM, *looking over the
food supply, gets worried.*)

WILLIAM: I say, Mistress Brewster,
Would we be prepared
To feed twenty Indians?

MISTRESS BREWSTER: Our feast may be shared
With ten or with twenty,
And there will be plenty.

WILLIAM: But what if there're *thirty?*

MISTRESS BREWSTER: I think we'll be spared.
Miles Standish thinks maybe
A dozen might come.

MISTRESS WINSLOW: We Pilgrims are fifty.
That makes quite a lot. (*Looks over food*)
But surely there's ample
For more than a sample
Of dozens of good things . . . (*Turns to* WILLIAM)
Just look in the pot.
(BOYS *come back with wood and water.* MISTRESS BREWSTER
*puts one in charge of fire, has another stir a bowl of batter,
sets the third to shucking dry peas.*)

1ST BOY: It keeps us all hopping,
This having a feast.

2ND BOY (*Hungrily, eyeing goodies*): My mouth starts to water.

3RD BOY: Mine never has ceased! (MILES STANDISH *hurries in, looks around anxiously.*)

MILES STANDISH: These lads—are they needed?
    Two boys must be speeded
    To gather more clams
    From the cove to the east.
    (*All the boys are eager to go.*)

MISTRESS BREWSTER: Two lads, Captain Standish?
    Well, if it seems fit . . .

MILES STANDISH: Two others should handle
    The meat-turning spit
    And keep the fires going
    So coals will be glowing
    For roasting the oysters.

MISTRESS BREWSTER: Grave tasks, I admit. (MISTRESS BREWSTER *nods to boys, dismissing them. They hurry out with* MILES STANDISH. MISTRESS WINSLOW *checks the list again.*)

MISTRESS WINSLOW: The wild geese and turkeys
    Are ready to stuff.
    The stuffing, Priscilla?

PRISCILLA: Will this be enough?

MISTRESS WINSLOW: Perhaps, but I doubt it.

PRISCILLA: Well, *I'll* go without it.

MISTRESS BREWSTER (*Nervously*): I'm hoping these dumplings won't sink and be tough. (*All work busily. In a few minutes the sound of shouting is heard offstage. The women and girls are startled.*)

GIRLS: What's that? Someone's shouting.

WOMEN: How lusty and loud!

GIRLS: It may be the Indians.
    It sounds like a crowd.
    (WILLIAM *rushes in excitedly.*)

WILLIAM: Our guests are arriving! (*He keeps looking out the door, turning back to report as more and more Indians arrive.*)
  The Indians! I'm striving
  To count. At least thirty
  Brave warriors and proud . . .
  Now forty . . . now fifty . . .
  Now *sixty* . . .

MISTRESS BREWSTER (*Unbelieving*): Don't joke!

WILLIAM: Now seventy crowding
  There under the oak.
  And still they keep coming!

MISTRESS BREWSTER: My poor ears are humming.

MISTRESS WINSLOW: How can we, how *can* we
  Feed so many folk?

WILLIAM: Eighty. No, *ninety!*
  Chief Massasoit too.

MISTRESS BREWSTER: We figured a dozen . . .
  Oh, what shall we do?

MISTRESS WINSLOW: For all our preparing,
  The food we'll be sharing
  Will scarcely be ample
  To last the day through.

DESIRE: And they were invited
  To stay for *three days*.

MISTRESS BREWSTER: My head's in a turmoil.

MISTRESS WINSLOW: My mind's in a haze.

GIRLS: We're all in a dither—
  From whence and from whither
  Shall we get more turkeys,
  More meat, and more maize?

WILLIAM (*Excitedly, from post at door*): There's Governor
  Bradford. He's coming.

MISTRESS BREWSTER: Poor man,
  He's probably worried.

Let's smile . . . if we can.

Gov. Bradford (*Hurrying in*):
Dear ladies, I wonder,
Would it be a blunder
To ask you a favor,
A slight change of plan?
The Indians are eager
To help and to share:
They want to bring deer-meat '
To add to our fare.
But after your labors
To feed our good neighbors
I felt I should ask you,
Dear friends, if you'd *care?*
They'll handle the roasting.
It might be a treat . . .
Unless you prefer
Our own foodstuffs to eat.

Girls (*Gaily*): With deer-meat aplenty
We'll feed eight times twenty!

Women (*Graciously*): Indeed, it will make our
Thanksgiving complete.

(Governor Bradford *nods, and goes out.*)

Girls (*Amused*): He asked if we minded!
These innocent men . . .

Women (*Amused*): You'd think we had *counted*
On ninety, not ten.

All: But now, as we're living,
We'll have a thanksgiving
To speak of with pleasure
Again and again . . .
A feast-day we'll treasure
Again and again!

THE END

Company Coming

MOTHER: Susan, have you put the salt
and pepper on the table?
Peter, find the pickle jar
with "Mustard" on the label.
Linda, is the lettuce washed?
Hurry, if you're able!

LINDA: Oh, what a jolly Thanksgiving Day.
Who cares if the weather outside is gray?
Everyone's busy and everyone's gay . . .
with company, company on the way.

MOTHER: Peter, put the place-cards on.
Don't you go forgetting.
Linda, send your father here—
carving knives need whetting.
Susan, have we finished now
with the table-setting?

SUSAN: The oven is sizzling a merry tune,
and savory tastes fill every spoon.
The clock on the cupboard says half-past noon . .
with company, company coming soon!

MOTHER: Linda, fill the glasses, dear.
Make the sideboard neater.
Susan, taste the pudding sauce—
shall we make it sweeter?
Would you like to take a peek
at the turkey, Peter?

PETER: Oh, what a wonderful time of year.
The cranberry jelly is firm and clear,
and everyone's busy and full of cheer . . .
with company . . .

MOTHER: Listen. The bell!

ALL: THEY'RE HERE!

Thanksgiving Everywhere

BOY: Oh, the sizzles in the kitchen!
          Close your eyes and take a sniff.
          Don't they set your nose to twitchin'?
          Did you get a proper sniff?
GIRL: And the spices in the dressing!
          And the fragrance in the air.
BOY: And the pie! No need for guessing:
          it's Thanksgiving, everywhere.
GIRLS: It's Thanksgiving,
BOYS: It's Thanksgiving,
ALL: It's Thanksgiving, everywhere.

GIRL: Oh, the oak leaves in the vases,
          and the dishes—Mother's best!
BOY: And the seven extra places,
          one for each invited guest.
GIRL: And the acorns down the middle
          of the table! I declare
          it's a day without a riddle:
          it's Thanksgiving, everywhere.
BOYS: It's Thanksgiving,
GIRLS: It's Thanksgiving,
ALL: It's Thanksgiving, everywhere.

GIRL: Oh, the merry, merry voices!

BOY: Glad to see you! How you've grown!

GIRL: Here's a day each heart rejoices
with a gladness all its own.

BOY: Out the window it is snowing—
there's November in the air.

GIRL: And indoors each face is glowing
with Thanksgiving, everywhere,

ALL: With Thanksgiving,
With Thanksgiving,
With Thanksgiving . . . everywhere!

A Thankful Heart

Grandma said that turkey,
cranberries, and pie
sometimes have a bitter taste,
and I asked her why.

Grandma said, "A banquet
fitting for a king,
eaten with a thankless heart,
isn't anything.

"And, you know," said Grandma,
"even what-is-least,
eaten with a thankful heart,
can be quite a feast."

Thanksgiving

You do not have
to use your eyes,

There is no "but" or "if":

Turkey roasting,
pumpkin pies—

You only have to SNIFF.

CHRISTMAS

Angel in the Looking-Glass

Characters

MISS PINSTER, *a dressmaker*
LUCY, *a young girl*
JIM YOUNG ⎫
ALICE YOUNG ⎭ *a married couple*
AUNT MARTHA, *a stern old lady*
CHARLES ⎫
RALPH ⎭ *her young nephews*
ZORLOVA, *a dancer*

TIME: *A week before Christmas.*

BEFORE THE CURTAIN: MISS PINSTER *is fitting* LUCY'S *angel costume. There is much pinning and adjusting as the two talk.
From time to time* LUCY *looks at herself in a large full-length
mirror placed at one end of the stage.*

LUCY: Are you sure I'll look like a real angel when you get
my costume finished, Miss Pinster?

MISS PINSTER: Yes, of course. Now hold still while I fix this
wing. I had to use cardboard underneath, you know, to
stiffen it.

LUCY: Do they look like real wings?

MISS PINSTER: Quite real, I think.

154

LUCY: I wish I could fly with them. I wish I could fly and fly
—way up above the town.

MISS PINSTER: Oh, that would be expecting too much. If I
could make wings that could fly, I shouldn't have to be a
dressmaker, you know.

LUCY: What would you be, Miss Pinster?

MISS PINSTER: Goodness, I have never given it a thought.
(*She stands dreamily for a moment with pins and tape measure
in hand.*) Oh, I think I should like to have a little shop and
sell hand-painted cups and things like that.

LUCY: And red-and-white-striped candy?

MISS PINSTER: Perhaps. Perhaps I could have a little glass
case of candy, too. (*She suddenly comes down to earth again.*)
But now, my dear, we must see how the halo fits. (MISS
PINSTER *picks up the halo.*)

LUCY: Oh, what a beautiful halo! It looks like a real one, all
gold and shiny.

MISS PINSTER: I am rather pleased with it myself. I just happened to have some gilt paint on hand, left over from the
time I touched-up the radiators. (*She adjusts the halo,
stands back and nods.*) You look more and more like an
angel, Lucy.

LUCY: Do I? (*Then hesitantly*) But . . . I don't always *feel*
like one, Miss Pinster. Do you think it's mean of a person
to buy another person a Christmas present and then not
want to give it away because it's so nice. I mean . . . I
know a girl who saved her money to buy her brother a set
of pencils with colored leads—twenty different colors in
all—and now . . . she wants to keep them for herself.

MISS PINSTER: Well, I wouldn't say she had much of the
Christmas spirit, would you? Now, let's see about the
sleeves, Lucy. Are they long enough under the wings?

LUCY: But wouldn't it be all right if she gave her brother

something else . . . that was cheaper? Oh, you can't imagine what beautiful pencils they are.

MISS PINSTER (*Intent on her work*): Yes, I think the sleeves are all right. My, I haven't made an angel costume in years! (*There is a moment or two of silence, as* MISS PINSTER *stands off and looks at the costume.*)

LUCY (*Slowly, thoughtfully*): Do you think if anyone saw me . . . walking down the hall of this apartment building, maybe . . . they would think I *was* an angel?

MISS PINSTER: They might! The effect is very good, I think.

LUCY: Would it make any difference to them if they *did* take me for an angel, Miss Pinster?

MISS PINSTER: Difference? What do you mean by that?

LUCY: I mean, would it make any difference in the way people acted? I think *I* would act different, if I saw an angel . . . maybe.

MISS PINSTER: Perhaps we all would. But, of course, we shall never really know, shall we? Not on this earth, at least. Now turn to the side a little, Lucy. I don't believe the hem-line is quite straight. No, it isn't.

LUCY: Do many people live in this apartment building, Miss Pinster?

MISS PINSTER: Oh, yes, quite a few. There are twelve apartments in addition to the janitor's. Hold still, now. I must pin up this side a little.

LUCY: Are they nice people?

MISS PINSTER: Yes, I think so—as nice as most people are. I have so little time to talk to them, of course. (*She pins at the hem, then stands back to see if it is straight.*)

LUCY: Are you coming to see our Christmas play, Miss Pinster? It's going to be Friday night, in the school auditorium, and it's free.

MISS PINSTER: Oh, I should like to come. Then I could see how the costume looks from the audience.

LUCY: I'm the only angel who speaks a part. The others just sing. I sing too, part of the time. Would you like me to recite my part for you?

MISS PINSTER: Yes, if you wish. Only you must turn around slowly, slowly, so I can be sure to get the hem right.

LUCY (*Turning very slowly*): Well, you see, the three shepherds are there on the stage, wondering about the star. It's not a *real* star on the stage, you know, but it looks like one. Then we angels come in singing. The shepherds are frightened, and they draw away. You know, they don't expect to see angels in the middle of the night. So then I say to them: "Fear not: for, behold, I bring you tidings of great joy, which shall be to all people. For unto you is born this day in the city of David a Saviour, which is Christ the Lord. And this shall be a sign unto you . . ."

MISS PINSTER (*Softly*): "Ye shall find the babe wrapped in swaddling clothes, lying in the manger."

LUCY: How did you know, Miss Pinster?

MISS PINSTER: Oh, I've known that for a long, long time.

LUCY: Well, then the other angels sing, and then I say: "Glory to God in the highest, and on earth peace, good will toward men." And the shepherds aren't afraid any more.

MISS PINSTER: You do it very nicely, Lucy. Now just a few more pins . . . (*The doorbell rings loudly. She looks at her watch.*) Oh, dear, that must be Mrs. Swishton coming for her fitting. She is a few minutes early, but she is always in *such* a hurry. Would you mind waiting a little while, Lucy? (*Doorbell rings again, loudly.*) I can take care of Mrs. Swishton in the other room.

LUCY: I don't mind, Miss Pinster. (MISS PINSTER *hurries out. For a moment* LUCY *stands still. Then she runs over to the mirror.*) Do you know who I am, looking-glass? I'm an angel. But, of course, you're Miss Pinster's mirror, so you knew it already. I wonder . . . if anyone else would

know who *didn't* know already. (*She looks around.*) I could
try! I could slip out the door, and go down the hall of the
apartment building, couldn't I, looking-glass? It wouldn't
take long. I could be back before Miss Pinster would miss
me at all. Are my wings all right? Is my halo straight? I
don't think anyone will notice the pins in the hem, do you?
(*Tiptoes across stage*) Good-bye, looking-glass. Don't tell.
(LUCY *exits, and the curtain rises.*)

*   *   *

SETTING: *The stage is divided into three "apartments": The*
YOUNGS' *apartment is on one side,* ZORLOVA'S *on the other,*
and AUNT MARTHA'S *in the middle. Each apartment is indi-*
cated by a small grouping of furniture. As one family talks,
the other two are silent.

AT RISE: ALICE *and* JIM YOUNG *are talking together in their*
apartment.

ALICE: I'm so glad you agree with me at last, Jim. It's much
more sensible to save the money for a new car than to go
to Mother Young's for Christmas. After all, we've gone
every year since we were married. *Four* times.

JIM: But Mother counts on it. It will be hard to tell her we
aren't coming.

ALICE: Oh, you can make up some excuse—too busy at the
office, or something. Just keep thinking of the new car,
and it will be easy.

JIM: Not so easy, Alice.

ALICE: If you write Mother Young today, she'll be all used
to the idea by Christmas.

JIM: I wonder.

ALICE: Now don't back down. Let's just think about *our-*
selves this year, for a change. Ourselves and the new car.
Let's forget about Christmas at Mother Young's.

JIM: I can't help thinking of Mother's face when she gets the letter. I'm afraid I won't have much peace of mind.

ALICE: Nonsense. (LUCY *enters down stage. She stops in front of the* YOUNGS' *apartment, hesitates, and then pretends to knock*.) I wonder who that can be.

JIM: I'll see. (*He goes to front of stage, pretends to open door, then steps back somewhat startled*.) Well . . .

ALICE (*Curious, going to door*): Why . . . who are you?

LUCY: I'm . . . (*Hesitates*) . . . "Behold I bring you tidings of great joy—peace on earth, good will toward men." (*She turns to go, then calls back*.) Merry Christmas! (*Exits*)

JIM: Well, I'll be . . . what do you make of it, Alice?

ALICE: I don't quite know. It's not one of the children from this building, I'm sure of that. Oh, Jim, it gives me the strangest feeling. There must be some reason why it happened just now . . . just when we were going to write the letter.

JIM: Did you hear: "Peace on earth!" Alice, I think that means peace of mind, too.

ALICE: She looked like one of the angels in the art gallery, didn't she? How strange. Jim, perhaps we can't just sit back and forget about Christmas, after all. Write to Mother Young that we're coming.

JIM (*Happily*): Do you mean it?

ALICE: Yes. You see, it came to me, when the angel was standing there: the new car can wait. But Christmas can't! (*They go in and close the door*.) You can't forget about Christmas. (*At* AUNT MARTHA'S *apartment*, CHARLES *and* RALPH *are talking. They seem to be quite unhappy*.)

RALPH: This is going to be the lonesomest Christmas we ever had. Now we've come to live with Aunt Martha I bet we won't ever have a real Christmas again.

CHARLES: She doesn't believe in any of the fun of Christmas, like other people.

RALPH: She says Santa Claus is nonsense, and giving presents is foolish, and a Christmas tree is a *heathen* custom. She thinks you should think about the Christ Child on Christmas . . . and nothing else!

CHARLES: Do you remember the big tinsel star we always had at the top of our Christmas tree? And all the colored balls?

RALPH: And the nice Foxy Grandpa?

CHARLES: Aunt Martha would say he was *heathen*. (*There is a moment's silence.*)

RALPH: We wouldn't dare ask for a Christmas tree, would we?

CHARLES: I should say not. (*Dreamily*) Oh, I wish we could have a great big Christmas tree, full of presents and lights and shining things. And I wish we could have someone for dinner—a big Christmas dinner.

RALPH: Sh! Aunt Martha's coming. (*The boys open books and read.* AUNT MARTHA *comes in with her knitting, and sits down primly. After a moment she looks up over the top of her glasses and speaks to the boys.*)

AUNT MARTHA: I have been meaning to tell you, boys, that I am pleased to see you taking such a sensible attitude toward Christmas. It's just a lot of fiddle-faddle. I am glad that you aren't begging for one of those heathen Christmas trees.

RALPH *and* CHARLES: Yes, Aunt Martha.

CHARLES (*Timidly*): Would it be heathen to want company . . . for Christmas dinner? The janitor's boy says he's never tasted turkey . . . and he's *nine* years old.

AUNT MARTHA: Turkey? Make a fuss over Christmas dinner! Why, Charles! (LUCY *comes on stage, stops before* AUNT MARTHA'S *apartment, hesitates, then pretends to knock.*) Christmas is all crusted over with foolishness these days. (*Hears* LUCY'S *knock*) What was that? Someone must be at the door. (AUNT MARTHA *goes to the door and pretends to*

open it. The boys come up behind her and peer out too.) Why
. . . why . . . who are you?

LUCY: I'm an . . . (*Hesitates*) . . . "Behold I bring you
tidings of great joy . . . peace on earth, good will toward
men." (*She begins to run off, then turns and calls out, "Merry
Christmas."*)

AUNT MARTHA: Well, of all things.

RALPH: It was an angel!

CHARLES: I never saw an angel before, did you, Aunt Martha?
(AUNT MARTHA *turns back into the room, closes the door,
sinks into her chair. Then she speaks slowly and dreamily,
as the boys sit down.*)

AUNT MARTHA: I was an angel once . . .

CHARLES *and* RALPH: You were!

AUNT MARTHA: I was an angel once . . . in a Christmas play
at the church. It was so long ago I had almost forgotten.
I wore a white costume with wings that had real white
chicken feathers sewn on. And after the play there was a
tall Christmas tree . . .

RALPH (*Surprised*): In the *church!*

AUNT MARTHA: Yes. It almost touched the ceiling. And
everyone got presents . . . and we all sang carols. Oh, it
was a wonderful Christmas.

RALPH (*Thoughtfully*): Aunt Martha, how can it be heathen
to have a Christmas tree, if there was one in church?

AUNT MARTHA (*Giving a start*): What's that? Why . . .
why . . . (*Hurriedly she changes the subject.*) Do you know
the angel's lines were the very ones I had to speak in the
play: "I bring you tidings of great joy . . ." It all comes
back to me now. (*Suddenly*) Boys, there must have been
some reason that angel knocked on our door just now. She
must have come to remind me. I am afraid I had forgotten
all about Christmas. About "good will toward men." (*She

looks at the boys eagerly.) Shall we have a Christmas tree, after all? A big one that will reach from the floor to the ceiling, with lights and presents on it?

RALPH *and* CHARLES: Oh, Aunt Martha.

AUNT MARTHA: And shall we have company for Christmas dinner? Goodness, I haven't cooked a turkey in years . . . I wonder if I remember how.

RALPH *and* CHARLES: Oh, Aunt Martha! (*At* ZORLOVA'S *apartment,* ZORLOVA *is sitting at her dressing table, primping. She begins to hum. Suddenly she gets up and tries a new dance step. She does it very well, and knows it! The telephone rings and interrupts her dance. She goes to answer.*)

ZORLOVA: Hello. . . . Yes, this is Zorlova, the dancer. (*She does a few steps as she holds the phone.*) Who? Oh, on the Community Christmas Tree committee. (*Her voice falls and she stops dancing.*) Next week—what night? . . . Well, I might be able to do it, but I'm very busy, you know. How much do you pay, by the way? . . . What! Give up the best part of an evening for nothing! Just to entertain the community? . . . Yes, I realize Christmas is coming. And I realize they haven't had much chance to see good dancing. But a person has to live. . . . No, I never attended a Community Christmas Tree program. Really, I am afraid I'm going to be very busy that evening. But if I *should* see my way clear to donating my talent, I'll let you know. Good-bye. (*She shrugs as if to say "What a nuisance." * LUCY *comes along and pretends to knock on the door.* ZORLOVA *looks at the door wonderingly.* LUCY *knocks again.* ZORLOVA *pretends to open the door.*) Oh! Who are you? How did you happen to come?

LUCY: "Behold, I bring you tidings of great joy which shall be to all people. . . ."

ZORLOVA: To all people. . . .

LUCY: "Peace on earth, good will toward men."

ZORLOVA: Oh! (LUCY *begins to run off, then turns and calls back*, "*Merry Christmas.*" ZORLOVA *speaks softly*.) To all people. . . . (*Slowly* ZORLOVA *goes back into her room. She stands silently for a minute, then grabs the telephone book, looks for a number, and picks up the phone.*) 549, please. (*She does a happy tap dance as she waits.*) Hello. Is this the Chairman of the Community Christmas Tree committee? This is Zorlova, the dancer. Forgive me, but I feel quite different now about dancing at the program. A strange thing has happened. I'll be very happy to do it, really, I will. . . . Yes, there *is* something about Christmas, isn't there? (*The curtain falls.* LUCY *enters and tiptoes across stage.*)

LUCY (*Going to mirror*): I'm back, looking-glass. (*Peers at herself*) Oh, I *do* look like an angel. (*She turns this way and that.*) It makes me feel all different inside, it really does. But the other people I saw just now . . . I couldn't tell if they felt different or not. How can you tell how people feel? You can only see their faces . . . you can't see what goes on inside of them! (MISS PINSTER'S *voice is heard outside.*)

MISS PINSTER: Good-bye, Mrs. Swishton. Remember, to-morrow at three. And I promise not to keep you waiting. Good-bye. (MISS PINSTER *comes on the stage again and sees* LUCY *at the mirror.*) What are you looking at, Lucy?

LUCY: An angel. I don't look like *me* at all, do I?

MISS PINSTER: Well, not exactly. Come now, just a few more pins in the hem and we'll be through for this afternoon. (*She starts to work on the hem again.*)

LUCY: Something happened while you were away, Miss Pinster.

MISS PINSTER: Oh, is that so?

LUCY: Yes. Something about Christmas.

MISS PINSTER: Really? Where?

LUCY: Right here in this apartment building.

MISS PINSTER: You don't say.

LUCY: Yes. You know that girl I told you about . . . the one who bought the beautiful box of color-pencils for her brother?

MISS PINSTER: Yes, I remember. Twenty pencils with different colored leads.

LUCY: Well, she's going to give them to him, after all. She isn't going to keep them for herself.

MISS PINSTER: Why, how nice! That's the real Christmas spirit. But how did it happen, Lucy?

LUCY: Well, you see, Miss Pinster, the girl got to feeling different . . . inside . . . because she saw an angel . . . in the looking-glass!

THE END

The Merry Christmas Elf

Characters

WRITER
SCHOOL CHILDREN
THREE GIRLS
CHRISTMAS ELF
MRS. FUDDY
TWO BIG BOYS
SMALL BOY
BROTHER
SISTER
NEWSBOY

SETTING: *Outdoors on Pine Street in Middleton.*

AT RISE: *The stage is empty for a moment. Then the* WRITER *comes in slowly. He looks at the snow on his coat sleeve.*

WRITER: Why, it's beginning to snow. Maybe that will be something to write about today, for my column in the *Middleton News*. For my daily bit of wisdom and wonder. Snow! (*Laughingly looks up at the sky and calls out*) Who's fluffing up the pillows of the sky, and sending down a shower of little white feathers? Who's dusting the ashes off the stars? Who's shaking down white petals from the wild

plum trees along the Milky Way? (*Looks at sleeve again*)
Who's cutting all these fancy shapes from tissue-paper ice?
(*Listens*) I guess they're all too busy up there to answer me.
(*To audience*) Yes, my friends, it's beginning to snow in
Middleton. In a little while the sidewalk here along Pine
Street will be white. When school is out (*Consults watch*)
in a few minutes, the children will be thinking of getting
out their sleds. Any time they see ten feathers of snow
coming down, they think of sleds. Maybe *that* will be something to write about . . . (*There is the sound of Christmas
music offstage, getting louder, then fading out.* WRITER *listens
intently.*) That must be Eddie Clark's sound truck. Eddie
owns the radio store on the corner of Main Street and
Fourth. He owns the only sound truck in town. He always
gets it out at this time of year and plays the proper music.
Maybe that's something to write about. . . . Every note
like a gaily-dressed dancer, whirling right out into the winter air, dancing up Pine Street and down Spruce, dancing
through the white petals falling from heaven, dancing into
your heart. Christmas music is like that, don't you think?
It waltzes around even after Eddie Clark's sound truck
turns the corner. (*Consults watch*) Well, today is the last
day of school before Christmas vacation. They're probably
all having parties and Christmas trees over at the school-
house. I remember how it used to be: A head full of jingle
bells! A heart full of tinsel and meadowlarks! A hand full
of (*Looks at snowy sleeve*) . . . of diamond dust! (*There is
a racket offstage.*) Hold on . . . here they come, the first
bunch of them. . . . (WRITER *backs out of the way as a
group of excited* CHILDREN *cross the stage.*)

BOYS *and* GIRLS: It's snowing! What did you get? I'll trade
you. . . . Let's go sliding on Randall's Hill. . . . Susie
says she believes in Santa Claus. . . . Look at it snow!
Christmas vacation . . . white Christmas! (*The* CHILDREN

exit, all except THREE GIRLS *who have come in at the end of the group. They have their arms around each other and are gaily singing "Deck the Halls." Every time they sing the "fa la la" refrain, they do a little jig in unison. At the end of the second verse, they see the* WRITER *and stop.*)

GIRLS: Oh! We didn't know we had an audience.

WRITER: That song makes me think of . . . of a flock of bright red birds perched all over a fir tree, singing of sunrise, singing of spring, in the midst of a winter world. Isn't there any more? Please!

GIRLS: There's another verse. (*They sing the third verse. At the end of the song, they laugh and run out.*)

WRITER (*Trying to do the little jig*): Fa la la la la, la la la la. It gets under your skin, doesn't it? It makes you feel good, doesn't it? (*He jigs again, then stops suddenly and looks around.*) Well. I'm certainly glad there wasn't anyone around to see me doing a thing like that . . . right in the middle of the sidewalk . . . in the middle of Middleton. Why did I do it? Maybe *that's* something to write about. What is there about Christmas coming?

CHRISTMAS ELF (*Dancing in gaily*): There's me. (*Whirls around and stops near the* WRITER) Maybe that isn't good English, but you know what I mean.

WRITER (*Staring at* ELF): No, I don't. Who are you?

ELF: I'm someone to write about! (*Teasingly*) Weren't you looking for something to write about?

WRITER: Have you been listening in on me, you rascal?

ELF: I've been watching you all the time, ever since you asked who was throwing down the snow. In fact, that's what drew me to you. (*Laughing*) Why didn't you think of the shepherd?

WRITER: What shepherd?

ELF: The one who makes the fleecy clouds. Maybe he lost some wool. (*Mimics tone of voice of* WRITER *and looks up at sky*) Who's throwing down some wool out of the fleecy clouds?

WRITER (*Laughing*): I guess I did forget about the shepherd. (*Looks* ELF *over*) Come on, who are you?

ELF: That's what you have to find out, Mr. Writer. But I'll give you a hint:

I'm not of this world, I'm sad to say,

Excepting once a year.

When Christmas is through I'm shut away,

With all my magic cheer.

Just once in a year, for a little while,

Folks think of the Christ Child's birth,

And open their hearts, and sing and smile,

And welcome me here on earth.

But I'm not telling you who I am!

You have to guess.

WRITER: You wouldn't be one of those dancers who seemed to hop out of Eddie Clark's sound truck, on a bar of music? You wouldn't be one of those bright red birds that seemed to flock around when the girls sang? You wouldn't be music . . . come to life? Wouldn't *that* be something to write about!

ELF: Guess again. Guess again. You're warm, but I can't say you're hot. (*Skips around, then stops and looks down the street*) Who's that coming?

WRITER: It looks like Mrs. Fuddy.

ELF: She doesn't look very happy.

WRITER: Oh no, not Mrs. Fuddy. She carries too much of the world around on her shoulders. But just wait till she sees you, all dressed up in red and green. That ought to cheer her up.

ELF: But she won't see me.

WRITER: You mean you're running away? You're going to hide?

ELF: I'm staying right here. But she won't see me. Nobody sees me! I'm invisible.

WRITER: But . . . *I* see you.

ELF: Oh, you're different. You believe in . . . (*Looks up at sky*) . . . in petals from the wild plum trees along the Milky Way. You're not afraid to think about magic things. (MRS. FUDDY *comes in looking tired and cross.*)

WRITER: Good afternoon, Mrs. Fuddy.

MRS. FUDDY: What's that? Just a moment, please. (*She opens her purse, takes out a pencil and pad, and makes a note.*) I just thought of something else I have to get for the church decorations. (*Replaces note and looks up*) What did you say?

WRITER: I said, "Good afternoon, Mrs. Fuddy."

MRS. FUDDY: Well, I don't know how good it is. Snowing and all. Look at it! Makes the walks so messy. I ought to have my galoshes on right now, but I simply haven't time to go home for them. So much to do! You're that writer who does a daily column for the *Middleton News*, aren't you? Why don't you write a piece about the busy, bothersome days before Christmas?

WRITER: Bothersome?

MRS. FUDDY: Yes, yes. All those things to do. Shopping, and baking, and worrying about costumes for the Christmas pageant, and writing cards, and making wreaths, and serving on the Christmas-basket committee, and . . .

WRITER: *Bothersome?* (ELF, *who has been listening, suddenly dances over to* MRS. FUDDY *and blows a kiss at her cheek.*)

MRS. FUDDY (*With a start, putting up her hand*): A snowflake . . . right on my cheek. Imagine. Only it seemed warm . . . not cold at all. (*She begins to smile.*) Well, I guess bothersome *isn't* the right word. (ELF *touches her other cheek.*) Another snowflake! And so warm. (*She is really smiling now.*) No, I'm *sure* it isn't the right word. Definitely not bothersome. We *want* to do all those things . . . to make Christmas bright and happy. It's really amazing, isn't it? All the things we can do. Oh, there's something wonderful about the holiday season.

WRITER (*Looking mischievously at the* ELF): You know, Mrs. Fuddy, a sprightly little elf, all dressed in red and green, just ran up and planted a Christmas kiss on each of your cheeks.

MRS. FUDDY: Oh, you writers! You're always making up stories . . . out of snowflakes. (*Laughing and happy, she exits.*)

WRITER: Well! *What* did you do to her? Who are you?

ELF (*Dancing around*): I'm not of this world for very long,

But if they'd let me stay,

I'd turn each frown to a merry song

And chase all cares away.

But I'm not telling you who I am.

WRITER (*Thoughtfully*): You're not like the rest of us, are you? The snow doesn't stay on your coat or cap at all.

ELF: That's because I'm invisible! (*There is a noise offstage, as if more children were coming from school.*)

WRITER: Careful. Here come some more children from school. (*Moves out of the way*)

ELF: They will not hear me make a sound,

Or see me here at all,

But they will *feel* me all around—

The big ones, and the small. (*Two* BIG BOYS *hurry in with a* SMALL BOY *tagging at their heels.*)

1ST BIG BOY: Look, it's snowing! Let's go coasting tonight.

2ND BIG BOY: Let's. Randall's Hill. There'll be enough snow by tonight.

SMALL BOY (*Eagerly*): May I go too?

1ST BIG BOY: Naw, you're too small. You stay home and go to bed like a good little boy!

2ND BIG BOY: You'd be a nuisance.

SMALL BOY: No, I wouldn't. Honest. I never went coasting at night. (ELF *skips over and taps the two* BIG BOYS *with his pointed cap.*)

1ST BIG BOY (*Suddenly pleasant*): Never went coasting at night? You better come along then. You don't know what you've missed!

2ND BIG BOY (*Cheerfully*): Sure. Come along. We'll show you the ropes. (*The* BOYS *exit.* BROTHER *and* SISTER *come in quarreling.*)

SISTER: It's not fair. You got six pieces of candy and I got only five.

BROTHER: Don't blame me. I didn't fill those Christmas stockings. Teacher did.

SISTER: It isn't fair. You've got to give me half the extra one.

BROTHER: I don't either.

SISTER: You do, too. (ELF *slips over and taps* SISTER *and* BROTHER *with cap.*)

BROTHER (*Suddenly merry*): Look, Sis. I'm going to give that extra piece to Mom.

SISTER: To Mom! (*Pleased*) Why, yes. And *I'm* going to give one of mine to Buddy.

BROTHER: I'll save one for Pop. Say, why didn't we think of it before? (*They exit happily. A noisy group of* CHILDREN *come in talking and shouting.* ELF *stands up like a musical director, using his cap for a baton, and starts to sing "Joy to the World." One by one the* CHILDREN *join in until all are singing. Toward the end of the song, they exit singing merrily.*)

WRITER: I've got it! (*Takes a pad and pencil from his pocket and begins to write*) I've got the angle! (ELF *tries to look over* WRITER'S *shoulder, but is too small. He runs to the wings and brings in a box, climbs up on it, and is able to see what* WRITER *is writing.*)

ELF (*Reading over* WRITER'S *shoulder*): "A strange thing happened this afternoon as I was walking along Pine Street, wondering what to write about. There was something in the air—something besides the soft white flakes floating down from heaven, something besides the jolly music tumbling out of Eddie Clark's sound truck. Something warming and wonderful . . ." (WRITER *moves on, writing as he goes.* ELF *has to get down from box and keep moving it along in order to read over* WRITER's *shoulder.*) "Did you ever feel as if your heart were full of April robins? As if a hundred candles were suddenly lit in your head? That's the way I felt this afternoon, my friends, when the strange thing happened. It was just as school was letting out. A group of children passed . . . and then, suddenly . . . I saw the Spirit of Christmas . . . in person! (ELF *excitedly jumps down from the box and runs to face* WRITER, *tugging at his coat.*) How did you *know?* How did you *know?*

WRITER (*Laughing*): I guessed from the very beginning, but I didn't want to let on. I guessed from the moment you said you were only allowed to come on earth once in a while. How did you say it exactly? I'd like it for my column.

ELF (*Slowly, as* WRITER *writes*):

I'm not of this world, I'm sad to say,

Excepting once a year.

When Christmas is through I'm shut away,

With all my magic cheer.

Just once in a year, for a little while,

Folks think of the Christ Child's birth,

And open their hearts, and sing and smile,

And welcome me here on earth.

WRITER (*Excitedly*): Wait till my story about you comes out in the paper. Maybe things will be different then. What a story! I'll rush it right around the corner to the *News* office

. . . so they can get out a special edition! (WRITER *exits, writing as he walks.* ELF *skips around him and exits too, leaving the box behind. For a moment the stage is empty. Then* MRS. FUDDY'S *voice is heard at the other side of the stage.*)

MRS. FUDDY (*Offstage*): Lovely. Just lovely! (MRS. FUDDY *comes in carrying Christmas greens. She is followed by* CHILDREN *with greens and small Christmas trees, wreaths, red bells, etc.*) We can start decorating the church right away. I never *saw* such lovely greens. And such heavy ones! (*She rests a minute, shifting her load in her arms.*) Where did you get them?

A BOY: Mr. Gentry showed us a place on his farm. He said the trees needed to be trimmed anyway.

A GIRL: He told us we could have all we wanted. My arms are breaking! (*She loses a bough and stoops to pick it up, but then loses another. Every time she retrieves one bough, she drops another. Other* CHILDREN *laugh. Then they too begin to lose part of their load.* ELF *comes dancing in. Since he is supposed to be invisible, the* CHILDREN *must act as if they do not see him at all. Everyone seems to be having a jolly time in spite of their troubles with the slippery greens.*)

MRS. FUDDY: So fragrant! I don't know *when* Christmas has been such fun. (*She sees the box the* ELF *left.*) Why, look, there's a box. Right in the street. I wonder how it got there.

GIRL: Let's put some of our decorations in it, so we won't keep dropping them. (*As* MRS. FUDDY *and* CHILDREN *put things in the box, the* SMALL BOY *comes in with his sled.* ELF *skips over and touches him on the shoulder.*)

SMALL BOY (*Calling out*): Want me to help? Want me to haul the box on my sled? I could do it . . . easy.

MRS. FUDDY: That would be fine. Do you think there is enough snow?

SMALL BOY: Sure. (*They lift the box on the sled.* SMALL BOY *beams.*) You know what? I'm going coasting tonight on Randall's Hill . . . with the big boys!

MRS. FUDDY: You are? That's splendid. (*They start out with sled and greens.*) Oh, isn't Christmas wonderful? (*The* THREE GIRLS *who sang "Deck the Halls" come in.*)

1ST GIRL: Maybe we could think of some new steps. (ELF *hurries over and taps them each lightly on the head with his cap.*)

2ND GIRL: I've thought of something better. Why don't we practice some carols . . . and then go out and sing them to the old folks at the County Farm . . . on Christmas Eve?

3RD GIRL: Why don't we? I bet they don't have much of a Christmas out there.

1ST GIRL: We could sing "Hark! The Herald Angels Sing."

2ND GIRL: And "The First Noel."

3RD GIRL: And "Silent Night." Let's. (*A* NEWSBOY *comes hurrying in with papers.*)

NEWSBOY: Extra! Extra! Read all about it. Strange Happenings on Pine Street This Afternoon. Extra! Extra! (ELF, *excited and pleased, dances around* NEWSBOY *trying to get a look at the paper.*)

GIRLS: On Pine Street? (*They look around them.*)

MRS. FUDDY (*Hurrying in*): Did I hear you say Pine Street, boy? Wait a minute . . . (*She gets a coin from her purse and buys a paper; starts to look at it eagerly.*)

SMALL BOY (*Running in with sled*): What happened?

NEWSBOY: Extra! Extra!

TWO BIG BOYS (*Hurrying in*): What's it all about? (BROTHER *and* SISTER, *and several of the* CHILDREN *who carried greens gather around.*)

A GIRL: Read it out loud!

A BOY: Read it, Mrs. Fuddy.

MRS. FUDDY (*Turning to children*): What do you think! The man who writes the daily column in the *News* says that he saw the Spirit of Christmas . . . in *person* . . . on Pine Street this afternoon. He says he actually saw the Spirit of Christmas. (*The* ELF *is having a wonderful time listening and watching.* NEWSBOY *exits, shouting* "*Extra! Extra!*")

A BOY: How can you see a spirit?

MRS. FUDDY: That's just it. That's what is so strange.

A GIRL: Maybe he made it up.

MRS. FUDDY: No . . . it doesn't sound like it. (*Suddenly*) You know, something *did* happen on Pine Street this afternoon. I don't mean to say that I saw the Spirit of Christmas, but I felt something. I definitely *felt* something. (*Puts hand to cheek*) I was coming along all tired and cross and hurried, and then suddenly something like a warm snowflake touched my cheek. And everything was different! (*She looks around her.*) It happened just about here, I believe. I wasn't tired or cross any more.

1ST BIG BOY: Yeah, that's right. I felt something too, somehow.

2ND BIG BOY: All of a sudden I thought it would be nice to take my little brother along sliding.

SISTER (*To* BROTHER): It was just about here you thought of giving Mom the extra piece.

THREE GIRLS: And suddenly we got the idea of going out to the County Farm to sing, on Christmas Eve. We were standing right here.

A BOY: What else does it say?

MRS. FUDDY (*Reading from paper*): "This afternoon I stood on Pine Street while the jeweler in the sky was sifting down diamond dust from heaven. I was wondering what to write about. And then, all of a sudden, with my own eyes, I saw the Christmas Elf—skipping and dancing around me. I saw the Spirit of Christmas, come to earth. And there, before me, as I watched, I saw the Elf turn frowns into smiles . . . like turning thistles into roses. I saw him change selfishness into kindness . . . like turning on the light of the sun in a dark corner. I saw him change worry into cheer . . . like turning cawing crows into canaries. I saw him change ill-will into good fellowship . . . like changing Scrooge into Santa Claus! (ELF *slips out to find the* WRITER.) With a kiss on the cheek, or a tap on the shoulder, or just a wave of his red arm, he changed everything in a twinkling. Why, oh why, do we shut away the magic of Christmas as soon as Christmas is over? Why do we close our hearts to the Spirit of Christmas as soon as the holidays end? Why don't we keep him with us—always?"

CHILDREN (*To each other*): Why? Why?

MRS. FUDDY: Why? (ELF, *pulling* WRITER, *comes in.* WRITER *stands far at side, listening.* ELF *dances around, then taps the* THREE GIRLS *gently. They step forward and begin to sing to the tune of "Jolly Old St. Nicholas.")*

THREE GIRLS:

Christmas comes but once a year,
Christmas cannot stay,
But its fellowship and cheer
Need not go away.
Let's all try to keep the elf
Of Christmas in our hearts
When the Old Year's on the shelf
And the New Year starts!

(ELF *dances out in front of the group, waves arms like a music director, and all sing "Deck the Halls" or some other appropriate Christmas carol.)*

THE END

Time Out for Christmas

Characters

LAST YEAR'S TEDDY BEAR
LAST YEAR'S RAG DOLL
TICK
TOCK } *who run the clock*
24 DAYS OF DECEMBER

SETTING: *The playroom.*

TIME: *Midnight, November 30.*

AT RISE: LAST YEAR'S TEDDY BEAR *and* LAST YEAR'S RAG
DOLL *are asleep against chairs, in rather awkward propped-up
positions. When the clock begins to strike midnight, they wake
up slowly. By the time the 10th stroke approaches, they are
fully awake. They jump up and rush to the clock, trying to
hold back its hands.*

TEDDY BEAR:
The magic hour of 12 o'clock!
Listen to us, Tick and Tock.
We must see you in a hurry!
Last year's toys are full of worry.

RAG DOLL:
Listen to us, Tock and Tick—

Stop the clock, and please be quick.

In a second, you remember.

You'll be ticking-in December.

And—boo, hoo!—with Christmas nearing,

We are much in need of cheering!

(TICK *and* TOCK *come from behind the clock. They always speak in quick, staccato voices, like the sound of a clock ticking.*)

TICK: What

TOCK: is

TICK: all

TOCK: the

TICK: noise

TOCK: and

TICK: clat-

TOCK: ter?

TEDDY BEAR: Something serious is the matter.

RAG DOLL:

   Last Year's Teddy Bear and I

   Are so worried we could cry.

   (*She takes out her handkerchief*)

TICK: Wor-

TOCK: ried,

TICK: Rag

TOCK: Doll?

TICK: Tell

TOCK: us

TICK: why.

RAG DOLL:

   Well, it's practically December

   (Two more ticks will end November)

   And that means that Christmas Day

   Isn't very far away,

   And—perhaps it may sound dumb

   But we wish it wouldn't come!

TICK: Wish

TOCK: it

TICK: would

TOCK: not

TICK: come!

TOCK: How

TICK: so?

TEDDY BEAR:
  Well, it's hard on us, you know:
  Christmas means that girls and boys
  Will be getting brand-new toys—
  Teddy Bears . . .

RAG DOLL: And Rag Dolls, too.

TEDDY BEAR:
  And, since we're no longer new,
  What will we old-timers do?

TICK: What

TOCK: will

TICK: last

TOCK: year's

TICK: old

TOCK: toys

TICK: do?

TEDDY BEAR (*To* TICK *and* TOCK):
  If you'll only help us out,
  We'll be saved—without a doubt.

RAG DOLL:
  Just forget to tick, you two,
  From Christmas Eve, until it's through,
  Then tick again the 26th,
  And all our troubles will be fixed.

TEDDY BEAR:
  If you forget to tick, you see,
  Christmas simply will not *be*.

And, with Christmas blotted over,
Last year's toys will be in clover.

RAG DOLL:

Then, of course, the girls and boys
Will gladly keep their last-year toys.
Oh, how happy we shall be!
(*She dances a wobbly dance just to think of it.*)

TEDDY BEAR: We'll dance the hornpipe merrily. (*He does a funny jig.* TICK *and* TOCK *point at the calendar.*)

TICK: But

TOCK: first

TICK: the

TOCK: days

TICK: must

TOCK: all

TICK: a-

TOCK: gree.

RAG DOLL:

December days should be delighted.
They must feel all snubbed and slighted.
They just tiptoe in . . . and go,
Christmas always steals the show—
It gets all the fame . . .

TICK: That's

TOCK: so.

TEDDY BEAR:

Don't let Christmas tick this year!
Then our standing will be clear—
We will rule the playroom still,
And be bubbling with good will.

RAG DOLL:

No new toys will take our places.
We will have the *gladdest* faces.

TICK: Ask

TOCK: the

TICK: days

TOCK: if

TICK: they

TOCK: are

TICK: will-

TOCK: ing.

RAG DOLL: Oh, their answers will be thrilling! (RAG DOLL *runs to the calendar, stands before it, and sings to the tune of "Jolly Old St. Nicholas.")*

Listen, you December days,
Do you think it's right
Christmas captures all the praise,
All the fame in sight?
Don't you think it would be best,
And adventuresome,
If old Christmas took a rest
And just didn't come?

TICK: Ev-

TOCK: 'ry

TICK: day

TOCK: must

TICK: have

TOCK: a

TICK: turn.

TEDDY BEAR: Oh, the secrets we shall learn! (TEDDY BEAR *runs to calendar and sings to tune of "Jolly Old St. Nicholas.")*

Christmas captures all the praise.
Christmas stands accused!
Listen, all you other days,
Don't you feel abused?
Step right out and have your say—
Is there any doubt
Christmas is a holiday

We could do without?

Dec. 1 (*Coming from behind calendar*): Do without Christmas? I should say not. I consider it a great honor to be the first day of the month in which Christmas comes. Christmas may be first in some ways, but it can never be the first of December! I'm perfectly satisfied with the part I play. (*Exits behind calendar, as* Dec. 2 *comes out.*)

Dec. 2: You think I'm jealous of Christmas? Why, without me Christmas wouldn't be what it is. Without me . . .

Dec. 3 (*Coming out*): And *me* . . .

Dec. 2 *and* 3: There would be two less days for getting ready for Christmas, for expecting it, and thinking about it, and shopping for it. Why, people *need us*. (*They exit, and* Dec. 4 *comes out.*)

Teddy Bear (*Mopping his brow*): It's getting rather warm in here!

Rag Doll:
At such a season of the year . . .
Something must be wrong, I fear.

Dec. 4: Who said Christmas gets all the praise? In some countries *I'm* the beginning of the holiday season. In France I'm called St. Barbara's Day. That's the day people float grains of wheat on plates of water and put them in a sunny window or near the fire. If the grain sprouts well, there will be a good harvest the coming year. And in Czechoslovakia on December 4, a twig of cherry is put in water. Everyone watches for it to bloom by Christmas Eve. If it does bloom, the girl who took care of it will marry during the coming year. So, you see, how important I am! (*Exits.*)

Rag Doll (*Subdued*): Perhaps we're rather out of date.

Teddy Bear (*Subdued*): We're out of luck, at any rate.

Rag Doll (*Hopefully*): The rest will side with us, just wait!

Tick: In

Tock: the
Tick: end
Tock: we'll
Tick: get
Tock: this
Tick: straight.

Dec. 5 (*Coming out*): Christmas has nothing on me. On the night of December 5th, which is the same as the Eve of December 6th, St. Nicholas comes to Holland! The children put out their shoes, and next morning. . . . (Dec. 6 *appears*)

Dec. 6: Next morning they find them full of candy and toys and treasures.

Teddy Bear (*Amazed*): December 6th! Well, I'll be jiggered.

Rag Doll: Nothing works the way we "figgered."

Dec. 5 *and* 6: Yes, we're the Festival of St. Nicholas in Holland. We don't envy anyone! (*They exit. Days of* December *from 7 through 11 come out separately at intervals, and all five are on the stage at once until after they have sung a carol at the end of their speeches.*)

Dec. 7 (*Skipping out*): I'd be lost without Christmas.

Dec. 8 (*Dancing out*): So would I.

Dec. 7: Along about now every year, school children are learning parts for the Christmas program. . . .

Dec. 8: And speaking pieces. . . .

Dec. 9 (*Coming in with half-finished present*): And making presents . . .

Dec. 10 (*In lilting voice*): And learning Christmas songs . . .

Dec. 11: And selling Christmas seals. . . .

Dec. 7, 8, 9, 10, 11: And singing carols! (*They join together and sing a lively carol, like "Joy to the World." When the song is finished, they exit.*)

Tick: They
Tock: don't

TICK: en-

TOCK: vy

TICK: Christ-

TOCK: mas

TICK: an-

TOCK: y.

RAG DOLL (*Sighing*): I feel cheaper than a penny.

TEDDY BEAR:

    All my fur is getting itchy.

    Guess our plan was not so litchy!

DEC. 12 (*Entering*): About this time of year, people are all excited about the community Christmas tree and the community toy shop. It's wonderful! (*Stares at* TEDDY BEAR *and* RAG DOLL) Why, you're perfect, Last Year's Teddy Bear and Last Year's Rag Doll. You're just what they need down at the toy shop. You'd make dandy new presents for someone who wouldn't get much otherwise. That is, if your master and mistress would give you up. Of course, some children are so fond of their last year's toys they'd never give them up.

TEDDY BEAR: Is that true or are you fooling?

RAG DOLL:

    Maybe we should have more schooling—

    Seems we have some things to learn.

TEDDY BEAR: Seems we acted out of turn.

DEC. 12: Just remember, Christmas has a place for *everyone*, somewhere! An important place. (*Exits*)

DEC. 13 (*Coming in*): I am the day of Santa Lucia in Sweden. On December 13, Santa Lucia, dressed in white, starts going from house to house to tell the Christmas story.

    And that's not all. On December 13, twelve days before Christmas, the peasants of France say that they are able to foretell the weather for the next twelve months. I don't feel abused. (*Exits*.)

DEC. 14 (*Hurrying in and out*): Am I having fun! Only nine more shopping days till Christmas!

DEC. 15 (*Hurrying in and out*): You should see the lines of people at the post office. If it weren't for me, I'm sure those Christmas parcels would never arrive in time!

DEC. 16 (*Coming in slowly*): On the night of December 16, the nine-day celebration of the Posadas begins in Mexico.

TEDDY BEAR (*Counting on fingers*):
That will bring us, swift as swift,
Right up to the 25th.

RAG DOLL: Our idea has fallen flat!

TICK: The

TOCK: Po-

TICK: sa-

TOCK: das?

TICK: What

TOCK: is

TICK: that?

DEC. 16: *Posada* means an inn or lodging house in Spanish. For nine days before Christmas, the people of Mexico act out the hardships Mary and Joseph had when they were trying to find an inn in Bethlehem. (DEC. 17, 18, 19, 20, 21, 22, 23, *and* 24 *enter carrying lighted candles. As they come in slowly they sing the Litany of the Virgin, or recite the Rosary; or, if either of these would be too difficult, they might sing an old carol.*)

DEC. 17 (*As if knocking on a door*): Open, please, to a stranger.

DEC. 16 (*As if answering the knock*): Who is it knocks at my door so late at night?

DEC. 17: We are poor pilgrims searching for a place to rest this winter night.

DEC. 18: We have traveled a long way from Nazareth, down the River Jordan.

DEC. 19: The night is cold and windy.

DEC. 20: And we are very tired. We are looking for a place to rest.

DEC. 16: But who are you, asking for shelter so late at night?

DEC. 21: I am a carpenter from Nazareth, Joseph by name.

DEC. 22: And I am Mary, his wife.

DEC. 16: Still, I know you not.

DEC. 23: You should know from the prophecy . . .

DEC. 24: Mary will be the mother of the Son of God!

DEC. 16 (*As if flinging open the door*): Ah, come into my home, then, and welcome. Come in. Come in. (*The* NINE DAYS *join in singing a glad Christmas carol, such as "O Come, All Ye Faithful." Then they exit one by one behind the calendar.*)

RAG DOLL:
Oh, I think our plan was dumb—
Christmas simply *has* to come.

TEDDY BEAR:
There is more to it than caring
How a few old toys are faring!

TICK: Christ-

TOCK: mas

TICK: is

TOCK: a

TICK: time

TOCK: for

TICK: shar-

TOCK: ing.

DEC. 24 (*Appearing again*): I am Christmas Eve. (*To* TEDDY BEAR *and* RAG DOLL) Do you still want Tick and Tock to forget to tick-in Christmas?

TEDDY BEAR: No, No . . .

RAG DOLL: No, No . . .

TEDDY BEAR *and* RAG DOLL:
No, No, No. (*They shake a finger at* TICK *and* TOCK.)
Back into the clock you go!

Don't you skip a single tick
Of December—now, be quick!
Lounging here like this is shocking—
It is time to start tick-tocking!
(TICK *and* TOCK, *laughing merrily, hurry back behind the clock
and begin to "tick-tock" loudly.* TEDDY BEAR *and* RAG DOLLS
do a happy wobbly dance, as DEC. 24 *looks on. As they dance
they sing to the tune of "Jolly Old St. Nicholas.")*
Jolly old St. Nicholas,
Lend your ear this way—
We have been "ridicolas,"
But forgive us, pray.
Though we acted pretty dumb,
Now we think it's clear
Christmas is for *everyone*
The best day of the year!

THE END

A Christmas Tree for Kitty

Characters

JANNIS
TODD
WILLA
THEIR MOTHER
CAROLERS (*any number of boys and girls*)
MARTHA
MIKE (*non-speaking*)

TIME: *The day before Christmas.*
SETTING: *An attractive living room.*
AT RISE: JANNIS *and* TODD *are decorating a tiny Christmas tree that stands on a table. The ornaments are small-sized, and most of them are hand-made.*

JANNIS: I guess no other kitten in the world will get a tree like this for Christmas. (*Stands off and admires it*) Isn't it *beautiful?* Where did you put the ball of catnip, Todd?
TODD: I haven't put it anywhere yet. (*Looks on table and finds it. Holds it to his nose and sniffs*) I can't figure out what a cat sees in catnip. Where shall we hang it?
JANNIS: Oh, near the top, next to the golden star. Can't you just see Kitty standing on her hind legs, trying to reach it?
TODD: And if she knocks anything off, it won't matter a bit.

(*Fastens catnip ball near the star*) There's not a thing on this tree that can break.

JANNIS: Not a single thing. (WILLA *comes in*)

WILLA: Haven't the carolers come to call for me yet? What are you doing? Oh, what a cute little tree. Who's it for?

JANNIS: We told you, Willa. We're trimming it for Kitty.

WILLA: Oh, yes, I remember. Where's Mother? (*Calls*) Mother!

TODD (*Hurrying to cover the tree with tissue paper*): We don't want Mother to see the tree till it's all finished. (MOTHER *comes in with Christmas ribbons and wrapping.*)

MOTHER: Did you call me, Willa?

WILLA: Do I look all right for a caroler? We're going to sing at the day nursery first, then at the rest home, then at the hospital. (MOTHER *makes a bow of red and green ribbon and pins it to* WILLA'S *coat.*)

MOTHER: I think it's a wonderful idea, to go caroling.

JANNIS: You ought to have Martha sing with you, Willa. She's got such a good voice.

WILLA: Martha? Oh yes, that girl you walk home with sometimes. The one who always wears a blue dress—the same one.

JANNIS: She doesn't have many dresses. But she can *sing!* (*The sound of* CAROLERS *is heard offstage.*)

WILLA: There they are! The carolers.

MOTHER: Do have them come in a minute, Willa. I'd like to hear how you sound together. I'll get some cookies . . . (*She leaves by one exit*, WILLA *by another.*)

WILLA (*Offstage*): Yoo-hoo! Come in a minute! My mother wants to hear how we sound. (WILLA *returns with a group of merry* CAROLERS.) What shall we sing? "O Little Town of Bethlehem"? (*She gives the key, and they begin to sing.* MOTHER *returns with plate of cookies and stands listening. When the song is over*, JANNIS *and* TODD *clap loudly.*)

MOTHER: That was lovely. I am sure you are going to give many people a great deal of joy this afternoon. I almost wish I were your age and could go along! Good luck . . . (WILLA *and* CAROLERS *exit with cookies in their hands. Calls of "Goodbye" and "Thank you."*)

JANNIS: Todd and I have almost finished trimming the little tree for Kitty, Mother.

TODD: But you can't see it till every last thing is on.

MOTHER (*Laughing*): I won't peek, I promise. Call me when you're ready. (*She goes out.* JANNIS *and* TODD *work on the tree again.*)

JANNIS: I wonder what Kitty will like most—next to the catnip.

TODD: The red yarn. She'll get all snarled up in it before you can say "Merry Christmas." That's her idea of fun.

JANNIS: Maybe she'll like the lollipops . . . they're so pretty, all red and green and yellow. (*Cocks her head and looks at tree.*) Or maybe she'll like the paper chains. Or the little cotton lamb.

TODD: I still think we should have used *wool* for the lamb. (*Looks at table*) Well, everything is on the tree now, Jannis.

JANNIS: Let's call Mother then. (*Loudly*) Mother!

TODD: All right, Mother. It's done. Come look! (MOTHER *comes in, looks eagerly at the little tree.*)

MOTHER: Why, it's lovely! I had no idea you were making it so fancy. Such gay colors! Won't Kitty be surprised!

TODD: Do you see our little woolly lamb . . . only it's *cotton*.

JANNIS: And the white-paper angels?

TODD: Not a single thing can break, no matter how rough Kitty is.

MOTHER: It's the prettiest little tree I've ever seen. Quite the prettiest. You ought to move it closer to the window, where it can be seen from the street.

JANNIS: Yes, let's. Kitty can't have it until tomorrow, anyway. Do you think she'll know what it is?

TODD: 'Course not. Cats don't know about Christmas. But that won't matter. (*As* JANNIS *and* TODD *move the table near the window*, JANNIS *suddenly stops and looks out eagerly*.)

JANNIS: Oh, look, there's Martha, coming down the street with her little brother Mike.

TODD: Wherever Martha is, Mike is. Or Johnny, or Freddy, or Millie.

JANNIS: I bet she's never seen a little Christmas tree like this one. They're too poor to have a tree, I guess—even a little one. Mother, will it be all right to have Martha come in and see Kitty's tree?

TODD: Mike will like it, too. But he won't say a thing. He'll just peek around Martha's skirt and never say a word.

JANNIS: Mother?

MOTHER: Why, yes . . . ask them in for a little while, Jannis.

JANNIS (*Running out, calling*): Martha! Martha!

TODD: Martha told Jannis they've got another baby at their house. It's a girl.

MOTHER: Another baby? Dear me, where do they put all the children, in that little house? What have they named it?

TODD: I don't know. Jannis told Martha they ought to call it *Mary*, because it came at Christmastime.

MOTHER: Mary is a nice name.

JANNIS (*Offstage*): Wait till you see, Martha! Wait till you see. You can't guess! Todd and I did it all by ourselves. (JANNIS *comes in with* MARTHA. MIKE, *a small bashful boy, clings to his sister's skirts*.)

MOTHER: Good afternoon, Martha. Is that Michael with you?

MARTHA: Yes, Ma'am. Mike. He's scared. I don't mean really scared, but . . .

MOTHER: Bashful?

MARTHA: Yes, that's it. He's bashful.

MOTHER: I'll go refill the cooky plate. Maybe that will help. (*Exits with plate*)

JANNIS (*Pointing at tree, eagerly*): There it is, Martha. On the table. (*For a moment* MARTHA *stares at the little tree in silence, fascinated.*)

MARTHA: Oh, I never saw such a cute little tree. (*She moves toward it, touching one of the angels reverently.* MIKE *follows, clinging to her.*)

TODD: Jannis and I made most of the ornaments.

MARTHA (*Awed*): Look, Mike. Look at the little woolly lamb. And the *real* little lollipops. (*At that* MIKE *really looks*) And the paper chains and stars and angels. And everything so cute and little.

JANNIS: It *had* to be little. (*Laughs*) You know why? It had to be little . . . because, you see, it's for Kitty.

MARTHA (*Astonished*): For Kitty?

TODD: Sure. For Kitty. That's why we didn't put on anything that could break.

MARTHA (*More astonished than ever*): But how did you *know*? Who told you? We didn't decide ourselves till this noon, at the dinner table. (JANNIS *and* TODD *look at each other, baffled.*)

TODD: What do you mean, you didn't decide?

MARTHA: You said *for Kitty.*

JANNIS: Yes, that's right.

MARTHA: But how did you know? How did you know we named the new baby Kitty? Katherine for real . . . but *Kitty* for short.

JANNIS: Oh, I . . . we . . . well, I guess people know a lot of things at Christmastime. Don't they, Todd? (*She nods at him eagerly, and he nods back.*)

TODD: Sure. At Christmastime!

MARTHA: A Christmas tree for Kitty. Oh, it's wonderful of you. It's like a birthday present and a Christmas present all in one.

TODD: It won't be hard to carry home, Martha, because nothing on it will break.

MARTHA: You even thought of that!

JANNIS: Wait. I'll write a card for it.

TODD (*Hurriedly taking off the catnip ball*): Here, tie the tag in place of this little ball . . . (*In* JANNIS'S *ear*) of catnip! (JANNIS *laughs as she slips the catnip ball in her pocket. She writes the tag.*)

JANNIS (*As she writes*): "A Christmas tree . . . for Kitty . . . from Santa Claus." (*Hangs tag where catnip ball was.*)

MARTHA: Oh, it's so wonderful . . . it makes me feel like singing.

JANNIS *and* TODD: We feel like singing too.

MOTHER (*Coming in with cookies*): Let's all sing! (MARTHA *starts* "O Tannenbaum" ("O Christmas Tree") *and others join in happily, except* MIKE *who is more interested in peeking at the little tree.*)

THE END

The Spirit of Christmas

Characters

READER
SPIRIT OF CHRISTMAS
1ST WOMAN
1ST GIRL
MILKMAN
GROCERYMAN
2ND WOMAN
2ND GIRL

TIME: *A few days before Christmas.*
SETTING: *No setting is necessary.*
AT RISE: READER *is standing downstage right, where he stays throughout the play.*

READER: The Spirit of Christmas
  Dances down the street,
  With his magic slippers
  On his magic feet.
SPIRIT (*Dancing in merrily, chanting*):
  Closed hands, closed hearts, send me away.
  Open hands, open hearts, make me stay.
READER: The Spirit of Christmas

Sees a yellow house
Slips through the keyhole
Quiet as a mouse,
Tiptoes to the kitchen,
Perches on a shelf
Near the cups and saucers
Talking to himself:

SPIRIT: Closed hands, closed hearts, send me away.

Open hands, open hearts, make me stay.

(1ST WOMAN *and* 1ST GIRL *come in, pantomime as* READER
speaks.)

READER: At the kitchen table

In the yellow house

Stands a frowny woman

In a checkered blouse,

Stands her greedy daughter

Nibbling crumbs and sweets

As they put the frosting

On their Christmas treats—

Cookies cut like circles,

Triangles, and bars,

Cookies shaped like angels,

Little moons, and stars.

(WOMAN *and* GIRL *work in silence for a moment.*)

Then there comes a rattle

On the stoop . . . (*Sound of milk bottles clinking off stage*)

1ST WOMAN: Dear me!

That must be the milkman.

Hope he doesn't see. (*Looks nervously from door to cookies.*)

GIRL: He will want a sample,

He will want a taste,

And we haven't any

Cookies here to waste.

1ST WOMAN: No, we haven't any

Sweets to give away . . .
These are meant for Christmas.
Cover up the tray!

1st GIRL (*In loud whisper as she covers tray*):
If we're very quiet
He will never know
We have all these cookies
Cooling in a row.

READER: The milkman leaves the bottles
At the door, and goes.
The Spirit of Christmas
Wrinkles up his nose.
And mother and daughter
Start to work once more.
(WOMAN *and* GIRL *work in silence for a moment.*)
Then there comes a clatter
At the kitchen door.

1st GIRL: That must be the order
From the grocery store.

1st WOMAN: Hurry, take a tea-towel,
Cover up the treats.
Grocerymen, I fear me,
Have an eye for sweets.

GROCERYMAN (*Off stage*): Order from the market!

1st WOMAN: Hide away the treats.

READER: Crack! goes a teacup
On the cupboard shelf.
Zip! go the slippers
Of the Christmas elf.
Whisk! through the keyhole,
(SPIRIT *hurries to front of stage.*)
Over the mat,
Before the girl and woman
Can say . . .

1st Woman (*Puzzled*): What's that?
   (*They look around and then go out*)

Spirit: Closed hands, closed hearts, send me away,
   Pity the people on Christmas Day
   Whose hands are closed and whose hearts are small.
   They won't be merry at all, at all, at all.

Reader: The Spirit of Christmas
   Sees another house,
   Brushes off his jacket,
   Straightens up his blouse
   Peeks inside the window,
   Squeezes through a crack,
   Perches on a platter
   On the china rack.

Spirit: Closed hands, closed hearts, send me away.
   Open hands, open hearts, make me stay.
   (*2nd Woman and 2nd Girl come in.*)

Reader: At the kitchen table
   In the second house
   Stands a jolly woman
   In a colored blouse,
   Stands her merry daughter
   Smiling at the sweets
   As they spread the frosting
   On their Christmas treats.
   (*Woman and Girl work at the cookies, having a good time.*)
   Then there comes a rattle
   On the stoop . . .

2nd Woman: I say,
   That must be the milkman. (*Calls out cheerfully*) Do not
     rush away!

2nd Girl (*Calling*): You must have a sample,
   You must have a bite
   Of our Christmas cookies,

Red, and green, and white.

(2ND WOMAN *and* GIRL *go to door with cookie trays.*)

MILKMAN (*At door*): Thank you. Thank you kindly.

Aren't they pretty, though!

2ND WOMAN: Put one in your pocket,

Munch it as you go.

2ND GIRL: Isn't Christmas jolly?

MILKMAN (*Merrily, munching cookie*): Guess I ought to know!

READER: The milkman goes off whistling,

Merry as a bird.

The elf atop the platter

Doesn't say a word,

But oh, there is a twinkle

Shining in his eye,

And oh, there is a chuckle

As the cooks go by.

(2ND WOMAN *and* GIRL *return to their work.*)

Mother and daughter

Start to work once more . . . (*Slight pause as they work*)

Then there comes a clatter

At the kitchen door.

2ND GIRL: That must be the order

From the grocery store.

2ND WOMAN: Is there any coffee

In the coffeepot?

2ND GIRL: Yes. I'll pour a cup full,

Nice and steaming hot.

2ND WOMAN: And we'll pass the cookies.

My, we've made a stack.

Grocerymen get weary

Rushing forth and back . . .

GROCERYMAN (*Off stage*): Order from the market.

2ND GIRL: Come and have a snack!

(2ND GIRL *and* WOMAN *go to the door with coffee and cookies.*)

READER: Zip! from the platter
   On the cupboard shelf
   Springs a merry fellow,
   Springs the Christmas elf,
   Dancing on his tiptoes,
   Talking to himself:
SPIRIT: Closed hands, closed hearts, send me away.
   Open hands, open hearts. . . . *Here I'll stay!*
   Here I'll stay for Christmas, here I'll dance and jig—
   Blessings on the people when their hearts are big!
   (*He dances a jolly jig.*)

THE END

The Christmas Cake

Characters

NARRATOR
MRS. McGILLY
MR. McGILLY
NEIGHBOR BOY

SETTING: *The McGilly kitchen.*

AT RISE: *The* NARRATOR *enters and stands at one side. As the* NARRATOR *speaks, the others pantomime their actions.*

NARRATOR: Mrs. McGilly was very proud,
   A very proud soul was she,
   She knew how to bake a holiday cake
   From a secret recipe. (MRS. McGILLY *comes bustling in, puts on apron, begins to mix cake.*)
MRS. McGILLY: Nobody else in the neighborhood
   Can make such a cake as mine:
   The cherries I canned will surely be grand
   To dress up my cake just fine.
NARRATOR: Mr. McGilly was slow and kind,
   As slow as his spouse was fast.
   He fancied to sit and whittle a bit

And dream as the hours went past. (MR. MCGILLY *comes in slowly and good-naturedly, and sits down to whittle.* MRS. MCGILLY *turns to look at him, her hands on her hips.*)

MRS. MCGILLY (*Scolding*):

Get me some kindling and fix the fire.
I'm making a Christmas cake—
It's specially nice with cherries and spice,
And specially hard to bake . . .

Take out the ashes and poke the coals,
Don't dawdle around and halt.
Go rustle some wood . . . if the cake's not good
It surely will be your fault! (MR. MCGILLY *puts down his whittling and goes to peer at the stove. He fusses around and pokes the fire.* MRS. MCGILLY *keeps one eye on him while trying to follow the recipe with the other.*)

Hurry, I'm almost ready now.
Why isn't that oven hot?
I soon must go down for groceries in town
That *you*, for a change, forgot.

MR. MCGILLY (*Shaking head over fire*):

Something's the matter. The fire's no good.
The oven is cold as stone.
If you have to flee, just leave it to me—
I'll tend to that cake alone. (*He puts in more paper and kindling.*)

MRS. MCGILLY (*Shaking her finger at him*): See you don't ruin our Christmas cake!

If anything turns out wrong
I'm sure to have fits, so use all your wits.
It's late. I must run along. (*She puts the batter in the pan ready for the oven, then takes off her apron and puts on wraps.* MR. MCGILLY *meanwhile continues to fuss with*

the fire. As MRS. MCGILLY *exits she turns in the doorway*
and shakes a warning finger at her husband. Then she goes
out.)

NARRATOR: Mr. McGilly meant well of course
(In spite of the looks he got),
Intending to bake the holiday cake
As soon as the fire was hot.
But how could he know that a boy would call,
A boy from the neighborhood,
And ask for a lift on a Christmas gift
He was whittling from maple wood? (*There is a knock on*
the door. MR. MCGILLY *leaves his job at the stove and goes*
to the door. A BOY *comes in with a half-finished carving.*
MR. MCGILLY *examines it, has the* BOY *sit down. Of course*
he completely forgets about the fire.)
Mr. McGilly sat down and showed
What grooves in the wood to make,
And, oh, he forgot when the fire was hot
To put in the Christmas cake!

MR. MCGILLY (*Helping the* BOY):
Whittle this rounder, and whittle this thin,
And whittle this end away.
The critter will stand on his legs just grand,
All ready for Christmas day.

BOY: Mr. McGilly, I knew you'd help!
There's nothing that you can't do.
(*He looks out of the window, and gives a start.*)
Oh, golly, your wife! She runs for her life . . .
I think I'll be running too! (MR. MCGILLY *remembers the*
cake and rushes to the stove. The BOY *gathers up his carving*
and knife and rushes for the door as MR. MCGILLY *rushes*
for the cake. At the door the BOY *and* MRS. MCGILLY *col-*
lide and almost knock each other over. BOY *hurries out*
with a frightened glance over his shoulder.)

MRS. McGILLY (*Frantically*):

Help me to rescue the cherry cake!

Help me to save my skin!

I boasted a lot, and then I forgot

To put any *cherries* in! (*She sees her husband holding pan with the unbaked cake in his hands.*)

Haven't you baked it? You darling man!

The cherries can go on top,

And no one will know my error, and so

My fame as a cook won't stop! (*She sighs with relief, takes the cake pan and puts cherries on top, poking them down in the batter. Then, smiling, she puts the cake in the oven and pats her husband lovingly on the back.*)

NARRATOR: Mrs. McGilly for once was glad

Her husband had dreamy ways.

She urged him to sit and whittle a bit

And showered him with words of praise.

Mr. McGilly looked up and grinned

And said to his spouse . . .

MR. McGILLY: My dear,

Nothing we'll get can compare, I bet,

With our holiday cake this year!

(*They smile happily at each other.*)

THE END

Where Is Christmas?

GIRL: It isn't in the tinsel,
the shining, twining tinsel,
the gleaming, beaming tinsel
that dresses up the tree . . .

BOY: It isn't in the shimmer
of colored lights that glimmer . . .

GROUP: Christmas is . . .

                  hmmmm, let's see . . .

BOY: It isn't in the presents,
the wrapped-so-brightly presents,
the tapped-so-lightly presents
we stand and wonder at . . .

GIRL: It isn't in the kitchen
where odors are bewitchin' . . .

GROUP: Christmas is

           more than that . . .

GIRL: It isn't in the spangles,
the baubles and the bangles . . .

BOY: It's not the jingle-jangles
that set the day apart . . .

GROUP: It isn't in the wrappings,
the showiness and trappings . . .
Christmas is

       IN THE HEART!

Christmas!

(BOYS *and* GIRLS *stand toward back of stage holding large cards with letters spelling* CHRISTMAS. *As each one speaks he takes a step forward.*)

C arolers, candles, chimes a-ringing,
H olly wreaths with berries clinging,
R eindeer, fairy-fast and tiny,
I   cicles all bright and shiny,
S tars and stockings, shoppers streaming
T hrough the town, and tinsel gleaming,
M istletoe in waxen glory,
A ngels from the Christmas story,
S anta with his sack to carry . . .

That spells CHRISTMAS. Make it merry!

The Christmas Mitten Lady

Once a dear old lady,
when Christmastime was near,
decided that a party
would fill her heart with cheer.
She gave her cat a loving pat
and murmured, "Girls and boys
are fun to see around a tree
with all their jolly noise.

"I truly love a party,"
she said. "I truly do.
I'd love to ask the neighbors—
not merely one or two,
but all the girls with bobs and curls
and pigtails down their backs,
and all the boys in corduroys
and overalls and slacks!"

The cat purred once in treble,
and once he purred in bass,
as if to say, "Sounds dandy."
And then he washed his face,
and in a heap he went to sleep
and dreamed of catnip tea.

While near at hand his mistress planned
her party Christmas tree.

Just then she heard a knocking.
A lad was at the door.
His face was full of freckles
(there wasn't room for more!).
"Hello," he said, and wagged his head,
"we hope you'll help this year.
We have a scheme that's like a dream
for spreading Christmas cheer:

"Our schoolroom plans a party
for Christmas, but, you see,
instead of getting presents
we'll trim a MITTEN TREE . . .
with woolly mitts of proper fits
for kids across the ocean
who haven't much to wear and such.
That's how we got the notion."

The dear old lady twittered:
"With mittens? I declare!
You'll trim a tree with mittens?
I'll gladly knit a pair."
And so she took her pocketbook
and hurried to the shops,
and bought a lot of yarn . . . with what
she'd saved for lollipops!

The mitts she knit were beauties.
The news spread very fast.
"I, too, am hunting mittens,"
said Jerry, coming past.

And Mary Ann, and Hugh, and Dan,
and Phyllis, and Louise—
all spoke of mitts of proper fits
for youngsters overseas.

The lady's party money
bought woolly yarn and gay!
Her dimes for Christmas candy
bought skeins of red and gray!
Till every cent was quickly spent . . .
her party plans were over,
but oh, the Tree, the Mitten Tree,
was certainly in clover.

"I truly love a party,"
the dear old lady said,
"but this year, seems I've chosen
a knitting spree instead!
The girls and boys will have their joys
at school some afternoon,
but I will sit, and knit, and knit,
and sing a mitten tune:

   "Bright mitts, light mitts,
   fit-just-right mitts,

   Blue mitts, new mitts,
   wool-all-through mitts,

   Gray mitts, gay mitts,
   good-for-play mitts,

   Long mitts, strong mitts,
   can't-go-wrong mitts . . .

Oh, how jolly it must be
to dance around a Mitten Tree."

And then an invitation
(all unexpected!) came:
"Dear Christmas Mitten Lady,
we hope you will be game
to dance with glee around our Tree
and join our party fun.
You've helped us more than twenty-four
times twenty folks have done!"

The dear old lady chuckled,
and hurried (with her cat)
to join the Christmas party.
She wore her nicest hat.
And oh, the glee she felt to see
the mitts on every twig,
and hear the joys of girls and boys.
Her heart felt awfully big.

"I truly love a party,"
she said. "I truly do.
I've been to quite a number,
and given quite a few . . .
a Christmas one is always fun,
it makes the heart-bells chime,
but, oh, my dears, I've not in YEARS
had such a lovely time!"

NOTE: This poem could be given as a pantomime for several
children, using a reader or narrator.

With Christmas in the Air

Ours is a house of mystery—
secrets are everywhere:
   Don't go peeking behind the chair!
   Don't look under the cellar stair!
   Close the closet—beware, beware!
Happens each year in history—
with Christmas in the air.

Ours is a house of mystery—
everyone acts so queer:
   Don't look back of the chiffonier,
   or into the basket of fishing gear!
   Don't peek under the chest—you hear?
Happens each year in history—
with Christmas almost here.

At Last It Came

I thought about a little wish
all by myself,
and it wasn't for the cookies
on the pantry shelf,
and it wasn't for an orange
or a candy cane
or permission to draw pictures
on the windowpane,
and it wasn't for a paint box
or a puzzle game . . .
it only was for CHRISTMAS,
and, at last, it came!

NEW YEAR'S DAY

Benjy Makes a Resolution

ALL: The old year was thinning,
        the New Year beginning,
        when Benjamin's wife made a plan:
WIFE: Some good resolution
        might be the solution
        of all of our troubles, my man.
        Let's take it upon us
        to make some good promise.
        Let's start the New Year with a bang!
BENJY: I'll start being judicious
        and act more ambitious,
        if *you* will not scold and harangue.

ALL: So Ben got ambitious!
        He helped with the dishes.
        Bang! bang! went the platters and pots.
        He vacuumed the rug
        with such vigor he dug
        a hole under each of the spots.
        He shook out the pillows
        till feathery billows
        of down covered dressers and chairs.
        Bang! bang! went the vases
        in dust-catching places.

Bang! bang! went the mop on the stairs.
But the worst came the day
Benjy polished away
at the glass of the old chandelier:
it tore from its socket
and fell like a rocket
on Benjy's bare noddle, poor dear.

WIFE: Such doings! Good gracious,
my plan was fallacious!
Let's give up our promises, Ben.
This pace is terrific.
To be more specific,
please, Benjy, get lazy again!

The Snowman's Resolution

The snowman's hat was crooked
and his nose was out of place
and several of his whiskers
had fallen from his face,

But the snowman didn't notice
for he was trying to think
of a New Year's resolution
that wouldn't melt or shrink.

He thought and planned and pondered
with his little snowball head
till his eyes began to glisten
and his toes began to spread;

At last he said, "I've got it!
I'll make a firm resolve
that no matter WHAT the weather
my smile will not dissolve."

Now the snowman acted wisely
and his resolution won,
for his splinter smile was WOODEN
and it didn't mind the sun!

LINCOLN'S BIRTHDAY

Abe's Winkin' Eye

Characters

ABE LINCOLN, *12*
SALLY, *his sister, 14*
TOM LINCOLN, *his father*
SARAH BUSH LINCOLN, *his stepmother*
MATILDA (*Tilda*), *about 8* ⎫
SARAH ELIZABETH (*Sarah Bets*), *15* ⎬ *his stepsisters*
JOHNNY, *his stepbrother, about 6*
NATTY GRIGSBY, *a friend*

TIME: *Late afternoon on a summer day in 1821.*
SETTING: *The interior of the Lincoln cabin on Little Pigeon Creek in southern Indiana.*
AT RISE: SALLY *is peeling vegetables for the soup kettle.* MRS. LINCOLN *is sewing on a jacket.*

MRS. LINCOLN: Just seems I can't ever get homey-close to your brother, Sally. 'Course I never let on as I'm tryin'. He's real polite and obligin' and all, and he never lies to me, or speaks an unkind word. Still, just seems I can't get close to him somehow. And I'd like to. The good Lord knows I'd like to. Heart close . . . winkin' close . . . if you know what I mean.

SALLY: Abe's queer that-a-way. He's got a mullin'-over streak, Abe has. He can't seem to shake things off, like me. Thinkin' about our mammy, now. Seems he can't get her out of his mind, though it's goin' on three years since we laid her over there in the clearin'. In the path of the deer-run, we laid her. She was always so fond of the deer comin' and goin' on their way to the salt-lick.

MRS. LINCOLN: Poor darlin', takin' the fever, and her still young and all!

SALLY: The week she was ailin', Abe'd just stand and look at her, solemn-like. Just stand a-lookin' at her lyin' under the bearskin in the corner with the fever-light in her eyes. Seems he can't forget that week our mammy was ailin'.

MRS. LINCOLN: Appears he'd rather keep rememberin' her than have me around tryin' to take her place. Not as I'm the kind of stepmother to hold it against him, though. He's got a deep-down feelin' for his mammy, and I say a deep-down feelin's somethin' mighty sacred to have.

SALLY: It was the time of year, too, made it bad. You know how late October is sometimes—with the leaves down, 'ceptin' on the oaks, and a bleak sky showin' through the branches, and gray cold after we'd been a-used to summer. That's the way it was when she took the fever. And nobody knowin' what to do, and the herb doctor thirty miles away.

MRS. LINCOLN: Poor darlin'.

SALLY: Wasn't much sun that week. And wasn't much time for Abe and Pappy and me to get used to the idea of her not up and doin'.

MRS. LINCOLN: I'd like to make it up to you-all for losin' her, I would.

SALLY: Oh, you do, Mammy! We never had things so good before. (*Looks around proudly*) Now we got a board floor and a rag rug, 'stead of just packed-down dirt. And a win-

dow! Pappy never got around to cuttin' through a window
before. And the bureau-chest you brought, and the feather
beds, and the hickory chairs, and the pots and pans, and
the books . . . Abe's plumb daffy about the books, though
maybe he's never thanked you, out loud, for lettin' him
read them.

MRS. LINCOLN: It's real nice the way he tells those Aesop
fables to my two young 'uns. Tilda, now, she'd like nothin'
better than to follow Abe around like a little yaller dog.

SALLY: He'd rather read or tell stories than eat, Abe would.
If only he could have a little more schoolin', Mammy. He'd
read real good then, like a preacher. I think Abe's smart,
don't you? Though Pappy says he's a lazy one.

MRS. LINCOLN: From the very first day your pappy brought
me and mine here from Kentucky, from the very first day
I set eyes on your brother, I put him down as a thinkin'
boy. Not just ordinary. There's something about Abe
that's different, Sally. I can't exactly put my finger on it,
but it's there.

SALLY: He never had much chance, but he's real good at
learnin'. We went to school some when we lived on the
Knob Creek farm. That's when Abe was seven. Since we
moved here to Pigeon Creek, we only went to school by
littles. It was nine miles each way to walk, and then pretty
soon the school closed up.

MRS. LINCOLN: I'd like to see Abe get more schoolin', I would
for certain sure. He's got somethin' in his head under that
mop of black hair. Anyone can tell just watchin' him
lookin' off into the distance, thinkin' and thinkin'.

SALLY: *Dreamin'*, Pappy says. He says Abe's got enough education to last his lifetime. He says now he's twelve years
old and so big for his age and strong, he can do a man's
work.

MRS. LINCOLN: Your pappy gets peculiar ideas sometimes. Only I wouldn't ever tell him, in so many words.

SALLY: Not in so many words. But you got other ways! The window, now. My mammy always hankered for a window, but Pappy said the door was enough. And the floor! He thought a packed earth floor was good enough for anyone . . . before he married you. You got ways!

MRS. LINCOLN: One of 'em is through that cookin' book I brought from Kentucky, Sally. And don't you forget it. Can't any man resist some nice tasty cookin'. (TILDA *and* JOHNNY *come running in.*)

TILDA: When's Abe a-comin' home?

MRS. LINCOLN: Land sakes, you pulled all the weeds out of the bean patch already?

TILDA: When's Abe a-comin'?

MRS. LINCOLN: You'd think you was a little banty hen, Tilda, the way you cluck around after Abe.

SALLY: He'll come as soon as he's through pullin' corn fodder for Jim Gentry. Maybe early, maybe late. Depends on how much there's left to finish up.

JOHNNY: He said he'd read to us.

TILDA: From "Robinson Crusoe."

JOHNNY: Robinson Crusoe, Robinson Crusoe!

MRS. LINCOLN: Then I'm thinkin' you'd better finish weedin' the beans so you'll be ready for him. (*Gets up and goes to cupboard*) Here's a piece o' corn pone if you're hungry.

JOHNNY (*With his mouth full*): Where's Sarah Bets?

MRS. LINCOLN: Don't you remember your sister's helpin' over at Mis' Romaine's today? Ought to be comin' home any minute, though, I should think.

TILDA: She won't play with us . . . now she's so grown up. Now she's got her head all full of Denny Hanks, like to burst.

MRS. LINCOLN: Why, Tilda.

JOHNNY: She won't play with us.

SALLY: Never mind, Tilda. And don't you mind either, Johnny. When your sister and my cousin get themselves married, we-all will be more related than ever.

TILDA: What'll I be to Abe then?

MRS. LINCOLN: Why, let's see—you'll be stepsister and cousin-in-law, I reckon, all at the same time.

TILDA: Is that good?

MRS. LINCOLN: 'Course it's good. Now go 'long with you and finish pullin' those weeds. (TILDA *and* JOHNNY *start out.* JOHNNY *turns back.*)

JOHNNY: Here comes Sarah Bets now.

TILDA: Comin' up the path from the road. Let's go meet her, Johnny. (*They are gone.*)

MRS. LINCOLN: Comin' home out of breath, like as not, so she'll have plenty of time to spruce up for Denny before supper. These young 'uns, how they grow up! Here's Sarah 'Lizbeth more'n fifteen already, and seems just a few years ago she was a babe in arms. She was a pretty baby, Sally. Mr. Johnston and I felt right smart havin' such a pretty baby, for our first one.

SALLY: She's still pretty, I think. Real pretty. Wish I was.

MRS. LINCOLN: Now, there's nothin' wrong with your looks, honey girl. You got your mother's dark complexion, your pappy says. And her gray eyes. And being a girl, you can be glad you didn't come out with a nose like Abe's. 'Course it's all right for a boy, a big nose like that, and a lower lip that likes to want to stick out. I always say looks don' make much difference with a boy. (*Thoughtfully*) There's somethin' about Abe's looks, though . . . somethin' I like . . . even if some folks say he's homely as a mud fence.

SALLY: It's been hard on Abe. That big nose . . . and him growin' so fast he's always a couple sizes too big for his britches. (SARAH BETS *comes in, sputtering.*)

Sarah Bets: That Abe! Couldn't anybody a-done it but Abe.

Mrs. Lincoln: Done what, Sarah Bets?

Sally: What's Abe a-gone and done now?

Sarah Bets: Wouldn't anybody else a-thought of it just like that. And right along the road too!

Sally: Along the road?

Mrs. Lincoln: How do you know Abe did it, whatever it is?

Sarah Bets: 'Cause it looks just like one of his pranks, that's why. Fresh cut on a poplar tree. Wasn't any knife but Abe Lincoln's did it, I can see that, easy as lickin' a dish. Initials cut out plain as day and big as life: "S. E. J." . . .

Sally: S.E.J. That'd be Sarah Elizabeth Johnston, I reckon.

Sarah Bets: And "D.H."

Mrs. Lincoln: Who'd that be now? D. H. Anyone around here with initials of "D.H.," Sally?

Sally: Couldn't be Dennis Hanks, could it? Couldn't be my cousin Denny?

Sarah Bets: Now you're a-makin' fun of me, you are. It's not that I'm objectin' to havin' my initials and Denny's set together, close-like. It's not that. It's just the way Abe did it, the old smarty.

Mrs. Lincoln: Two hearts linked together, your initials in one and Denny's in the other? That what you mean, Sarah Bets? And what's wrong with that, honey child? It's been done since the beginnin' of time.

Sarah Bets (*Mournfully*): But it's *not* two hearts, Mammy. I wouldn't be objectin' to hearts. Like as you say, that's been done since the beginnin' of time. But that Abe has to think up somethin' different. The smarty!

Mrs. Lincoln (*Teasingly*): Just as I was tellin' Sally a mite ago—Abe's a thinkin' boy, he is.

Sally: What'd he go think up now, Sarah Bets?

SARAH BETS: If it was hearts, I wouldn't be mindin'. But *eyes!*

SALLY: Eyes?

MRS. LINCOLN: You mean Abe went and carved eyes atop your initials, 'stead of hearts around 'em?

SARAH BETS: Yes, he did. Wouldn't anybody else be so teasin' mean. Two eyes. And one of 'em *winkin'*. That's the worst!

MRS. LINCOLN (*Laughing*): One of 'em winkin'? Well, now, Sarah Bets, I call that real clever, I do. One of 'em winkin'!

SARAH BETS: Well, it's not very funny to *me*. Folks passin' by, seein' that, what'll they think? Oh, Mammy . . .

MRS. LINCOLN: There, there, honey, don't you go feelin' bad. You're not even sure it was Abe did it, though I must say as it sounds like him. He's got a prankin' streak, that's all. Tell you what. When Sally gets through a-peelin' the vegetables, you both go 'long with the parin' knife, and I'm bettin' you can turn those eyes into hearts easy as a cat can lick her paw.

SALLY: 'Course we can, Sarah Bets. (*Giggles*) That'll give Abe somethin' to think about next time he passes by that tree.

SARAH BETS: Wish I could think up some way to get even with him. He's always up to tricks. But it's hard to get even with Abe. He could talk a duck out of its webbed feet!

SALLY: He's got a smooth tongue in his mouth, all right.

SARAH BETS: And a lucky piece in his pocket. Ever since he found that lucky stone, he's been ridin' a high horse. Thinks he can get away with anythin'! If only I could get that lucky stone away from him, maybe he wouldn't act so smart-like.

MRS. LINCOLN: Sarah Elizabeth Johnston, what a way to

talk. Abe sets great store by that lucky piece. You leave him be. (*Goes to cupboard*) Here, have a bit of corn pone and yaller honey, and you'll be feelin' better. (*Chuckles as she gets cornbread*) One of 'em winkin'! (*There is a shrill whistle outside. The women stop to listen. The whistle is repeated.*)

SALLY: Sounds like Natty Grigsby. Come to see if Abe's home, likely.

SARAH BETS (*Looking out the door*): It's Natty, all right. With his fishin' pole. Wonder how he got off work so early.

MRS. LINCOLN: Might be his pappy's hankerin' for a taste of fish for supper. A good change from pork, I say. Have Natty come in and set, Sarah Bets. Till Abe gets home.

SARAH BETS (*Calling*): Abe's not home yet, Natty. Come in and set a minute. (*Pause*) Oh, I reckon he'll be back pretty soon. Come on, we won't take a bite outen you. (*In a minute or two NATTY, a boy of 12, rather small for his age, comes in shyly.*)

NATTY: When'll Abe be home, Mis' Lincoln?

MRS. LINCOLN: Shouldn't be too long now. He figured he might finish up at Gentry's around four.

SARAH BETS: If he didn't get himself mixed up in too much mischief.

SALLY: Or if he didn't get a-hold of a book to read. Did you come along the road, Natty?

NATTY: No, through the woods. Maybe I better not wait. Maybe Abe could meet me at the rapids . . .

MRS. LINCOLN: What's your hurry, Natty? Set still a minute and tell us the news. What's been happenin' over your way?

NATTY: Nothin' much. Aaron's cow had a calf. Twins!

MRS. LINCOLN: Twins! You don't say. That doesn't happen often with cows.

NATTY: They're pretty small, but Aaron thinks they'll be all right.

SALLY: How's Aaron? I haven't seen him for a dog's age.

NATTY: He's all right.

MRS. LINCOLN: And how's your folks?

NATTY: They're all right.

MRS. LINCOLN: And your mammy?

NATTY: She's all right. Only she broke one of her china cups last week and she felt real bad.

SARAH BETS: Well, I should think she would. China cups don't grow on bushes along Little Pigeon Creek. Not that I can see.

SALLY: How's the summer been treatin' you, Natty?

NATTY: All right. You know what? Last week, the day it was Friday the thirteenth, I killed a rattlesnake. Thirteen rattles!

MRS. LINCOLN: What do you think of that? Thirteen! On the thirteenth. And folks let on as Friday the thirteenth is unlucky.

NATTY: Maybe it wasn't unlucky on the thirteenth, but it was afterward.

SALLY: What do you mean, Natty?

NATTY: Come winter, Azel Dorsey's a-goin' to start a school, and Mammy says we've got to go, all us kids. 'Cept maybe Aaron is too old.

MRS. LINCOLN: A school? Is that what you said, Natty?

NATTY: Yes'm. Over at Azel Dorsey's.

MRS. LINCOLN: Where's that?

SALLY: About four miles from here, I think. Abe and I went over once or twice.

NATTY: I wish I was as big as Abe. Then maybe they wouldn't make me go.

MRS. LINCOLN: If Abe was to go, you wouldn't mind it so much, would you, Natty?

NATTY: No'm. It would be fun if Abe went. Do you think Mr. Lincoln would let him?

MRS. LINCOLN: I'd like for Sally to go too, and Tilda and Johnny. I certain sure would. (*She gets up suddenly and puts sewing away.*) Sally, I'm a-goin' to make that special spoon-bread your pappy likes so well. It just came to my mind, all of a sudden. See if the hens have laid any new eggs, will you?

SALLY: The special spoon-bread! (*Smiles at her stepmother*) Oh, Mammy . . . can't any man resist some nice tasty cookin', I've heared tell! (*She runs out.*)

MRS. LINCOLN: A school!

NATTY: Just one of those old blab schools. Everybody talkin' at the same time, learnin' his lessons.

MRS. LINCOLN: Well, I say anybody ought to learn double in a school like that, gettin' educated through his eyes and ears both, at the same time. Sarah Bets, whyn't you go for the winter term yourself?

SARAH BETS: Me? I'm too old, Mammy. Besides . . . (*She picks up the paring knife.*)

MRS. LINCOLN: Besides . . . one of 'em winkin'. (*She chuckles. In a moment* SALLY *comes hurrying back with eggs.*)

SALLY: Here's enough eggs for the best special spoon-bread you ever made, Mammy. Now can Sarah Bets and I go tend to that business with the parin' knife?

MRS. LINCOLN (*Teasing*): I wouldn't have the *heart* to say you couldn't. (SALLY *and* SARAH BETS *go out giggling.* NATTY *looks after them.*)

NATTY: Guess I'd best be goin' too, Mis' Lincoln. Abe can meet me at the crick.

MRS. LINCOLN: I reckon there's a charge for goin' to that school, Natty?

NATTY: Yes'm. I don't know how much, though. And there's books to get. Spellin' book, 'rithmetic book, and singin' book, anyway. You really think Mr. Lincoln will let Abe go?

MRS. LINCOLN: I wouldn't be *too* surprised as he would. But I'm not one to go around countin' chickens till they're well hatched out and walkin'.

NATTY (*Looking out the door*): Holy fishhooks, there comes Mr. Lincoln himself. I'm a-goin'! You tell Abe . . . (*He ducks out the door.* MRS. LINCOLN *busies herself at the fire-place, poking up the fire, getting out the iron skillet. In a few moments* TOM LINCOLN, *dressed in backwoods costume, comes in.*)

MR. LINCOLN: 'Evenin', Sairy.

MRS. LINCOLN: 'Evenin', Tom. Come, set right down and rest yourself. Did you have a hard day workin'?

MR. LINCOLN: Hard enough. Trees get tougher every day they get older. Harder to cut.

MRS. LINCOLN: 'Course they do. Just set and get a good rest for your feet before supper.

MR. LINCOLN: Where are the young 'uns?

MRS. LINCOLN: Johnny and Tilda are weedin' in the bean patch. Leastwise they're supposed to be. Sally and Sarah Bets just went for a little walk. Gets stuffy, bein' indoors too long, you know. 'Specially when you're young.

MR. LINCOLN: And Abe?

MRS. LINCOLN: Abe's not home from Gentry's yet.

MR. LINCOLN: I've been wonderin' about Abe.

MRS. LINCOLN: Why for, Tom?

MR. LINCOLN: Big strappin' boy like that—ought to put more work behind him than he does. I'm afeared he's more than a mite lazy, Sairy.

MRS. LINCOLN: He's only twelve. And he's got his thoughts to think about.

MR. LINCOLN: Goin' on big as a man, Abe is. Could almost turn out a man's work if he'd a mind to. Trouble with Abe, he'd rather lie on the woodpile readin' than get down and split a little kindlin', to earn his salt.

MRS. LINCOLN: He's a readin' boy, all right. And he's got a good head on his shoulders. You know, Tom, if he had a little more schoolin' he'd make something out of himself. Preacher, maybe.

MR. LINCOLN: He's got enough education already. Folks in the backwoods don't need any more than to know how to write a little, figure a little, and read a little. Too much education gives a fellow ideas, Sairy. Like as if he's too good for his folks.

MRS. LINCOLN: Abe'd never be like that.

MR. LINCOLN: 'Pears to me you spend a lot of your time standin' up for Abe. I can't see he shines up to you much.

MRS. LINCOLN: I'm just thinkin' what his own mother would be thinkin', Tom. (*Busies herself with mixing bowl*) Had a little extry time this evenin'. Thought I'd mix up some of that special spoon-bread you fancy. That is, if you still fancy it.

MR. LINCOLN (*Pleased*): Can't ever have too much of that spoon-bread. (*In a moment his pleasure turns to a sigh*) Might help me take my mind off Squire Carter.

MRS. LINCOLN: He been after you again?

MR. LINCOLN: Still wantin' me to sell him that little piece of land.

MRS. LINCOLN: I don't trust him, Tom.

MR. LINCOLN: Says he's got everythin' down in black and white. I just got to sign. We could use the money, Sairy.

MRS. LINCOLN: You read what's down in black and white, Tom?

MR. LINCOLN: It's lawyer talk. I can't make much out of it. Lots of big words beatin' around the bush, seems to me.

MRS. LINCOLN: Too bad Abe couldn't a-had more schoolin'. He could of helped you figure it out.

MR. LINCOLN: Hmmm.

MRS. LINCOLN: Maybe he could even be a lawyer himself, if he had more education. Never can tell.

MR. LINCOLN: Oh, Abe'll make out all right. He's big and strong, and can't anyone swing an ax better than he can already.

MRS. LINCOLN: Reckon I'll put in an extry egg. Give it a nice rich yeller color, that-a-way. (*After a pause*) I heard some news this afternoon, Tom.

MR. LINCOLN: Did you?

MRS. LINCOLN: It'll mean more work for me, gettin' the children's clothes in shape and all.

MR. LINCOLN: For what?

MRS. LINCOLN: They'll all be needin' new wool socks for one thing. But I'm glad to do it as a hen settin' on eggs.

MR. LINCOLN: What you talkin' about, Sairy?

MRS. LINCOLN: Natty Grigsby was over this afternoon. Says Azel Dorsey is fixin' to open a school this winter.

MR. LINCOLN: School, eh?

MRS. LINCOLN: Reckon I'll put in a little more shortenin' too, while I'm at it. And sweetenin'. Can't make good spoonbread unless you put plenty of good things inside. (*She works industriously over the mixing bowl.*) Yes, Azel Dorsey's a-goin' to open a school this winter. Can't think of anythin' could pleasure me more. The young 'uns ought to be in school, all of them. Even Sally. She's not too old—only fourteen. She'll be needin' a new linsey-woolsey dress, I reckon. And Abe'll need a new jacket. His is worn all frazzle-tazzle and out at the elbows.

MR. LINCOLN: Abe?

MRS. LINCOLN: He's just a boy yet, Tom, though he's so strappin' big. And he's got a deep-down hankerin' to larn. He's walked miles just to borrow a book!

MR. LINCOLN: Might spoil him to get more education.

MRS. LINCOLN: Not Abe. I'll make him a homespun jacket, and plenty big . . . so his arms won't go a-danglin' out of the sleeves.

MR. LINCOLN: What you so all-fired concerned over Abe for, Sairy?

MRS. LINCOLN: Could be with a mite more schoolin' Abe could read the fancy words Squire Carter got beatin' around the bush.

MR. LINCOLN: Well . . . could be.

MRS. LINCOLN: 'Pears I never mixed up a better-lookin' spoon-bread batter. And, land sakes, there's so much you'd think I'd a-doubled the receipt! (*Pause*) Wouldn't anythin' pleasure me more, Tom, than if you'd tell Abe he could go to Azel Dorsey's school.

MR. LINCOLN: Well . . .

MRS. LINCOLN: It's only for the winter. There's plenty of time for Abe to work the rest of the year.

MR. LINCOLN: There's the cost.

MRS. LINCOLN: Abe'll be glad to work to pay for it. And he won't be dreamin'-slow about *that* kind of work, I'm a-thinkin'.

MR. LINCOLN: Well . . .

MRS. LINCOLN: You tell him, Tom. Walk out with him for a piece and tell him. Tell Abe when he gets home, this very day . . . (ABE, *a tall, gangling boy of 12, ambles in.*)

ABE: Tell me what, Pappy?

MR. LINCOLN (*Shrugging*): I'm not full minded to tell you anythin' . . . not yet, leastwise.

ABE (*To* MRS. LINCOLN, *with reserved politeness*): 'Evenin', ma'am.

MRS. LINCOLN: 'Evenin' to you, Abe. I hope you didn't go leave your appetite over at Gentry's place. We're a-havin' your pappy's special spoon-bread for supper.

ABE (*Smiling, then becoming reserved again*): Reckon I better tote you some spring water before supper. (*Turns to his father as he picks up bucket*) I got somethin' I'm full minded to tell *you*, Pappy.

MR. LINCOLN: Ye have?

ABE: It's about Squire Carter. Happened to mention to Allen Gentry while we were pullin' fodder that the Squire is dickerin' to buy a piece of your land. Allen says he heard his pappy say he'd trust Squire Carter just about as far as a rattlesnake. Says the Squire is tricky as a red-tailed fox when it comes to puttin' words down on paper.

MR. LINCOLN (*Standing up*): Reckon I'll walk a ways with you to the spring, Abe. Got somethin' I'm minded to tell you, after all. (ABE *and* MR. LINCOLN *exit.* MRS. LINCOLN *watches them from the door. She smiles as she turns back to work. In a moment* TILDA *and* JOHNNY *hurry in, look around.*)

TILDA: Didn't I see Abe a-comin' across the clearin'? Where's he at?

MRS. LINCOLN: He's gone to the spring for water, Tilda.

TILDA: Come on, Johnny, we'll follow him. (*Eagerly*) We'll go part way and hide behind the trees like Indians . . .

JOHNNY: Like Indians.

TILDA: And jump out and scare him when he comes back.

JOHNNY (*Jumping*): Like Indians!

MRS. LINCOLN: Not so fast there, Matilda Johnston. You'd better think of tendin' to your p's and q's. Abe's pappy is a-walkin' with him on the spring path.

TILDA *and* JOHNNY: Oh!

TILDA: I reckon we won't be Indians and scare Abe then.

MRS. LINCOLN: Sarah Bets and Sally will be comin' home along the road soon. Why don't you meet them instead?

TILDA (*Always ready for anything*): Come on, Johnny.

JOHNNY (*Suddenly distracted*): Where's my stone? (*He feels his clothes, looks in pocket of shirt.*)

MRS. LINCOLN: What stone, honey boy?

JOHNNY (*On the verge of tears*): My lucky stone. Like Abe's.

TILDA: It isn't either like Abe's. It's not near as good.

JOHNNY: It is too.

TILDA (*To her mother*): Just a silly little flat stone he found near the crick. Doesn't have a hole in it like Abe's.

JOHNNY (*Whimpering*): I lost my lucky stone.

TILDA: You can find another.

JOHNNY: No, I can't. It was just as flat as Abe's, Mammy.

TILDA: But it's not lucky without a hole, silly.

JOHNNY (*Crying*): It is so.

MRS. LINCOLN: Be a honey-child, Tilda, and go with Johnny back to the bean patch. Like as not he dropped it there.

TILDA (*Pouting as she goes out with* JOHNNY): But it's no good. (MRS. LINCOLN *begins to set the table, humming as she moves around. In a moment* ABE *comes back, with an empty water pail.*)

MRS. LINCOLN (*Surprised*): Why, Abe. You been clear to the spring and back already?

ABE: Pappy told me before we got past the fence. I couldn't tote the water without thankin' you first.

MRS. LINCOLN: Thankin' me? For what, Abe?

ABE: I reckon you heard about the school?

MRS. LINCOLN: Well, yes . . .

ABE: And you brought Pappy 'round to thinkin' I should go.

MRS. LINCOLN: Whatever makes you think that, now?

ABE: I know Pappy. He never took much stock in education. But you. . . . (ABE *hesitates, as if wanting to show affection without quite knowing how.*)

MRS. LINCOLN: I'll be glad as a duck in the rain to make you a new jacket and some wool socks, Abe. And maybe I can do somethin' to lengthen your britches . . . so you'll look right pert to go to Azel Dorsey's school.

ABE (*Much touched*): If I wasn't so ganglin' big, I'd like to cry, I'm that pleased.

MRS. LINCOLN: I'm that pleased myself, Abe.

ABE: It's what I wanted more than anythin', to go to school again.

MRS. LINCOLN: I reckoned you wouldn't be like Natty Grigsby and not want to.

ABE: I can't see how you talked Pappy into it, though.

MRS. LINCOLN (*Chuckling*): As I was tellin' your sister Sally, I brought me some good cookin' receipts from Kentucky.

ABE (*Puzzled*): Can't quite figger that out . . .

MRS. LINCOLN (*Winking*): Your pappy's a great hand for likin' his vittals nice and tasty. I notice it makes a big difference how he feels, what he gets to eat. Maybe that's why I told him about this special spoon-bread for supper tonight . . . after Natty was here tellin' about the school.

ABE (*Grinning*): 'Pears like you got your two eyes open to what goes on around, all right enough.

MRS. LINCOLN: Not two, Abe. Only one open. The other one's a winkin' eye!

ABE (*Taken aback*): A winkin' eye?

MRS. LINCOLN: Above my initials, sort of like.

ABE: Where'd you . . . how'd you . . . ?

MRS. LINCOLN: Anythin' so queer about a winkin' eye, Abe?

ABE: Nothin' queer. Just funny . . . laughin' funny. (*He laughs loudly, and* MRS. LINCOLN *joins in. After a bit he sobers, takes the lucky stone from his pocket, flips it and catches it.*)

ABE: Ever heard tell of a lucky stone?

MRS. LINCOLN: 'Course I have.

ABE: This is a real good one. There's a hole plumb in the middle . . . well, maybe a *little* to one side. (*Holds it out*) I'd be pleasured to give it to you.

MRS. LINCOLN (*Blinking off a tear*): Thank you, Abe. That's real nice of you. It's a heart-close thing for you to do, son. Real heart-close.

THE END

Abraham Lincoln Speaks

BOY: "With malice toward no living soul
for malice makes man small,
and what is greater than a heart
with charity for all?"
GROUP: Abraham Lincoln speaks.

GIRL: "I am not bound to win, succeed,
but only to be true,
and so I stand with those who stand
for what is right to do."
GROUP: Abraham Lincoln speaks.

BOY: "Democracy? A way of life
to save us from disaster:
As I would not be made a slave,
I would not be a master."
GROUP: Abraham Lincoln speaks.

GIRL: "My great concern is not if God
is on my side. Instead,
my great concern is: Am I on
His side, with Him ahead?"
GROUP: Abraham Lincoln speaks.

BOY: "Let us have faith that right makes might
         and, in that faith, to dare
         to do our duty as we see
         our duty—anywhere."

GROUP: Abraham Lincoln speaks.

         Abraham Lincoln speaks to us
         across the bridge of years,
         giving us strength to carry on,
         and faith to still our fears.

         Abraham Lincoln speaks.

Young Abe Lincoln

TOM LINCOLN: "Lazy as all get out, I'm feared,"
                 his father said, and scratched his beard,
                 watching his gangling son stand still
                 with dreamy eyes on a distant hill.
                 "Lazy . . . yet Abe'll sprint ten miles
                 after a book, and be all smiles."

SALLY: "Solemn and deep," his sister thought,
                 "knowin' more sorrow than he ought."
                 Could he forget his mother lying
                 humped in the corner, fevered, dying?
                 "Yet . . .," Sally said beneath her breath,
                 "yet he can tease me half to death!"

DENNIS HANKS: "Peculiarsome," his cousin said,
                 watching the black-haired, shaggy head
                 bend to the fire to catch the light
                 darting across his book at night.
                 "Peculiarsome" that Abe should keep
                 straining his eyes when he might sleep!

SARAH LINCOLN: "Brainy," his second mother saw,
                 hearing his yarns with pride and awe.

"Abe must go back to school again,
though I'm not knowin' how, or when.
Brainy! And yet he makes me laugh
till I 'most split my sides in half."

ALL: That was the lad on Pigeon Creek—
            wind in his hair, sun on his cheek,
            ax in his hand as the round year rolled
            winter to warmth, summer to cold.
            That was the lad who grew to be
            living proof of democracy!

There Was a Lad Who Hungered

There was a lad who hungered,
but it was not for bread.
He hungered for a printed page
he had not six-times read.

There was a lad who thirsted,
but nothing he could drink
could quench his thirst for finding
a page that made him think.

There was a lad whose cupboard
was singularly bare:
not half a loaf, not half a fish,
not half a cup was there.

And yet he feasted, somehow,
with firelight in his eyes,
and patience made him humble
and hardship made him wise.

VALENTINE'S DAY

New Hearts for Old

Characters

WARREN
CAROL
KENNETH
SHARON
MOTHER
FATHER

TIME: *Late afternoon on Valentine's Day.*
SETTING: *A living room.*
AT RISE: WARREN, CAROL *and* KENNETH *are at the living room table looking over the valentines they received at school.*

WARREN: Here's a beauty.
CAROL: Look at this.
KENNETH: Here is one you shouldn't miss.
  Read the rhyme on this one, Sis.
  (*He hands* CAROL *a valentine and she reads it and smiles.*)
CAROL: Valentines give lots of pleasure,
  Maybe more than we can measure.
  Here is one I surely treasure. (*Hands one around*)
  Oh, I *wish* we could have bought
  That fancy heart for Mom . . .
WARREN: We thought

237

That Dad would help us out. He ought!

CAROL: But we have been afraid to speak.

　　We had it on our minds all week . . .

KENNETH: But, somehow, Father makes us meek!

CAROL (*Resolutely*): When he comes home we can't delay,

　　We've got to ask him right away—

　　A Valentine's good just *today*

　　And now it's almost dinner time!

WARREN: He won't agree, I bet a dime:

　　Dad and Valentines don't rhyme!

CAROL: I won't give up until we've tried.

KENNETH (*Dreamily*): That Valentine is deep and wide

　　And full of chocolate creams inside . . .

　　Don't you think that Mom would love it?

WARREN: I don't think! I'm *certain* of it.

CAROL: Such a nice red bow above it,

　　Tied around the big red heart . . . (*Stops suddenly*)

　　Say, we aren't so very smart—

　　Let's let Sharon have a part!

WARREN: Sharon? She's too little yet.

KENNETH: Don't forget she's Father's pet.

　　She could turn the trick, I bet.

CAROL (*Going to kitchen door and calling*): Sharon! Will you
come a minute?

WARREN: Well, perhaps there's something in it.

　　With her help we'll, maybe, win it. (SHARON *comes hopping
in, singing a nursery rhyme in a singsong voice.*)

SHARON: "Handy Pandy, Jack-a-dandy,

　　Loves plum cake and sugar candy.

　　He bought some at a grocer's shop,

　　And out he came, hop, hop, hop."

CAROL: Sharon, listen, we've a plan

　　To make Mom happy.

KENNETH   If we can.

CAROL: We'll buy a big red Valentine,
  And you can help with it just fine.
WARREN: A Valentine all full of candy,
  So Mom can feel like Jack-a-dandy.
SHARON: Candy Valentine? That's funny!
WARREN: All we need is just some money.
  The box is waiting at the store.
KENNETH: There's nothing Mom would care for more.
CAROL (*To* SHARON):
  You tell Father when he comes
  Our money is in *little* sums,
  And we just need a paper dollar.
WARREN: I can hear him give a holler!
CAROL: Just a dollar, and we'll hop
  Like Handy Pandy to the shop,
  And buy the Valentine non-stop.
SHARON: Candy Valentine?
CAROL: Yes . . . from
  The four of us, with love to Mom! (SHARON *nods happily,
    and looks at the valentines on the table.*)
WARREN: I bet that Father won't recall
  What day it is today, at all.
  He'll think it's just like any other.
CAROL: I'm sure that's not the case with Mother.
KENNETH: I think a certain heart-shaped gift
  Would really give her quite a lift. (*There is a noise outside,
    and a door bangs. Children look up.*)
WARREN: Guess that must be Father now.
KENNETH: I'm full of butterflies, and how.
CAROL: Sharon, don't forget to ask . . .
WARREN: I'm glad that *I* don't have the task. (FATHER
  comes in briskly with newspaper. He nods at the children.)
FATHER: Good evening, children.
CHILDREN: 'Evening, Father.

FATHER (*Setting himself in his favorite chair*):
　Hope you haven't been a bother.
　Have you all been good? Where's Mother?

CAROL: Making some dessert or other. (FATHER *begins to read. Children look at each other. Then* CAROL *nudges* SHARON *and nods.* SHARON *hops over to* FATHER, *singing as she goes, to the "Handy Pandy" tune.*)

SHARON: Mom is just like Handy Pandy,
　Loves plum cake and sugar candy.
　Can't we hurry hop, hop, hop,
　And buy it at the candy shop?

FATHER (*Not paying any attention*):
　Of course. Of course. And now be quiet.
　Father's tired—and won't deny it.

SHARON: You mean you'll let us go and buy it?

FATHER: Buy it? (*Puts down paper*) What?

CHILDREN: You said "of course."

FATHER (*Frowning*):
　I'll have to track this to its source:
　What's this nonsense anyway?
　Buy it . . . ?

CAROL:　　　　It's a *special* day.

FATHER: Special? Special? News to me.
　There's nothing special *I* can see. (SHARON *runs to living-room table and brings back a pile of valentines.*)

SHARON: Valentines! Just look at these.

FATHER (*Making a face*):
　Don't suggest I read them, please.
　Valentines are pretty silly.

CAROL: Some are beautiful and frilly.

FATHER: Just a foolish waste of money! (*The children look at each other with foreboding.*)

SHARON: Daddy, now you're talking funny:
　You just said of course we could . . .

FATHER (*Impatiently*): Something I misunderstood!

SHARON: You said *of course*, about the candy
  For our special Handy Pandy.

FATHER (*Raising his voice*):
  What's this all about? I say,
  Is everybody daft today?

SHARON: Now we only need the dollar.

FATHER: Dollar!

WARREN (*Aside to* KENNETH): See, I knew he'd holler.

SHARON: Yes, to get Mom's Valentine—
  A candy one that's extra fine.

FATHER (*Almost beside himself*):
  Carol, will you explain this, please?

CAROL: We *could* get Valentines like these, (*Points to valentines*)
  But we wanted Mom's more dandy:
  There's a heart-box full of candy
  Down the street, but we are low
  On cash for *such* a heart, you know.

FATHER: And so you thought that I'd supply it?

SHARON: We'll go hop, hop, hop, and buy it.

FATHER: So. Well, listen—get this straight:
  Valentines don't carry weight
  With a grown-up like your mother.
  One's more foolish than another.
  She knows you love her well enough,
  Without a lot of silly stuff.
  She outgrew that *long* ago.
  As for candy . . . well, I know
  She shouldn't have it. Makes her fat!
  I have to watch a thing like that.
  I have to keep this family sane.

CAROL: But Father . . .

FATHER: Can't I make it plain
  That since I was a ten-year-old

Valentines have left me cold?

Now I'll thank you to keep quiet. (*Goes back to paper*)

SHARON: We can't hop, hop, hop, and buy it? (MOTHER *comes in from the kitchen with her apron on. She is surprised to see* FATHER *home so soon.*)

MOTHER (*To* FATHER):

Good evening, dear.

How nice you're here.

FATHER: I got home good and early. (*Smiles at* MOTHER)

MOTHER: Oh, Valentines! (*Goes to table to look at them*)

How this one shines . . .

SHARON: The edge is cut all curly.

MOTHER: And look at this!

I wouldn't miss

Inspecting all these rhymes. (*She pores over the valentines.*)

FATHER: What's that you say?

MOTHER: How sweet! How gay!

It brings back good old times.

I always thought

That people ought

To send their friends a greeting.

CAROL: And so do I. (*Glances at* FATHER)

FATHER: What nonsense. Why?

I'd rather take a beating.

MOTHER: These new designs

For Valentines

Are different from the old ones:

I have a few

I'll show to you . . .

Some ancient pink-and-gold ones

I found today

All stored away

In mothballs, in the attic.

WARREN: You saved them, Mom?

KENNETH: Whom were they from?

FATHER: Such conduct is erratic!

MOTHER: Just wait for me
  And you will see . . . (*She hurries out hall door*)

KENNETH: What did she find, I wonder?

CAROL: She *does* still care.

FATHER: Well, I declare.
  I may have made a blunder.

WARREN: Let's decorate
  Around Mom's plate
  With Valentines, for dinner.

CAROL (*Picking up scissors and red paper*):
  Let's cut some darts
  And bright red hearts.
  Here's one for a beginner.

SHARON: I'll cut some too.

KENNETH: It's hard to do.

SHARON (*Running to* FATHER *with paper and scissors*):
  You'll help me, won't you, Father?

FATHER: What's that? Who, me?

SHARON: Just two or three . . .

CAROL: Don't, Sharon, be a bother.
  I'll help you cut. (SHARON *hesitates.* FATHER *reaches for
  scissors and paper.*)

FATHER: A heart? Tut . . . tut . . .
  Of course, there's nothing to it. (*Begins to cut*)

SHARON: But, Daddy, look!
  You've cut a crook.

FATHER: That's where a dart went through it! (MOTHER
  comes back with a cardboard box. FATHER *quickly gives*
  SHARON *the scissors and paper and shoos her away. He
  buries his nose in the paper. The children are curious to
  see what is in the box.*)

MOTHER: I've saved this, dears,

For twenty years . . . (*Lifts out an old-fashioned valentine*)
It's really quite a treasure.
I still recall
The boy and all . . .
It gave me so much pleasure.

FATHER: What's that you say?
Who was it, pray? (*Clears throat*)
I find this most distressing.

MOTHER: A charming chap.

FATHER: Some silly . . . sap!

MOTHER: Why don't you all start guessing?

CAROL: You mean we *know?*

MOTHER: Oh, yes. Although
He's older now, and fatter,
And quite sedate.

FATHER: At any rate
He's not around to matter.

MOTHER: Your error, dear.
He lives right here!
(*The children look puzzled. Then* CAROL *blurts out.*)

CAROL: You mean that *Father* sent it?

KENNETH (*Reading verse on valentine*):
It says, "Be mine,
Sweet Valentine." (MOTHER *looks at* FATHER *with a mischievous smile.*)

MOTHER: I hope, my dear, you meant it.

FATHER: Of course I did.
A kid's a kid!

MOTHER: You must have been near twenty. (MOTHER *smiles, and the children look at* FATHER *with amusement.*)

FATHER (*Gasping*):
I sent you that!
I'll eat my hat.

WARREN: You must have loved her plenty.

MOTHER (*Holding up a heart-shaped box*):
  And next year, this.
KENNETH: Too good to miss!
FATHER: I feel . . . a . . . little harried.
MOTHER: And after a while.
  This perfume vial, (*Holds up a little bottle*)
  The year before we married.
FATHER (*Weakly*): I've had enough.
  You *saved* that stuff?
MOTHER: This box is full of riches.
SHARON: Let's see some more. (*Eagerly the children bend over*
  MOTHER's *box, looking at the contents.* FATHER *stealthily*
  gets up and tiptoes out the hall door.)
WARREN: What's this thing for—
  All full of little stitches? (MOTHER *picks up something that*
    looks like a little satchet bag and smells it dreamily. She
    smiles. Then she passes it to each of the children to smell.)
MOTHER: Just sniff, and guess.
CAROL (*The last one to take the satchet*): Rose petals?
MOTHER: Yes!
  From every gift of roses.
  Oh, Valentines
  Are treasure-mines
  Much more than one supposes.
SHARON (*Looking around*): Where's Daddy?
WARREN: Say,
  He's gone away!
MOTHER: He seemed a little harassed.
CAROL: He tiptoed out
  Without a doubt
  Because he felt embarrassed:
  He was so *sure*
  You'd not endure
  A Valentine. Oh, never!

MOTHER: He's very dear,
  But I've a fear
  He isn't always . . . clever.
KENNETH: If only we
  Could make him see
  That Valentines aren't folly,
  Not dull and dumb
  And wearisome,
  But gay and bright and jolly. (MOTHER *nods, and goes out to the kitchen.*)
WARREN: And even yet
  His wife would get
  A lift from such a greeting . . .
CAROL: To know that she
  Is prized, and he
  Does not just think of eating! (*She is silent for a moment, then bursts out suddenly.*)
  Let's make a fine
  Big Valentine
  For Father, and surprise him.
KENNETH: He may not know
  We love him, so
  Perhaps we should advise him.
WARREN: And then he may
  Admit this day
  Is really an occasion,
  And next year get
  The best heart yet
  For Mom, without persuasion.
  (*Eagerly the children set to work at the living-room table, making* FATHER'S *valentine.*)
CAROL: He'll swell with pride
  To read inside
  This heart, of our affection.

KENNETH: He'll grunt and blush
  And say, "Tush, tush,"
  But make a close inspection.
CAROL: He *can't* be mad.
SHARON: He'll be so glad
  He may give us the money.
WARREN: Then we could get
  The candy yet. (*Sighs*)
  But Father . . . well, he's funny.
  (MOTHER *comes back with a plate of heart-shaped tarts.*)
MOTHER: The King of Hearts
  Shall have some tarts!
  I'll fix them on the table. (MOTHER *works at the dining
    table, her back to the hall door.*)
  I'll trim his plate.
  He'll dine in state.
  I'll please him, if I'm able.
  (FATHER *appears at the hall door with a big red heart-
  shaped candy box. He gestures frantically and comically at
  the children. They are too busy to notice.*)
SHARON (*Proudly, to* MOTHER):
  This Valentine,
  So big and fine,
  We're fixing up for Father. (FATHER *gives a start.* MOTHER
    keeps trimming the table.)
MOTHER: You're fixing, too?
  How nice of you
  To go to all that bother. (FATHER *finally catches* SHARON'S
    eye and beckons to her, signaling her to be quiet. SHARON
    *slips over to him and he gives her the candy box, gesturing
    at the other children. No one else notices.* SHARON *tiptoes
    back to the living-room table with the box and puts it down.
    The other children look at it with their mouths open. Then
    they see* FATHER, *who warns them to keep quiet. He takes*

a tiny package from his pocket and holds it up for children to see. They can't figure out what it is.)

Almost done!

It's always fun

To have a few surprises.

CAROL: Aren't you right! (*She is excited but tries to sound calm.*)

I think tonight

They come in several sizes. (*The children sign a card to put on the candy box.* FATHER, *still at the door, tries to make the children understand that he has bought* MOTHER *a little bottle of perfume. He points to* MOTHER, *holds up bottle, sniffs, smiles, sniffs again. He is so funny the children finally burst out laughing.* MOTHER *turns to look at them.*)

MOTHER: Why so gay?

CAROL: Because today

Is such a nice invention. (CAROL *jumps up and runs to* MOTHER, *holding her hands over* MOTHER'S *eyes.*)

CHILDREN: Close your eyes! (SHARON *runs to the dining table with the candy box and puts it at* MOTHER'S *place.* WARREN *hurries to get the little perfume bottle from* FATHER. *He puts it at* MOTHER'S *place on the table.* KENNETH *quickly fixes big valentine at* FATHER'S *place.*)

CHILDREN *and* FATHER: Surprise! Surprise! (CAROL *takes hands from* MOTHER'S *eyes.*)

CAROL: Now, Valentines, attention!

The King of Hearts (*Nods at* FATHER)

Will find his tarts

And message of devotion.

The Queen (*Nods at* MOTHER) will find

Another kind

Of token, we've a notion.

FATHER (*Looking at table*):

What's this I see?

Er . . . er . . . for *me?*

I . . . I feel I'm going to smother.

MOTHER (*Looking at table, picking up candy box and reading card*):

How super-fine!

"A Valentine

From all of us to Mother." (*She picks up the perfume bottle and opens the wrapping.*)

And perfume! Oh, (*Looks lovingly at* FATHER)

How *did* you know?

ALL (*Dancing around*): Today beats any other!

THE END

Hearts, Tarts, and Valentines

Characters

READER
QUEEN
KING
MESSENGER
GUARD
JACK OF HEARTS
A MAN
A WOMAN
A CHILD
TOWNSPEOPLE

TIME: *A day in early February.*

SETTING: *The kingdom of the King and Queen of Hearts. The throne is near the back of the stage.*

AT RISE: *The* READER *is turning over the pages of a large book of fairy tales. He stands or sits on one side of the stage.*

READER: Hmmmm. (*Turns over pages*) "Hearts, Tarts, and Valentines." I never read that before. I wonder what it's like. (*In a reading tone of voice*) Once upon a time, as everybody knows, the Queen of Hearts made some tarts, all on a summer day. But as everybody does *not* know, the Queen of Hearts also made some tarts on a winter day. On a day in February. And someone stole them all away. Now it happened that the King of Hearts (KING *comes in and goes to sit on his throne*) was almost as fond of tarts as he was of his son, the Jack of Hearts. And so, on this February day, the King called for some of his wife's tarts as a special treat. Imagine his surprise and anger when he learned that all the Queen's fresh tarts had just been stolen. (*The* QUEEN *comes rushing in, in a flurry.*)

QUEEN:

My tarts! My tarts have all been taken.

They stole the tarts but left the bacon!

KING (*Rising from his throne and shaking his fist*):

That house of cards across the river

Is back of this, I bet a sliver.

The King of Diamonds and his court

Would do a thing of *just* this sort.

(*Clasps hands loudly*)

Messenger! Messenger! (MESSENGER *runs in.*)

Hurry, my man, and tell all the guards on duty

They must capture the thief who stole the Queen's tarts and return all the booty! (MESSENGER *salutes and runs out.*)

QUEEN (*Almost weeping*):

To make matters worse they were your favorite tarts,

Full of cocoanut and tutti-frutti!

KING (*Holding his hands to his heart*):

Cocoanut and tutti-frutti!

Oh, cocoanut and tutti-frutti.

(*He staggers out with the* QUEEN *holding his arm.*)

READER: The King's Messenger lost no time broadcasting the news of the theft. First he turned his loudspeaker in the direction of the river, where most of the Guards of Hearts were stationed. You see, the river was the boundary between the Hearts and Diamonds, who had been mortal enemies for more than a year. Formerly they had been quite good friends. They belonged to the same clubs. They were alike in calling a spade a spade, and all that. In fact, it had even been rumored on more than one occasion that the two houses might be united in one pack, so to speak. For the Jack of Hearts had lost his head to the Princess of Diamonds. But that was before the unfortunate episode of the lace handkerchief. That changed everything! All the friendship between the Hearts and Diamonds got lost in the shuffle. We will explain about the lace handkerchief in a moment. (*The* MESSENGER *is heard calling offstage, then he comes running in with a megaphone.*)

MESSENGER:

Warning, warning, everyone!

A frightful deed has just been done.

Catch the thief who stole the tarts

Concocted by our Queen of Hearts!

(*A* GUARD *approaches.* MESSENGER *turns to* GUARD.) Have you seen any suspicious-looking Diamonds around? Any Diamonds in the rough? The thief who stole the tarts is undoubtedly a Diamond.

GUARD: Do you think so?

MESSENGER: Of course. Who but a Diamond would stoop so low? Remember the lace handkerchief . . . (MESSENGER *exits.*)

GUARD (*Putting his hand over his heart*): The lace handkerchief! How can I ever forget it? (MESSENGER *is heard calling "Warning, warning" off stage.* GUARD *exits.*)

READER: No one on either side of the river could forget about the lace handkerchief. The Hearts could not forget about it because their King was sure a Diamond stole his lace handkerchief the day of the Tournament of Shuffles. At least, the King rode over the bridge with his handkerchief, and came back without it. The Diamonds could not forget about the lace handkerchief because their feelings were hurt to think the King of Hearts could accuse them of such a deed. You would think that such a trivial thing as a handkerchief could be ironed out without much difficulty. But no. Instead of getting better, dealings between the Hearts and Diamonds got worse with every day that passed. And now, on top of the lace handkerchief, came this matter of the stolen tarts. (*The* JACK OF HEARTS, *carrying a platter covered with a napkin, tiptoes in, looks around stealthily, and prepares to cross the stage. Just then the* GUARD *returns.*)

GUARD: Halt! Who goes there?

JACK (*Putting up his arm to hide his face*): M-m-m-me.

GUARD (*Threateningly*): Who are you and what are you carrying on that plate? (*Looks at* JACK'S *face*) Ah, the Jack of Hearts! (*Peeks under the napkin*) You knave! Are those the Queen's tarts?

JACK: Y-y-yes.

GUARD: Well, what have you to say for yourself?

JACK (*Beseechingly*): Have pity on me, Guard. I am in a terrible state. Heart trouble! And of the worst kind. Ever since the episode of the lace handkerchief my parents have forbidden me to see the Princess of Diamonds. And I left my heart in her keeping. (*Clutches his heart*) My poor heart!

GUARD: So? What has that got to do with stealing the Queen's tarts?

JACK: My parents will not even allow me to write to the Princess. And so I thought . . . I hoped . . . if I could bribe a Guard of Diamonds on the other side of the bridge to take these tarts to the Princess . . . she would know I still loved her. You see, these are specially nice tarts— cocoanut and tutti-frutti.

GUARD (*Licking his lips*): Cocoanut and tutti-frutti? (MES-

SENGER *is heard off stage calling:* "*Warning, warning, everyone,*" *etc.* GUARD *remembers his duty.*)

Sorry, Jack, but it's my bounden duty

To take you to the palace with your booty.

Cocoanut, you say, and tutti-frutti?

JACK (*Looking at the tarts*):

Surely no one can accuse me of wanting to waste them.

If only the Princess of Diamonds were able to taste them,

She'd know that my love wasn't cold or worn down at the
heel,

That all would be well if we only could get a fair deal!

But how can my father, the King, see that I want to wed—

At the tiniest mention of Diamonds, my father sees red.

GUARD:

I know. And the culprit's in danger of losing his head.

Which all goes to show that some things are much better
unsaid.

(GUARD *puts hand over heart. Then he takes* JACK *out.*)

READER: And so the Guard brought Jack and the platter of
tarts back to the palace. As might be expected, the King
and Queen were astonished to find it was their own son,
and not a Diamond, who had stolen the tarts. There was
only one consolation. Not a single tart was missing! Poor
Jack. He took his scolding without saying a word. He did
not *dare* explain how he planned to send the tarts across
the river to the Princess of Diamonds. Ever since the episode of the lace handkerchief, no one in the kingdom had
the courage to mention a Diamond in the King's presence.
And of course, things were just as bad on the other side
of the river. No one dared mention a Heart to the royal
house of Diamonds for fear of losing his head. The common
people, both Hearts and Diamonds, wondered if it were in
the cards for the quarrel ever to be patched up. They
thought the whole affair very foolish. Who wanted a lace

handkerchief anyway? What use was it? What difference
did it make? As punishment for stealing the tarts, Jack was
sentenced to guard duty for one week on the river bank.
He found himself stationed right next to the guard who
had caught him with the tarts. The two struck up a great
friendship, and it must be said, they spent much more
time talking to each other than guarding the river. Mostly
they talked about the foolish quarrel over the lace handkerchief. They wondered what they could do to patch
things up. How could they play their cards to turn the
trick? (GUARD *and* JACK *enter, and pace slowly back and
forth.*)

GUARD:

It's only the high uppy-ups
Who sit with their tarts and their cups
Who argue and stew and make a to-do.
It's only the high uppy-ups.

I've talked to a number of men—
We'd like to be friendly again,
We're tired of fuss—seems foolish to us.
We'd like to be friendly again.

JACK:

But how can you do it, I ask?
It seems an impossible task.
I wish you could trace that small piece of lace . . .
But how can you do it, I ask?

If Diamonds would own to the theft
And send back whatever is left
And say they regret and hope we'll forget,
No cause for a grudge would be left.

GUARD (*Putting his hand over his heart*):

But what if they're innocent, Jack,
And haven't the lace to send back?

It may be a *Heart* picked it up from the start,
All trampled and ragged and black.

And that wouldn't fix things, I fear.
The King would say, "Well, it is clear
They trained a trick horse to do it, of course."
No, that wouldn't fix things, I fear.
(*The* GUARD *takes a rumpled piece of lace from his pocket
over his heart and hands it to* JACK.)
JACK (*Amazed, looking at the lace*):
The lace! It's all soiled and abused.
But *Diamonds* cannot be accused
Of having it now. You got it—but how?
I'm certainly very confused. (*They go out.*)
READER: Quickly the Guard explained how it happened.
On the day of the Tournament of Shuffles he noticed a piece
of lace lying in the dirt on the other side of the river. It
was torn and trampled on, for the cavalry of both Hearts
and Diamonds had galloped that way. The Guard picked
it up, for his mother had taught him always to pick up pins
and string and anything that might have the slightest value.
He stuffed the bit of lace in his pocket and thought no more
of it. The next day he heard the Town Crier reading a
proclamation accusing the House of Diamonds of dealing
a mean trick. The King of Hearts had gone to the Tournament with his best lace handkerchief. He had come home
without it. Proof enough that some Diamond had stolen
it from his pocket during the Tournament! Diamonds
were not to be trusted! The Guard never once imagined
that the trampled bit of lace he found could be the King's
best handkerchief. Days passed. The bad feeling between
the crowned heads of Hearts and Diamonds grew worse and
worse. Finally the Town Crier announced that anyone in
the kingdom of Hearts who so much as mentioned a Dia-

mond to the King would lose his head. It was not until two months after the Tournament, when the Guard was emptying out his coat pockets before sending his uniform to the cleaner, that he came across the torn bit of lace. Absentmindedly he smoothed it out, and then—to his dismay—he could see it had a border of tiny hearts, with a larger heart on a coat of arms in the middle. There was no doubt about it, it was the King's lost handkerchief! The cause of all the trouble! (*The* GUARD *and* JACK *enter again.*)

GUARD: I didn't want to lose my head
   . . . I didn't want to lose my head. . . .

JACK:
Oh, something must be done and soon.
Let's start this very afternoon:
Let's spread the news—the King won't hear,
And think of trumps and tricks to clear
The cold and hostile atmosphere.

GUARD:
Let's gather up some eager people
And meet beneath the old church steeple
And try to figure out a way
To get both kingdoms feeling gay. (*They go out quickly.*)

READER: And so that very afternoon there was a meeting of townspeople in the shadow of the steeple of the church. (*Townspeople begin to come in, some alone, some in groups or pairs.*) Everyone was anxious to do something to patch up the quarrel between the two royal houses. The Guard took charge of the meeting (GUARD *and* JACK *come in*), with Jack as his trump card. First of all, the Guard explained that Jack had lost his heart to the Princess of Diamonds, and she had lost her heart to him. What is more she wore his diamond. All they needed was a fair deal. Then the Guard explained that nobody had stolen the lace handkerchief. It was all a mistake. The Diamonds had been unjustly accused. The King's handkerchief had merely fallen from his pocket and been trampled on by the cavalry of both kingdoms. There was a great chorus of "Ohs" and "Ahs" among the townspeople as the Guard finished his story and held up the bit of lace he had found.

A MAN: Quarrels are mostly just that silly.

GUARD: The King won't listen, willy-nilly.

JACK: Even I could not compel him . . .

A MAN: We dare not risk our necks to tell him.

A WOMAN:

My relatives across the river
Also have to shake and shiver:
They think this quarrel a silly thing
But dare not go and tell their King.

A CHILD: There must be something we can do.

GUARD: Has anyone a plan? A clue?

A WOMAN:

To *write* the rulers might be better—
They can't behead a headless letter!
(*A shout of approval goes up from the crowd.*)
Two days from now is just halfway
In February. On that day
Let's all send letters, not of fear
But love and friendliness and cheer,
Messages of merry sorts
To both the Kings of both the courts.
Let February 14th stand
For kindliness—a special brand.
(*Shouts of approval again*)

A MAN:

We needn't sign our names at all.
The stack of mail will be so tall.
The Kings will *have* to pay attention.

A WOMAN:

I've hit upon a good invention:

Let's deck our notes with doves and darts
And cut them in the shape of hearts.

A CHILD:

And mount them gracefully in place
Upon a piece of paper lace!
(*More shouts from crowd*)

GUARD:

The hearts, of course, will stand for us,
The lace for what provoked the fuss,
With diamonds on the edge . . . and thus
With all united each to each
We'll have this little truth to teach:
United we shall stand and flourish,
Divided we shall fall and perish;
Divided we shall not survive,
United we shall stand and thrive!
(*Applause and shouts from crowd as they exit.*)

READER: And so the news spread among the commoners in both kingdoms that February 14th was to be a day of forgiveness and love. Everyone on both sides of the river, old and young, fat and thin, tall and short, began to write loving messages on bright red hearts mounted on paper lace with diamonds around the edge. Never had the townspeople had more fun. And *never* did the King of Hearts and the King of Diamonds receive as much mail as on that fourteenth day of February. (KING OF HEARTS *comes in with an armload of mail and sits on his throne. He seems to be very happy, as he looks over the messages. In a moment* JACK *comes in with more mail.*)

JACK: These are from across the river.

KING (*Looking at some of the letters* JACK *brings*):

They're so nice they make me quiver.
(KING *reads aloud.*)
Let's be buddies, let's be pards,
Let's dismiss the border guards.

Don't you see, it's in the cards!

(KING *reads another*.)

Friendship never questions whether

It is spring or winter weather—

Hearts and diamonds go together . . . always.

QUEEN (*Coming in with plate of tarts*):

Have another tart, my love.

KING:

What are they concocted of? (*Takes one, looks at it*)

This one surely is a beauty.

QUEEN (*Beaming*):

Cocoanut and tutti-frutti!

READER: At the same moment the same things were happening on the other side of the river in the royal house of Diamonds. The King of Diamonds was enjoying all the lovely messages the mailman kept bringing. And he was munching his Queen's tarts at the same time and feeling very pleased with the world. As might be expected, with such an abundance of love and good nature overflowing the boundaries of both kingdoms, the two royal houses soon got together for a grand reunion. Jack and the Princess of Diamonds fell into each other's arms. The two Kings exchanged tarts and the two Queens exchanged recipes, and everyone had a wonderful time. Needless to say, all hard feelings were quickly forgotten. But just to make sure some silly thing (like a lace handkerchief) would not disrupt the peace and happiness again, the two Kings proclaimed February 14th as a day of forgiveness and love, to be observed each year without fail by all the people of both kingdoms. And from that day to this, everyone has exchanged bright red hearts mounted on paper lace. And without doubt the custom will be continued until doomsday . . . because, as you have seen, it's in the cards!

THE END

What's in a Name?

(BOYS *and* GIRLS *hold bright cards with large letters as they speak their lines*)

GROUP: What do we need for Valentines?
GIRL: A *V* . . . that stands for verses,
         some so gay
         they're tucked away
         in bureau drawers and purses!

GROUP: What do we need for Valentines?
BOY: An *A* . . . that stands for arrows,
         for shooting hearts
         with paper darts—
         instead of shooting sparrows.

GROUP: What do we need for Valentines?
GIRL: An *L* . . . for love a-plenty:
         here's love for you,
         although it's true
         I'm also loving twenty!

GROUP: What do we need for Valentines?
BOY: Some envelopes to hide them.
         They start with *E*.

as you can see,
and oh, the fun inside them.

GROUP: What do we need for Valentines?
GIRL: An *N* . . . for novel notions
       of how to say
       a different way,
       "I love you, dear—just oceans."

GROUP: What do we need for Valentines?
BOY: A *T* . . . that stands for target:
       a tempting heart
       and well-aimed dart
       addressed to Ann or Marget.

GROUP: What do we need for Valentines?
GIRL: An *I* . . . for "I-love-you"-ing!
       For "I implore"
       and "I adore"
       and "I am yours for wooing."

GROUP: What do we need for Valentines?
BOY: An *N* . . . for nonsense, maybe:
       a funny rhyme
       to pass the time
       for John or Jane or Abie.

GROUP: What do we need for Valentines?
GIRL: An *E* . . . for emblems showing:
       for Cupid's darts
       and flowers and hearts
       and other signs as knowing.

GROUP: What do we need for Valentines?
BOY: An *S* . . . to stand for sender,
       and secrets, too:
       Is this from you?
       This sentiment so tender!

GROUP: *That's* what we need for Valentines,
       for fancy ones and clever,
       and here's a cheer
       from far and near
       to Valentines . . . forever!

Valentines!

Valentines crimson through and through,
Valentines full of I-Love-You,
frilly ones, shiny,
silly ones, tiny,
middle-sized, big, and please-be-mine-y,
Valentines sweet as sugar and spice,
Valentines, Valentines—aren't you nice!

Valentines winsome as can be,
Valentines gay with love-from-me,
tricky ones, clever,
full of endeavor,
arrows, and Cupids, and love-forever,
Valentines HEARTY—every one,
Valentines, Valentines, aren't you fun!

Valentine's Day

The aspens and the maples now
have lacy frost on every bough,

And through the woods the shadows go,
writing verses on the snow.

The tops of weeds are sealed up tight
in little envelopes of white,

And listen! in the frosty pines
snowbirds twitter Valentines.

WASHINGTON'S BIRTHDAY

Washington Marches On

(*A Living Newspaper*)

Characters

Scene 1: AUGUSTINE WASHINGTON, *Virginia planter*

Scene 2:
{
BETTY WASHINGTON, *13*
GEORGE WASHINGTON, *14*
SAMUEL WASHINGTON, *12*
MARY BALL WASHINGTON, *their mother*
}

Scene 3:
{
LORD FAIRFAX
LAWRENCE WASHINGTON
GEORGE WASHINGTON, *almost 16*
}

Scene 4:
{
ANNE FAIRFAX WASHINGTON
GEORGE WASHINGTON, *20*
}

Scene 5:
{
GENERAL BRADDOCK
GEORGE WASHINGTON, *23*
1ST SOLDIER
2ND SOLDIER
3RD SOLDIER
}

Scene 6:
{
BETTY WASHINGTON LEWIS, *25*
MARY BALL WASHINGTON
}

Scene 7:
{
VOICE FROM AUDIENCE
GEORGE WASHINGTON, *43*
JOHN ADAMS
}

266

Scene 8: { 1ST SENTRY
2ND SENTRY
MESSENGER

Scene 9: { MARTHA WASHINGTON
GEORGE WASHINGTON, *46*
ORDERLY
MARQUIS DE LAFAYETTE

Scene 10: { 1ST NEWSBOY
2ND NEWSBOY

Scene 11: { GEORGE WASHINGTON, *52*
NELLY CUSTIS, *5*

Scene 12: { CHANCELLOR LIVINGSTON
GEORGE WASHINGTON, *57*
VOICES FROM AUDIENCE

Scene 13: SCHOOLMASTER

Scene 14: BOYS *and* GIRLS *with flags.*

CHORUS: *Any number of boys and girls.*

NOTE: *This play may be staged as simply or as elaborately as desired, with or without costumes.* CHORUS *may sit on one side of the stage, or in the audience. If the play is given in front of a classroom, blackboard may be used for dates. Otherwise, large date-cards should be lined up against back wall as play progresses.*

SETTING: *On stage are two chairs and a table holding paper, ink and quill pen. Any scenes requiring furniture take place near these furnishings. All other scenes take place at other parts of the stage.*

CHORUS:

When was he born, George Washington?
What was the place and date?

Solo

(*Holding up card or writing on blackboard: Born—1732*):

> Seventeen hundred thirty-two.
> Virginia, the State.

Scene 1

AT RISE: AUGUSTINE WASHINGTON, *a Virginia planter, comes in excitedly, goes to table, takes paper and quill and begins to write.*

AUGUSTINE (*As he writes*): Wakefield on the Potomac
                                          February 22, 1732

To Lawrence and Augustine Washington

Appleby School. England

My Dear Sons: It is with great pleasure that I inform you that you now have a half-brother, born this very day. The baby and his mother are doing well. We have decided, after some discussion, to name him George. Unfortunately it may be some years before you will be able to make his acquaintance.

I trust you are doing well in your studies and working diligently. I trust also that you are enjoying this acquaintance with our mother country. Enclosed you will find a draft of money for your use, over and above expenses, in celebration of the happy event that has taken place today. Your affectionate father, Augustine Washington.

(*He nods with satisfaction, seals letter, hurries out with it.*)

CHORUS: Washington marches on!

*   *   *

Chorus:

How did he grow, George Washington?

SOLO:

Strong as a sturdy tree.

CHORUS:

Did he have hopes and youthful dreams?

SOLO:

(*Holding up card or writing on blackboard: 1746—To Sea?*):

He wanted to go to sea!

SCENE 2

AT RISE: GEORGE, BETTY, *and* SAMUEL *hurry in with packet of mail.*

BETTY: *What* will Uncle Joseph's letter say, I wonder . . . about your going to sea, George? I hope he doesn't say you should.

GEORGE: When I want to go so badly, Betty?

BETTY: But I don't *like* to think of you going so far away. And it's so *dangerous*. That's what Mama says.

SAMUEL: George isn't afraid of danger. Are you, George?

BETTY: I wonder if Uncle Joseph knows how *anxious* we've been waiting to hear from him? (*Takes up letter, tries to look through envelope.*) It certainly takes a long time for a letter to get from London, England, to Fredericksburg, Virginia.

GEORGE: Too long. I've had my things packed for weeks. And Lawrence has the promise of a commission in the Navy for me. All I need is for Mother to say *yes*. (*Sighs*) I wish she'd listen to brother Lawrence, instead of asking Uncle Joseph.

BETTY: She thinks Lawrence is too young to give advice.

SAMUEL: He's twenty-eight. That's old!

GEORGE: And he's married to Anne Fairfax, and he's been in the Navy fighting in the West Indies, and he's master of Mount Vernon, and . . .

BETTY: Still, Mama thinks Uncle Joseph knows best. You know how she has depended on him, ever since Father died.

GEORGE: Well, there's a good chance he'll say yes, anyway. (*Calls*) Mother! Mother! The letter has come from London. From Uncle Joseph.

MRS. WASHINGTON (*Hurrying in excitedly*): The letter! Did I hear you say the letter has come? At last. (*She takes it, hesitates*) I *trust* your Uncle's judgment is the same as mine. (*Opens letter*) Hmmmm. (*Reads to herself while others watch.*)

BETTY: What does he *say*, Mama?

GEORGE (*Anxiously*): May I go?

MRS. WASHINGTON: Listen to this: "I understand that you have some thoughts of putting your son George to sea. I think he had better be put apprentice to a *tinker*. The common sailor has no liberties . . . they will use him like a dog." (*To* GEORGE) Do you hear, George? It is not only dangerous to go to sea, but they'd use you like a dog! So . . . it is decided. After this excellent advice from your Uncle, assuredly you must not go to sea. What else is there in the post, Betty? (*She and* BETTY *exit one side, looking at mail.* GEORGE *and* SAMUEL *start out other side.*)

GEORGE (*Obviously disappointed*): Want to drive stakes for me, Sammy? I suppose there's nothing to do now but practice with Father's surveying instruments. (*Brightens*) There's something like an ocean . . . an endless sea . . . about the wilderness. If I could be a surveyor in the wilderness, I wouldn't mind not going to sea . . . very much. (*They exit.*)

CHORUS: Washington marches on!

* * *

CHORUS:

When did he help survey the lands
that rich Lord Fairfax had?

SOLO:

(*Holding up card or writing on blackboard: 1748-52—Surveyor*):

Seventeen hundred forty-eight . . .
when he was still a lad.

SCENE 3

AT RISE: LORD FAIRFAX *and* LAWRENCE *enter.* LAWRENCE
takes a paper from his pocket, holds it out.

LAWRENCE: What do you think of this, Lord Fairfax?

LORD FAIRFAX: What is it? (*Peers at paper, takes small magnifying glass from pocket*) A map?

LAWRENCE: Do you recognize it?

LORD FAIRFAX (*Studying paper*): A map of the South Meadow here at Mount Vernon, is it not? Very carefully done. Neat. Accurate, as far as I can judge. Excellent workmanship. Did your young brother George do it? I have seen him with his instruments, again and again.

LAWRENCE: Yes, George did it. Amazing, how serious he is about his maps. For a lad not quite sixteen . . .

LORD FAIRFAX: He has skill. Ambition. Patience. Self-discipline. I have been wondering, Lawrence, about the thousands of acres of wilderness I own west of the Blue Ridge Mountains. Settlers are moving in, taking what land they want, cutting timber, building cabins. I feel I should have my boundaries marked, to establish ownership. Do you think George would care to help?

LAWRENCE: Do I think . . . ! There he comes now, Lord

Fairfax, over the hill. I am sure he can answer your question better than I. (*Calls*) George! Over here, George!

LORD FAIRFAX (*Looking at map again*): A nice piece of work. Very nice indeed. (GEORGE *enters with tripod.*)

GEORGE: Good morning, Lawrence. And Lord Fairfax, sir.

LAWRENCE: Lord Fairfax has a question to ask you, George.

GEORGE: To ask *me?*

LORD FAIRFAX: And not about fox-hunting, either. Or horses. (*Clears throat*) You are interested in surveying, I notice . . .

GEORGE: Yes, sir. Very much, sir.

LORD FAIRFAX: And how far along are you?

GEORGE: I still have a great deal to learn. But I'm not *too* bad, am I, Lawrence?

LORD FAIRFAX: Would you be able to start in three weeks? On March 11, say?

GEORGE: Start what, sir?

LORD FAIRFAX: I am planning to have my wilderness lands surveyed. Would you care to be one of the party? I will pay you well.

GEORGE (*Eagerly*): Would I! Would I, sir! Oh, let me get some of my maps to show you . . . (*He runs out.* LAWRENCE *and* LORD FAIRFAX, *amused, follow.*)

CHORUS: George Washington marches on!

* * *

CHORUS:

When did Mount Vernon come to him—
his brother's large estate?

SOLO:

(*Holding up card or writing on blackboard: 1752—Gets Mt. Vernon*):

Seventeen hundred fifty-two,
dropped from the hands of fate.

Scene 4

At Rise: Anne Fairfax Washington *and* George *enter, talking earnestly.*

Anne: I need your help, George.

George: You know I will do anything I can, Anne. But I cannot bring Lawrence back . . . or your little daughter. To think of losing them both, so close together!

Anne: Within a few weeks of each other. That was July. Now it is November, and the ache is still in my heart. They say that time heals all sorrows. But, oh, how slowly, George.

George: I know. I miss Lawrence too, more than I can say. He was so much more to me than a half-brother. Had he been full brother and father combined, I could not have loved him more.

Anne: I am glad you had those months with him in the Bahamas last winter . . . though I missed him terribly at the time.

George: We were so hopeful the mild air would help him. And for a while it did, you know. But (*Giving gesture of despair*) . . . And so young, only thirty-four.

Anne (*After a pause*): George, I want your advice—as a brother-in-law, not as one of the executors of the estate. Lawrence left you a large interest in Mount Vernon, and you have always loved the place. Don't you think you should take it over? I have no wish to be burdened with so many acres of farm land. I know nothing about farming.

George (*Figuring on back of envelope*): No place in the world means more to me than Mount Vernon. But, as Lawrence's wife, you must have a fair return. (*Figures*) How would it be if I paid you eighty thousand pounds of tobacco yearly?

Anne: Isn't eighty thousand pounds of tobacco a great deal, George?

GEORGE: I would gladly pay it.

ANNE: You are more than fair. You are generous! And it will be such a load off my mind to know you are here, carrying on as master of Mount Vernon. You will be very busy, George . . . with all those acres, and Lawrence's wish for you to enter the militia . . . and the House of Burgesses.

GEORGE: Yes, I shall be very busy. But that is exactly what I like. And now, shall we go check the accounts? (*They exit*)

CHORUS: Washington marches on!

*   *   *

CHORUS:

When did he fight in what is called
the French and Indian War?

SOLO:

(*Holding up card or writing on blackboard: 1754-8, French & Indian War*):

Seventeen fifty-four to eight,
with hardships by the score.

SCENE 5

AT RISE: GENERAL BRADDOCK, *brandishing his sword, crosses stage excitedly.*

BRADDOCK (*Shouting*): Hold ranks! Hold ranks! Take the fire of the enemy like men. I command you to hold ranks. (GEORGE WASHINGTON *rushes in to catch up with* GENERAL BRADDOCK.)

WASHINGTON: General Braddock! General Braddock . . . if you will order the men to scatter, sir . . . Let them meet the enemy under cover instead of out in the open. I know how these Indians and French fight, from behind trees . . .

BRADDOCK (*Striding out*): My men will stand in ranks, Washington, as they are bidden, without breach of discipline. (*Exits*)

WASHINGTON: But, sir . . . (*Exits after* BRADDOCK. *Three* SOLDIERS *stagger in.*)

1ST SOLDIER: Let's get out of here, anywhere. Anywhere!

2ND SOLDIER: Where did the shots come from? Did you see the enemy?

3RD SOLDIER: The shots come from all directions. No one sees the enemy.

1ST SOLDIER: We make easy targets in our red coats.

2ND SOLDIER: Did you see Braddock's aide-de-camp, Colonel Washington? He strode among us soldiers, calm as ice, trying to get us to retreat in orderly fashion. His horse was shot out from under him.

1ST SOLDIER: Aye, and he mounted another.

2ND SOLDIER: Men were slaughtered all around him, but he wasn't even wounded.

3RD SOLDIER: I could follow a man like that! Would to heaven he were in charge here. (*They stagger out.*)

CHORUS: Washington marches on!

*   *   *

CHORUS:

When did he marry, settle down
on the land he loved so well?

SOLO:

(*Holding up card or writing on blackboard: 1759-75, Farmer*):

Seventeen hundred fifty-nine,
a happy date to tell.

SCENE 6

AT RISE: MARY BALL WASHINGTON *comes in with sewing, sits and works. Soon* BETTY WASHINGTON LEWIS *hurries in with newspapers. She greets her mother affectionately, and takes off wraps as she talks.*

BETTY: Oh, Mama, have you seen the papers—from Fredericksburg and Alexandria? I was afraid you hadn't, so I took the ferry over . . . I couldn't wait to show you.

MRS. WASHINGTON: About George's wedding?

BETTY: Yes, look! (*Shows a paper*) A long account, and so glowing, Mama. The charming and beautiful young widow, Martha Custis, and the handsome and gallant young officer, George Washington!

MRS. WASHINGTON (*Looking at paper*): She will be a great help to George in many ways. Perhaps I should not say it out loud . . . but I can't help thinking that her fortune will not come amiss. I hear it is a large one.

BETTY (*Sitting down*): And, imagine, a ready-made family for George! Jacky six, and Patsy four. I can imagine how he loves them.

MRS. WASHINGTON (*Reading*): "In the church where the wedding was solemnized there was a bright show of resplendent uniforms with their gold lace and scarlet coats. Later the bridegroom, himself clad in shining blue and silver and scarlet, rode beside the coach that bore his bride homeward . . ." (*Looks up*) George has done well, Betty. I always knew he would.

BETTY: And remember how he wanted to go to sea? And how Uncle Joseph agreed with you that he shouldn't?

MRS. WASHINGTON: Indeed I remember. How different his life would have been! Come, let us move closer to the grate. There is a January chill in the air today. (*They exit.*)

CHORUS: Washington marches on!

*   *   *

CHORUS:

When did the Revolution start—
that placed him in command.

SOLO:

(*Holding up card or writing on blackboard: 1775-83, Commander-in-chief*):

Seventeen seventy-five. In June
he took the task in hand.

SCENE 7

AT RISE: JOHN ADAMS *enters, takes place behind table.*

VOICE FROM AUDIENCE: Sh! John Adams is about to speak. Sh!

ADAMS: Gentlemen of the second Continental Congress,— We are agreed that we must prepare to defend ourselves against British tyranny immediately. To my mind the choice of commander of the continental armies is easy enough. There is no soldier in America to be compared with Colonel George Washington of Virginia, either in experience or distinction. He is gallant, straightforward, earnest. (*Looks up*) Did I glimpse the Colonel leaving the room in confusion just now? Run after him, attendant. Bring him back! (*Resumes speech.*) I move that Congress, meeting here in solemn assembly in Philadelphia, put the gentleman from Virginia in charge of the American army! (*Cheers, shouts of "Aye, aye" from audience.*) His skill and experience as an officer, his independent fortune, great talents, and excellent universal character, would unite the colonies better than any other person in the union." (*More cheers from audience, calls for "George Washington!" and "Colonel Washington." WASHINGTON enters slowly. JOHN ADAMS steps up, escorts him to table, then sits down.*)

WASHINGTON: I beg it to be remembered by every gentleman in this room, that I this day declare with the utmost sincerity I do not think myself equal to the command I am honored with. I cannot refuse a call to serve my country. As to pay, I will have none of it. I do not wish to make any profit from the war. I shall keep an accounting of my expenses, and that is all I desire. (*Cheers from audience. JOHN ADAMS grasps WASHINGTON'S hand, and they exit together.*)

CHORUS: Washington marches on!

*　　*　　*

CHORUS:

Month after month the army fought,
and often on the run!
Month after month of toil and trial,
and never a battle won.

SOLO:

(*Holding up card or writing on blackboard: 1776, Crosses Delaware*):

Then on a bitter Christmas night
Washington staged a famous fight.

SCENE 8

AT RISE: *Two* SENTRIES *enter, pace back and forth.*

1ST SENTRY: No morning ever has gone more slowly. (*Slaps arms to keep warm.*) How soon do you think they will send back news?

2ND SENTRY: For the hundredth time, don't expect news till noonday, at the earliest. (*Looks at watch*) Eleven o'clock. Calm down, brother.

1ST SENTRY: If only I could have gone along.

2ND SENTRY: Someone had to stay behind to guard the camp. You and I are as good as the next. (*Stomps feet*) It's blasted cold.

1ST SENTRY: Noonday at the earliest?

2ND SENTRY: Look here. They didn't leave till after midnight. (*He shudders*) And *what* a Christmas midnight! Sleet. Bitter cold. The Delaware choked with cakes of floating ice. Do you think it a quick and easy task to transport 2400 men across the river on such a night? Even with the best planning?

1ST SENTRY: They say General Washington had it all worked out to the smallest detail.

2ND SENTRY: Naturally. Still, after the crossing, they had to march nine miles through snow and cold to Trenton. You think that can be done in a moment?

1ST SENTRY: No . . . ooo.

2ND SENTRY: I say if they arrived at Trenton an hour after sunrise they did well. And *then*. You expect they could march right in and take the town? Against those well-armed German soldiers the British hired to guard it? (*Pounds hands together*) You expect too much.

1ST SENTRY: I am counting on Christmas. I am counting on those Hessians drinking too much, and celebrating too much, last night.

2ND SENTRY: Even so, taking a town is not easy. And have you reason to suppose our luck has changed? Retreat. Retreat. Retreat. That has been our record. Have we won a battle yet—answer me that?

1ST SENTRY (*Grudgingly*): No . . . ooo. But this! We are

all fired with the wish to give General Washington a Christmas present. A victory—at last.

2ND SENTRY: A wish. That's all very well. But wishes don't win battles. Though heaven knows a victory is a Christmas present that would warm all our hearts. (*Bitterly*) They need warming. (*Stomps*) And not only our hearts.

1ST SENTRY: Noonday!

2ND SENTRY: Remember, a messenger would have to get back the nine miles from Trenton, and cross the river again. After the battle.

1ST SENTRY (*Stubbornly*): If the victory were a quick one . . . (*They pace back and forth in silence. In a few moments a* MESSENGER *runs in.*)

SENTRIES (*Challenging him*): Halt! Who goes there?

MESSENGER (*Saluting*): Messenger from General Washington in Trenton.

SENTRIES (*Eagerly*): Speak up, lad. What news?

MESSENGER: We crossed the river on the barges without mishap, in spite of the sleet and bumping ice.

1ST SENTRY: Yes, yes, you crossed the river. But the battle? Do we hold Trenton?

MESSENGER: We marched the nine miles without mishap, arriving after sun-up, deploying to enter by different roads.

2ND SENTRY: Naturally, by different roads. We know the General had it all planned. But the Hessians? Did they put up a good fight?

MESSENGER: There was no place for them to run. They were dazed, drugged from too much celebrating last night. We had no losses to speak of.

SENTRIES: And the Hessians?

MESSENGER: They lost their commander and forty-one others —dead. It was all over in less than an hour. We captured thirty officers and more than a thousand men.

SENTRIES (*Throwing up their hats*): A victory! A victory!

A Christmas present for General Washington! Come, let's tell the others. (*Go out with* MESSENGER) Our first victory in the war . . .

CHORUS: Washington marches on!

* * *

CHORUS:

Success was brief. Then more retreat
through countryside and gorge.
What was the time that tried men's souls?

SOLO:

(*Holding up card or writing on blackboard: 1777-8, Valley Forge*):

The winter at Valley Forge.

SCENE 9

AT RISE: MARTHA WASHINGTON *enters with knitting, sits and works busily.* GENERAL WASHINGTON *enters, paces back and forth deep in thought.*

MARTHA: You are worried, George. (*Pause*) Are you angry with me for coming? After you wrote that I would be much more comfortable at Mount Vernon?

WASHINGTON (*Going to her affectionately*): No. No. I am not angry with you, Martha. Assuredly you *would* be more comfortable at Mount Vernon. Valley Forge is not re- nowned for its comforts! But you have been a cheering note in a bleak landscape ever since you came, my dear. The soldiers feel it. Especially the sick and wounded you so kindly visit.

MARTHA: Oh, I'm glad.

WASHINGTON: And the ones who get the socks you knit think you are an angel from heaven! I wonder if you realize how much a pair of warm socks means in Valley Forge?

MARTHA: I think so, George.

GEORGE (*Bursting out impatiently*): Socks . . . mittens . . . coats . . . shoes . . . uniforms . . . *why* don't we get our supplies? Bread . . . meat . . . ammunition . . . guns . . . we need everything, Martha. Everything! That's why I am worried. Congress is so disorganized and inefficient. Why, these days, we scarcely have what can be called a government.

MARTHA: I suppose the British moving into Philadelphia didn't help matters. You say Congress is in exile at York. It has probably lost heart. (*Hastily*) Though, of course, I understand nothing about politics.

WASHINGTON: Lost heart! Lost head, I should say. (*Paces angrily*) And to think that just twenty miles from here General Howe and his officers are having a gay winter social season in Philadelphia! His men are warm and well-fed. They live in ease and comfort. While my men are starving and freezing! Yet naked as they are, Martha (*There is a catch in his voice*) . . . they show incomparable patience and loyalty. Ah, Thomas Paine is right . . . this is indeed a time that tries men's souls. Mine included.

MARTHA: Is there no way out?

WASHINGTON: None that I can see at the moment, unless Congress can pull itself together. How can we have an army without supplies? And the men have not been paid for months! (ORDERLY *enters, salutes.*)

ORDERLY: The Marquis de Lafayette to see you, sir.

WASHINGTON: Lafayette! Show him in immediately.

MARTHA (*Rising*): Perhaps I should leave . . .

WASHINGTON: Not until you have greeted our young friend, Martha. He, too, is a bright light on a bleak horizon. (LAFAYETTE *enters, salutes. He and* GENERAL WASHINGTON *greet each other affectionately.*) My dear Lafayette!

LAFAYETTE: General Washington!

WASHINGTON: You have met my wife once before. (*She and*

LAFAYETTE *bow*) The soldiers here call her Lady Washington.

MARTHA (*Smiling at* LAFAYETTE *as she exits*) : It is my reward for darning their socks, Marquis!

LAFAYETTE: I could not wait to bring you the news, sir.

WASHINGTON: News?

LAFAYETTE (*Taking letter from inner pocket*) : A secret letter, from friends in France. There is every reason to believe that France will soon declare war on England, and support our cause with money and supplies.

WASHINGTON: Can it be true! Soon, you say?

LAFAYETTE (*Showing letter*) : Very soon. Indeed, I am informed that a handsome sum of money is already on the way.

WASHINGTON (*Much relieved*) : What is it they say . . . that it is always darkest just before the dawn? Come, we must tell Martha. (*They exit.*)

CHORUS: Washington marches on!

* * *

CHORUS:

Year after year the war dragged on,
the verdict still not won.
And then the battle of Yorktown came.

SOLO:

(*Holding up card or writing on blackboard: 1781, Yorktown*) :

Seventeen eighty-one.

SCENE 10

AT RISE: NEWSBOYS *run across stage shouting, waving papers.*

1ST NEWSBOY: Extra! Extra! Cornwallis surrenders after three-week siege. Washington takes 8000 men. Victory! Victory! (*Exits*)

2ND NEWSBOY: The most decisive battle of the war. Washington wins at Yorktown. The war is over! (*Exits*)

CHORUS: Washington marches on!

* * *

CHORUS:

But still a treaty to be signed
before our land was free!

SOLO:

The General had to keep command
till seventeen eighty-three.

CHORUS:

And then, at Christmas, home again!
Mount Vernon. Home, at last.

SOLO:

(*Holding up card or writing on blackboard: 1784-8, Farmer*) :

Seventeen eighty-four to eight.
And, oh, the time went fast.

SCENE 11

AT RISE: WASHINGTON *enters, sits at table, begins to write.*

WASHINGTON (*Writing*): To the Marquis de Lafayette, many greetings. At length, my dear Marquis, I am become a private citizen on the banks of the Potomac; and under the shadow of my own vine and my own fig-tree, free from the bustle of a camp and the busy scenes of public life, I am solacing myself with those tranquil enjoyments of which a soldier can have very little conception. I have not only retired from all public employments, but I am retiring within myself . . . (NELLY CUSTIS *comes in a little tentatively.*)

NELLY: Grandfather. Grandfather, you promised to show me the new little colt . . . (WASHINGTON *smiles, puts down quill, and goes out with* NELLY.)

CHORUS: Washington marches on!

*   *   *

CHORUS:

When was he called to serve again?
Washington, President!

SOLO:

(*Holding up card or writing on blackboard: 1789-97, President*):

Seventeen hundred eighty-nine.
Two terms, eight years, he spent.

SCENE 12

AT RISE: CHANCELLOR LIVINGSTON, *carrying a Bible, and* GEORGE WASHINGTON *enter.*

LIVINGSTON (*Holding out Bible*): Do you solemnly swear that you will faithfully execute the office of President of the United States, and will, to the best of your ability, preserve, protect, and defend the Constitution of the United States?

WASHINGTON: I do solemnly swear that I will faithfully execute the office of President of the United States, and will, to the best of my ability, preserve, protect and defend the Constitution of the United States. (*Bends to kiss Bible. Then, solemnly, with bowed head . . .*) So help me, God.

LIVINGSTON (*To audience*): Long live George Washington, President of the United States!

AUDIENCE (*Cheering*): Long live George Washington. Long

live the father of our country. Hail to the first President of the United States. (WASHINGTON *and* LIVINGSTON *exit*.)

1ST VOICE FROM AUDIENCE: Did you hear? He won't accept a salary as President.

2ND VOICE: Nor did he take a salary all those years he was commander-in-chief.

3RD VOICE: Imagine, he fears he is not good enough for the post!

4TH VOICE: Who *would* be good enough if he isn't?

SEVERAL: No one. No one in our thirteen States.

5TH VOICE: Poor man, we snatch him away from Mount Vernon again. We demand much of him.

SEVERAL: We need him. We need him!

AUDIENCE: Long live George Washington, President of the United States!

CHORUS: Washington marches on!

* * *

CHORUS:

When did he die, George Washington?

SOLO:

(*Holding up card or writing on blackboard: 1799—Died*):

Seventeen ninety-nine.

CHORUS:

But he still lives on in our minds and hearts, and will till the end of time!

SCENE 13

AT RISE: SCHOOLMASTER *enters, with books.*

SCHOOLMASTER: Boys of the Latin School of Fredericksburg, sad news has just reached us from Mount Vernon, this

December day. George Washington is dead! The father of our country is dead.

He was our friend . . . almost our neighbor, when he lived across the river at Ferry Farm years ago. And many of you remember his mother when she lived on Charles Street next door to her daughter and grandchildren.

George Washington is dead. In him were united such qualities of greatness as seldom appear in one man. How long he served our country! How well he served it—as soldier, patriot, statesman, citizen!

Boys, open your copy books and write these words on the title page where you will see them often: "George Washington—first in war, first in peace, and first in the hearts of his countrymen."

Our beloved commander-in-chief, our first President, is dead. But he will never be forgotten. Other heroes, other statesmen, will come and go, but the memory of George Washington is here to stay. (*Nods solemnly, and exits*)

CHORUS: Washington marches on!

* * *

SCENE 14

BEFORE CURTAIN: *A procession of boys and girls of the present generation march across the stage carrying flags, chanting:* "Washington marches on!"

THE END

That Spells Washington

BOYS *and* GIRLS *stand toward back of stage holding large cards with letters spelling* WASHINGTON. *As each one speaks he takes a step forward.*

W   for wisdom shown
       in war and peacetime, too.

A   for the ability
       to act and carry-through.

S   for service, year by year,
       with pen as well as sword.

H   for a heroic heart
       unheedful of reward.

I   for insight, and ideals
       in all his different roles.

N   for nobleness of mind
       in times that tried men's souls.

G   for gallantry and grit,
       for guidance, soon and late.

T   for his untiring toil
       to make our country great.

O   for obstacles he met
       and staunchly overcame.

N   for nation's need of him
       who never sought for fame.

GROUP: That spells WASHINGTON—the man
who, time and time again,
was *first* in playing many parts
in war, and peace, and in the hearts
of all his countrymen.

George Washington, Farmer

I

1ST BOY: "I think a farmer's life," he wrote,
          "the most enjoyable of all.
          To watch the wheat and barley sprout
          and see the trees grow strong and tall
          is best of all pursuits, bar none."
          He signed the words:
                              "G. Washington."

GROUP: And yet this man who loved the farm
          was quick to heed the call to arm:
          he stayed away four years and more
          to fight the French and Indian war.

II

2ND BOY: "The more I learn about the land,"
          the better I am pleased," he wrote.
          "A farmer's satisfactions grow
          like crops . . . I'd happily devote
          my life to seeds and soil and sun."
          He signed the words:
                              "G. Washington."

GROUP: And then the Revolution came.
    Again his country made its claim.
    He drilled the troops and held command—
    eight years away from crops and land!

III

3RD BOY: "No sight delights me quite as much,"
    he wrote, "as farmland, thriving, neat.
    I've added to my coat of arms,
    quite suitably, some spears of wheat.
    A farmer's work is mostly fun."
    He signed the words:
          "G. Washington."

GROUP: But, once again, the years were spent
    away from home—as President.
    Two terms, eight years away again,
    handling the strained affairs of men!

IV

4TH BOY: "At last," he wrote, "I can enjoy
    the shadow of my fig and vine.
    At last I have my heart's delight:
    a farmer's life again is mine.
    But now my days are almost done . . ."
    He signed the words:
          "G. Washington."

GROUP: Two final years of "heart's delight"
    this Farmer had, who, overnight,
    had heeded every beck and call
    to do his duty, big or small . . .
    though he loved farming best of all!

Washington at Valley Forge

(December, 1777)

ALL: A wooded valley and a frozen creek,
the hills surrounding, high and cold and bleak;
a little forge for melting metal down,
a valley forge—the kernel of a town,
a dreary place with Christmastime so near . . .

1ST BOY: The General called a halt: "We're camping here.
We'll need some huts as shelter from the cold.
Work quickly, men, the year is growing old."

ALL: The General watched his soldiers chop and saw.
Their feet were bleeding and their hands were raw.
They lacked supplies and clothes and shoes and
food,
but, like their leader, they had fortitude.

2ND BOY: The General stood upon a rise of ground.
His heart was heavy as he looked around:
"My unpaid men are weary, hungry, cold,
while twenty miles away the Redcoats hold
fair Philadelphia and live in state,
and sit in comfort near a blazing grate!

The snow at Valley Forge is stained with red.
My soldiers dream of boots and gloves and bread."

ALL: The General thought of home—Mount Vernon's
            charm.
        His soldiers wintered, what would be the harm
        in going home? The cold had months to run!
        He turned and looked into the puny sun,
        and chose the hardship—as he'd always done—
        the General by the name of Washington.

At Mount Vernon

(1798)

General Washington? He's around—
down by the grove he may be found,
or riding beyond that rise of ground,
with a hickory switch in a hand that's browned.

What is he wearing? Something plain,
with an umbrella, sir, for rain,
hung from his saddle like a cane.
He'll have his eyes on grass and grain.

What is he like? He's sixty-six,
thinking of bushels, bales, and bricks,
glad to be through with politics,
glad to be home with barns to fix.

Look for a man who stops to chat
of crops and trees and such as that,
pointing out sights to marvel at.
Look for a broad-brimmed, old, white hat.

Look for a man with his battles won,
weathered by time and trial and sun,
thinking a farmer's life is fun—
that, sir, is . . . General Washington.

St. Patrick and the Serpent

I

NARRATOR:	St. Patrick drove the serpents out
	of Ireland (so 'tis said),
	from here and there and roundabout,
	from Cork to Malin Head
	he banished all the snakes there were . . .
A GIRL:	Except for one that wouldn't stir!
A BOY:	Except for one that wouldn't leave!
GROUP:	And, sure, it made St. Patrick grieve.

II

NARRATOR:	St. Patrick drove the serpents out
	of Ireland (so they claim).
	From here and there and roundabout
	it brought St. Patrick fame.
	He cast the serpents in the sea . . .
A BOY:	Except for one that wouldn't flee!
A GIRL:	Except for one that wouldn't drown!
GROUP:	And, sure, it made St. Patrick frown.

III

NARRATOR:	St. Patrick was a canny man,
	a prudent man (they state),

	and so he conjured up a plan—
	he built a box-like crate,
	and sweetly asked the serpent in.
A Girl:	The serpent stroked its satin skin,
	and wouldn't try the box at all.
	But said,
Serpent:	For me, it's much too small.

IV

Narrator:	St. Patrick was a learnéd man
	and subtle (so they tell).
	He coaxed the serpent:
St. Patrick:	Faith, you can
	fit very, very well.
	I'm sure you can, with room to spare.
Serpent:	I can't, you know I can't, so there.
St. Patrick:	You can.
Serpent:	I can't.
St. Patrick:	I know I'm right.
Serpent:	You're wrong.
Narrator:	They argued day and night.

V

Narrator:	St. Patrick had a mighty voice,
	persuasive (so they state)—
	it made the Emerald Isle rejoice
	to hear the great debate:
St. Patrick:	You'll fit the box.
Serpent:	I won't at all.
St. Patrick:	It's plenty big.
Serpent:	It's pinchy small.
St. Patrick:	Unless you prove it, I am right.
Serpent:	I'll show you, then. The box is tight!

VI

NARRATOR: St. Patrick watched the serpent glide
            into the box ('tis told),
            and when it mostly was inside
            the canny Saint made bold
            to close the lid, and tie it tight,
            and throw the box with all his might
            upon the waves that rolled away.
GROUP: And, sure, it made St. Patrick gay.

VII

NARRATOR: St. Patrick drove the serpents out
            of Ireland (so 'tis said),
            he scoured the country roundabout
            from Cork to Malin Head,
            and banished all the snakes there were . . .
A GIRL: Including one that wouldn't stir.
A BOY: Including one that left the isle
            all boxed and tied, in state and style!
GROUP: And, sure, it made St. Patrick smile.

Sure, Don't You Know?

GIRL: Oh, what's the smile for, Paddy boy,
that goes from ear to ear?
PADDY: Sure, don't you know what day it is?
St. Patrick's Day is here!

BOY: And what's the green for, Paddy boy,
the wearing of the green?
PADDY: It's tokening the Emerald Isle—
the greenest place you've seen.

GIRL: And what's the shamrock, Paddy boy,
with leaves that come in three?
PADDY: And don't you know that illustrates
the Holy Trinity?

BOY: And what's the song for, Paddy boy,
that sets the day apart?
PADDY: 'Tis just the Irish joy in me
a-bursting from my heart.

Wearing of the Green

It ought to come in April,
or, better yet, in May
when everything is green as green—
I mean St. Patrick's Day.

With still a week of winter
this wearing of the green
seems rather out of season—
it's rushing things, I mean.

But maybe March *is* better
when all is done and said:
St. Patrick brings a promise,
a four-leaf-clover promise,
a green-all-over promise
of springtime just ahead!

Easter Morn

GROUP: Now everything is born again
all up and down the earth,
for it is Easter morn again—
the morning of rebirth.

BOY: The grass is turning green again,
with frosty winter over.
GIRL: And dandelions are seen again,
and daffodils, and clover.
BOY: And all the roots and all the shoots
and all the seeds are stirring.
GIRL: And in the trees, the willow trees,
sit pussywillows, purring!

GROUP: Now everything is new again
all up and down the land,
for Easter has come true again
and hillsides understand.
BOY: The wind is bright and warm again
in all the open places.
GIRL: The meadow larks perform again.
And daisies show their faces.
BOY: And all the leaves on all the trees
are starting to unfold.

300

GIRL: While, on the run, the Easter sun
           shakes out its living gold.

GROUP: Now everything is bright again
           all up and down the world.
           The tendrils that were tight, again
           are magically uncurled.

BOY: And voices start to sing again.

GIRL: And eyes begin to see
           the worth of everything again,
           as Easter turns the key.

BOY: And mankind feels the pull again
           of Something from above.

GIRL: And everyone is full again
           of faith, and hope, and love.

GROUP: And everyone is full again
           of faith, and hope, and love.

Easter's All Dressed Up Today

BOYS: Easter's all dressed up today!
        I wonder if she'll see
        the puddle in the pasture
        near the weeping-willow tree.

GIRLS: She doesn't! Oh, she stumbles,
        and skids and slips and tumbles,
        and, getting splashed, she mumbles:
        "Now *would* you look at me!"

ALL: Easter frowns beneath her bonnet:
        "Oh! My dress has splashes on it.'

BOYS: The sun says, "What a sorry sight."
        The clouds say, "Goodness, yes."
        The rain says, "Come, let's rescue her,
        this maiden in distress."

GIRLS: So, with some silver tinkles,
        the clouds send cleaning sprinkles,
        and sun irons out the wrinklᵣ
        that rumpled Easter's dress.

ALL: And Easter smiles beneath her bonnet:
        "Look! My dress has sunshine on it."

Easter Tulip

I planted a tulip,
put it in a pot,
put it in the shadow
where the sun was not,
watched it, watered it,
never once forgot.

The tulip was a slow-poke.
It wasn't to be seen.
But up popped a pale weed,
thin, and yellow-green,
looking like the periscope
of a submarine.

The periscope took bearings:
"Pretty nice, I'd say."
Reported to the tulip:
"Hurry, don't delay."
And so the tulip hurried . . .
and bloomed for Easter Day.

ARBOR DAY

On Strike

Characters

OWL
SQUIRREL
ROBIN
WOODCHUCK
BAT
MOLE
SKUNK
RABBIT

SCENE 1

TIME: *A summer day.*

SETTING: *A clearing in the woods.*

AT RISE: *All except* RABBIT *are gathered together at a meeting place under a tree. The* OWL, *looking very wise in his glasses, is chairman of the meeting. He has a book under one arm.*

OWL (*Rapping on the tree for order*): The meeting will come to order. Is everyone here? Squirrel?

SQUIRREL (*Standing up quickly*): Here. (*Salutes*) At your service.

OWL: Robin?

ROBIN (*Chirping*): Here.

304

OWL: Woodchuck, otherwise known as Groundhog?

WOODCHUCK (*Puffing because he is so fat*): P—p—present.

OWL: Bat? (*There is no answer. In a moment, louder*) Bat!

BAT (*Very sleepily*): Y-e-s . . . your Honor. (*Yawns*)

OWL: Are you awake?

BAT (*Yawning*): Oh, yes . . . your Honor.

OWL: Mole?

MOLE (*In a small voice*): Here.

OWL: Skunk?

SKUNK (*Standing up and strutting, showing off beautiful coat*):
Here.

OWL: Rabbit? (*No answer*) Rabbit!

RABBIT (*Timidly peeking from behind a bush, looking around
cautiously, then speaking in a hushed voice*): Here.

OWL: Come on, Rabbit, show yourself. I think we are quite
safe here at the edge of the woods, out of sight of the farm-
house.

RABBIT (*Looking around*): I never harm anyone . . . but
someone is always trying to hurt me. (*Sighs, then timidly
comes from behind the bush*)

OWL: Now that we are all here, we can proceed with the
business in hand. (*Clears throat*) Ladies and gentlemen of
the Grievance Committee, we are gathered here today to
decide on ways and means of combating the great conspiracy against us.

SKUNK (*Indignantly*): Farmer Dullard's conspiracy. The old
dullard!

OWL (*Rapping for order*): No interruptions from the floor,
please. As I was saying, we are meeting today to air our
grievances against Farmer Dullard, and to decide what can
be done. For countless generations our families have lived
here on the farm now owned by Farmer Dullard. For countless generations we have lived in comparative peace with
the human race.

RABBIT (*Timidly*): We have always had to be . . . (*Looks around*) very cautious . . . though.

OWL: Of course, we have had to use our wits. But until Farmer Dullard moved here last year, our lives went along quite smoothly. Am I right. Yea or nay?

ALL (*Except* BAT): Yea. Yea.

BAT (*Coming in sleepily at the end*): Yea.

OWL: Farmer Dullard is making life unbearable. The time has come for the Grievance Committee to decide on a course of action. Our homes are being destroyed. Our food is being taken from us. Our lives are constantly in danger. Evidence is mounting that Farmer Dullard is deliberately trying to get rid of us. Robin, will you please state your case.

ROBIN (*Standing, tipping back and forth in birdlike fashion*): I live in the orchard, as my family has for more years than I can count. It has been a wonderful place to live until . . . until lately . . . (*Chokes up*)

OWL: Please control yourself, Robin. We realize this is a painful matter for you to discuss, but the Committee must know the facts. What has happened?

ROBIN: Ever since Farmer Dullard moved in, the orchard hasn't been the same. We robins are in constant danger. Maybe we *do* eat a few of his cherries now and then, but is that any reason . . . (*Gets out handkerchief and wipes eyes*)

OWL: Any reason for what, Robin?

ROBIN: For . . . for hiding behind the grape arbor and shooting at us. Yesterday my Aunt Elizabeth and Cousin Charley got hit. I'll never see them again. (*Sits down and buries face in handkerchief*)

OWL (*Consulting his book*): "Insect pests do untold damage to fruit crops every year. Birds are the greatest insect destroyers. Without birds, farmers would have to go out of the fruit business." (*Looks up*) I guess this is one book Farmer Dullard never has read. (*Reads again*) "Scientists have found as many as 250 tent caterpillars in the stomach of one bird."

ROBIN: And what about weed seeds?

OWL: Hmmm. (*Turns pages*) Oh yes, here we are: "Birds eat not only insects, but they eat quantities of weed seeds. Scientists discovered that a bobwhite ate 1,700 weed seeds at one meal, and that a snowbird ate 1,500 pigweed seeds." (*Turns pages*) Robins . . . robins . . . (*Reads*) "The robin as an insect destroyer more than makes up for any injury he does to fruit crops."

ROBIN: There now!

SKUNK: If Farmer Dullard weren't such a dullard, he'd know that himself.

SQUIRREL: I shudder to think what his orchard would look like without robins.

OWL: Does anyone wish to make a motion?

MOLE (*Squeakily*): I do. I move . . . that the Committee move . . . that every move of Farmer Dullard against the robins . . . is . . . is . . .

OWL: Wicked, cruel, and unreasonable. Excellent! All in favor say "Aye."

ALL (*Except* BAT): Aye.

BAT (*Coming in at end again*): Aye.

OWL: Now, Skunk, do you wish to state your case?

SKUNK: I certainly do. And the facts don't smell very sweet, I can tell you. Farmer Dullard is after me and my family. Not only with a gun, but with traps. And he is cutting out the brush along the creek where we have lived for generations. Maybe we *do* take an occasional egg from his hen-house, but is that any reason . . .

OWL: No reason at all, considering how many rats and mice you skunks eat around the barns.

SKUNK (*Smacking lips*): Ummmm, rats and mice! We like them much better than eggs, if Farmer Dullard only knew it. To say nothing of liking grasshoppers and beetles. He just doesn't realize how much good we do around the place. I accuse him of . . .

OWL: Of cruel, wicked, and unreasonable conduct! All in favor . . .

ALL (*Except* BAT, *interrupting*): Aye.

BAT (*Yawning*): Aye.

OWL: Woodchuck, can you think of any good you woodchucks do around the farm?

WOODCHUCK: G . . . g . . . good? Well, I should s . . . s . . . say. Don't we go after the J . . . J . . . June beetles? Don't we eat them by the h . . . h . . . hundreds?

OWL: And how does Farmer Dullard treat you, may I ask?

WOODCHUCK: Like c . . . c . . . criminals. That's how. He is always sicking his d . . . d . . . dogs after us, or hiding near our b . . . b . . . burrow with a gun, or trying to d . . . d . . . dig us out. He makes life m . . . m . . . miserable for us. Maybe we d . . . d . . . *do* eat a few things from his g . . . g . . . garden once in a while, but . . .

OWL: But his action is uncalled for and unwarranted. Is everyone agreed?

ALL (*Except* BAT): Agreed.

BAT (*Sleepily*): Me too.

OWL: All right, Bat. Better late than never. Just where do *you* stand, by the way? (BAT *has fallen asleep again.* MOLE *nudges him.*)

BAT: Huh?

OWL: I said where do you stand? (*Shakes* BAT *gently, and stands him on his feet*)

BAT (*Still sleepy*): Stand? I don't, you know. I always hang when I sleep. (*Gets a thought that rouses him*) Oh, and that's the trouble. I'm in danger of losing my den tree!

MOLE: Your *what?*

BAT: My den tree. The tree where I live. The tree with the nice hollow in it where I hang with my family and sleep . . . (*The thought makes him sleepy again*) . . . all day long. (*Yawns*) Oh, it's a wonderful tree. But Farmer Dullard is clearing out the woods, and he marked our tree to cut down. Our wonderful tree! It's been in the family for years. (*Wipes eyes, yawns*)

OWL: I know just how you feel. My hollow tree is in danger, too.

SQUIRREL: And so is mine. Of course, in summer I live in a nest of sticks and bark high up in the branches. But for winter I *do* like a hollow tree. Farmer Dullard just doesn't understand about forestry and trees. Why, his woods will be overrun with insects if he cuts down our den trees and drives us all out.

BAT: Mosquitoes . . . (*Rouses himself*) Ummmm, mosquitoes!

OWL: What are you talking about?

BAT: We bats dote on mosquitoes. If Farmer Dullard cuts down our tree, I move . . . (*Yawns*) that mosquitoes . . . (*Yawns*) sting him all to *pieces.*

WOODCHUCK: I s . . . s . . . second the motion.

OWL (*Rapping on tree for emphasis*): The motion about mosquitoes is carried . . . unanimously. Now, Mole, what is your grievance against Farmer Dullard?

MOLE: Oh dear, life has never been so hard. We moles don't know which way to tunnel! Farmer Dullard is always trying to dig us out and block our doorways. Maybe we *do* hump up his lawn a little, but is that any reason . . .

OWL: Decidedly not. (*Thumbs through book.*) Moles . . . moles. Here we are. "Although moles disturb lawns with their tunnels and eat earthworms which are beneficial to the soil, more than half their diet . . ." (OWL *looks up*) take note of this, my friends . . . "more than half their diet consists of harmful insects like cutworms which cut off little cabbages and corn plants at the ground and kill them."

MOLE: Ummm, cutworms! (*Smacks his lips*)

OWL: Farmer Dullard is outvoted . . . (*Quickly counts noses*) eight to one!

ALL (*Except* BAT): Yea.

BAT (*Yawning*): Yea.

OWL: Now, Rabbit, do you think you could step up before the Committee and tell how you have been treated? Nobody's going to bite you.

RABBIT (*Coming out timidly*): Yes, sir. (*Keeps looking around cautiously*)

OWL: First, explain your service to humanity.

RABBIT: I don't understand, please.

OWL: In other words, what good do you do in the world?

RABBIT (*Sighing*): I'm afraid not very much, sir. I don't (*Looks at* BAT) eat mosquitoes. I can't say (*Looks at* WOODCHUCK) I like June bugs. I haven't the right kind of teeth (*Looks at* SKUNK) for eating rats and mice and grasshoppers. I can't (*Looks at* ROBIN) sit up in the cherry and apple trees and eat pests. I have no taste for (*Looks at* MOLE) cutworms or grubs. (*Sighs humbly*) I guess I'm not much good for anything.

SQUIRREL: Why, you are too! You're awfully nice to look at!

OWL: I must say everyone admires the way you can jump.

MOLE: And your ears—they're most unusual, you know.

BAT (*Dreamily*): Mosquitoes . . .

RABBIT: My fur is of some value, I understand. But, without my fur, I'd never be here to tell the tale . . .

OWL: I think we are all agreed that rabbits have a definite . . . shall we say *artistic* . . . value for mankind.

RABBIT: Farmer Dullard doesn't seem to think so. He is always after us, he and his dogs. And he is cutting away the briar patch where we have lived for generations. Maybe we *do* eat some of his clover and alfalfa, but is that any reason . . .

OWL: Emphatically not.

SKUNK (*Strutting*): Emphatically *not*.

OWL: Motion carried. And now, friends, I too have a case. We owls like mice and insects quite as much as skunks do. But Farmer Dullard does not seem to realize it. (*Looks around*) It is obvious from the evidence that we are all victims of a conspiracy. Innocent victims of a cruel conspiracy. Now the question before us today is—what shall we do about it?

RABBIT (*Timidly*): All I know is . . . I can't go on like this. I'm a nervous wreck.

SKUNK: We can't any of us go on like this. It isn't *dignified*.

ROBIN: It isn't just.

MOLE: Or intelligent.

WOODCHUCK: Or h . . . h . . . healthy.

OWL: Ladies and gentlemen of the Grievance Committee, as Chairman, I say there is one thing for us to do.

ALL (*Except* BAT): What? What?

BAT: Where?

OWL: The only thing for us to do is to beat Farmer Dullard at his own game. Since Farmer Dullard insists on taking unfair advantage of us, we must strike for our rights—all of us, all at the same time.

ALL (*Except* BAT): Strike?

BAT (*Yawning*): I second the motion.

OWL: Farmer Dullard has been making life miserable for us. All right then, we strike. We pack up and move out on him, in a body. Let the rats overrun his granary! Let the mice overrun his hay mow! Let beetles and cutworms and grasshoppers and other pests take over his garden and orchard. Let mosquitoes . . .

BAT (*Waking up*): Mosquitoes! (*Smacks his lips*)

OWL: Let mosquitoes sting Farmer Dullard right and left!

ALL (*Except* RABBIT): When do we strike?

OWL: The sooner, the quicker.

RABBIT (*Fearful*): But . . . to move to a strange place . . . think of the danger. I am so fond of my briar patch.

OWL: I have an idea we won't have to strike very long. We'll need a picket, though. Someone who can keep an eye on things and report to us while we're off the job. Who will volunteer for picket duty?

SQUIRREL (*Quickly*): I will. I'll stay here and keep you posted on everything that happens. I can hide in the treetops and see without being seen.

OWL: Providing you can remember to scold to yourself and not out loud!

SQUIRREL: Who, me?

SKUNK: I second the motion. I think Squirrel will make a very good picket.

WOODCHUCK: P . . . p . . . peach of a p . . . p . . . picket.

OWL: We'll set up strike headquarters out of sight of the farm, and whenever there is news, Squirrel can make a report. Everyone in favor say "Aye."

ALL (*Except* BAT): Aye.

BAT (*Rousing*): . . . my, mine, me, we, our, ours, us.

MOLE (*Nudging* BAT): Wake up, you're dreaming again.

OWL: All right, then. It's agreed. We strike. We move out immediately and set up strike headquarters nearby, with a picket on duty. And in six weeks, to a minute, (*Consults watch*) we'll meet here again, under this same tree, to decide what to do next.

RABBIT (*Jumping up excitedly*): I hear dogs! Way off in the distance, I hear dogs. Farmer Dullard must be coming. Run . . . run for your lives.

Owl (*Calling out as all scatter in different directions*): In six weeks. Remember! Six weeks, to the minute.

CURTAIN

* * *

Scene 2

Time: *Later.* (*A curtain does not have to be used at the end of the first scene, since the passage of time is indicated in the speeches. This scene should start slowly and speed up gradually.*)

Setting: *Same as Scene 1.*

At Rise: Owl *is sitting on a stump as* Skunk *saunters in.*

Skunk: Hoo, hoo, Owl. Are you there?

Owl: Hoo, hoo.

Skunk: We've been on strike four weeks today, brother Owl. I wonder what Squirrel will report when he comes again. He's been a pretty good picket, hasn't he?

Owl: Excellent. Hoot! There he comes now.

Squirrel (*Coming in importantly*): Hear ye, hear ye. Farmer Dullard is in a dither. He can't begin to catch all the rats in the barn. He can't begin to catch all the mice in the hay mow. (*Exits, calling "Hear ye, hear ye."*)

Owl: Did you hear that Skunk?

Skunk: Did I? Mice in the hay and rats in the barn. It looks as if we're winning the strike.

Owl: Hoot and ahoy. All we need is patience. Everything comes to him who waits. (*Yawns, ducks back behind foliage.* Skunk *goes back behind stump. In a minute* Squirrel *comes in again a little faster than before.*)

Squirrel: Bulletin! Bulletin! The cutworms are cutting off

the cabbages. The cutworms are cutting off the corn. The June beetles are eating the garden. A million new grubs have been born. (*Exits calling "Bulletin," etc.*)

WOODCHUCK (*Crawling out of burrow, behind bush*): M . . . m . . . mole. Mole!

MOLE (*Sticking head out*): Woodchuck. Woodchuck!

WOODCHUCK: D . . . d . . . did you hear the news?

MOLE: I did indeed. The cutworms! The grubs!

WOODCHUCK: The J . . . J . . . June beetles. (*Chuckles*) W . . . w . . . wonder what Farmer Dullard thinks now. (*Goes back to burrow*)

MOLE (*Backing behind bush*): Plenty, brother. You can be sure of that. (SQUIRREL *comes in again, a little faster.*)

SQUIRREL: Extra! Extra! Insects are swarming over the orchard, eating the leaves, eating the fruit. Mosquitoes are driving Farmer Dullard frantic. Zooommmm, zzzzzz. (*Exits, calling "Extra!" etc.*)

ROBIN (*Hopping in*): Bat, Bat. Where are you? (*No answer*) Bat! (*There is a feeble, sleepy answer from behind a tree.*) Bat!

BAT (*Sticking head out*): Oh, it's you, Robin. What's up? Or down?

ROBIN: Did you hear the news? Insects are swarming over the orchard. Mosquitoes are driving Farmer Dullard frantic.

BAT (*Smacking lips*): Mosquitoes—ummmm. Aren't they wonderful? (*Yawns*) Wonder . . . ful. (*Retires to sleep again.* ROBIN *hops out. From here on* SQUIRREL *comes in faster and faster, to show passage of time. Heads of other animals bob back and forth.*)

SQUIRREL: Farmer Dullard can do nothing to stop the invasion of rats and mice. They are eating all his hay and grain. They are even chewing up the harness. (*Exits and soon returns*) Farmer Dullard can do nothing to stop the invasion of cutworms and June beetles, to say nothing of grasshoppers and other insects. His garden will soon be in ruins. (*Exits and returns quickly*) Farmer Dullard is in despair over his orchard, which is swarming with pests. He can't do a thing . . . except scratch his mosquito bites. (*Exits, re-enters almost at once*) Extra special! Extra special! Farmer Dullard admits his mistake! He regrets he drove us out on strike. He is willing to call off the whole conspiracy. He sees now that it hurts him more than it hurts us. Extra special! (*Exits*)

OWL: What did I tell you, folks? Tomorrow the six weeks are up. The Grievance Committee will meet at the meeting place.

CURTAIN

* * *

SCENE 3

TIME: *The next day.*

SETTING: *The same.*

AT RISE: OWL *is again in charge of the meeting, which is already in progress.*

OWL: Everyone seems to be here except Rabbit. Rabbit! (*Calls out*) Rabbit!

RABBIT (*Hopping in excitedly*): Pardon me for being late. But I'm so excited. (*Looks around*) Is it safe to talk?

OWL: Quite safe.

RABBIT: I was so lonesome for my old briar patch this morning I slipped back at dawn to take a look. And what do you think?

SQUIRREL: I could have told you. Instead of cutting down the last of the briars, Farmer Dullard is letting them grow again. He's discovered that rabbits are worth looking at. That's one of the things I had to report. (*Holds up list*)

RABBIT: It's wonderful. My nice safe briar patch. Now I'm sure I won't get a nervous breakdown.

OWL (*Rapping for order*): Fellow strikers, we are all assembled . . .

ROBIN (*Eagerly*): May I say a word?

OWL: Robin has the floor.

ROBIN: I was feeling very lonely for the old orchard this morning. And so I flew back, at dawn, to have a look. And what do you think. That old grapevine is so eaten up with insects Farmer Dullard can't hide behind it with his gun any more.

SQUIRREL: I was going to report that too. And something you couldn't see, Robin! Farmer Dullard *hasn't* a gun any more. He sold it to the junk man.

ROBIN, WOODCHUCK, SKUNK *and* RABBIT: No gun! No gun! (*They do a joyful dance.*)

SQUIRREL: He sold his traps too.

WOODCHUCK *and* SKUNK: Whee! (*They dance together*)

OWL (*Rapping for order*): Order! Order! Dancing is out of order. Squirrel, we couldn't have picked a better picket. Have you anything else to report?

SQUIRREL: Since Farmer Dullard came to his senses, things have been happening thick and fast. (*Looks through his notes*) He wants to make things pleasant for us, so we'll call off the strike. Now he won't cut down all our den trees in the woods.

MOLE (*Nudging* BAT): Bat, did you hear that?

BAT (*Sleepily*): Gnat? (*Smacks lips*) Gnat!

MOLE: No, den tree.

BAT (*Waking up*): Den tree? My den tree—where I used to hang and sleep?

SQUIRREL: It's still there, Bat. Waiting for you. And swarms of mosquitoes too.

BAT (*Dreamily*): Ah . . . isn't life wonderful?

OWL: And is my tree all right too?

SQUIRREL: Your tree is still there, Owl. Unfortunately mine got cut down before Farmer Dullard saw the light. But I'm not worried. I can find another, before winter.

WOODCHUCK: What about my b . . . b . . . burrow?

SQUIRREL: It's there waiting for you. Farmer Dullard decided it was better to have you and your family eat a little of his garden than have the June beetles and their relatives eat *all* of it.

WOODCHUCK: Ah . . . June b . . . b . . . beetles. (*Sighs with happiness*)

SKUNK: And what about me?

SQUIRREL: Oh, you don't have to worry any more, Skunk. Farmer Dullard has decided to leave a nice lot of brush along the creek where you like to live. He's even put out a garbage pail for your benefit . . . behind the barn.

SKUNK: He has! Well, what do you know!

SQUIRREL: And will you get fat cleaning up on those rats and mice! You too, Owl.

OWL: I can do with some rats and mice, I will admit.

MOLE: And me? How about me?

SQUIRREL: Farmer Dullard isn't such a dullard any more. In fact, he's thinking of changing his name to Dillard. He understands now who kept the cutworms and grubs under control. He's not going to worry about a few humps in his lawn.

MOLE: Ummm, it will be good to get my teeth in a cutworm again.

SQUIRREL: A cutworm. You can get your teeth in a million, more or less.

OWL: Well, fellow strikers, it looks as if we can all go back to our jobs. Farmer Dullard . . . Dillard . . . realizes he needs us as much as we need him.

WOODCHUCK: I second the m . . . m . . . motion.

SKUNK: I third it.

OWL: And may we never have to strike again, as long as we live. All in favor say "Aye."

ALL (*Except* BAT): Aye.

BAT (*Dreamily*): Me too.

THE END

. . .   . .

Let's Plant a Tree

ALL: It's time to plant a tree, a tree.
      What shall it be? What shall it be?

1ST: Let's plant a pine—we can't go wrong:
      a pine is green the whole year long.
2ND: Let's plant a maple—more than one!
      to shade us from the summer sun.
3RD: Let's plant a cherry—you know why:
      there's nothing like a cherry pie!
4TH: Let's plant an elm, the tree of grace,
      where robins find a nesting place.
5TH: Let's plant an apple—not too small,
      with flowers in spring and fruit in fall.
6TH: Let's plant a fir—so it can be
      a lighted outdoor Christmas tree.
7TH: Let's plant a birch, an oak, a beech,
      there's something extra-nice in each.

ALL: It's time to plant a tree, a tree.
      What shall it be? What shall it be?
      It doesn't seem to matter much—
      they all have special charms and such
      in winter, summer, spring or fall.
      Let's plant a . . .
                    look, let's plant them *ALL.*

Planting a Pine

NOW I'm twice as tall as you,
little tree. You're tiny.
I am four feet, you are two,
with needles green and shiny.

I am twice as big, but oh,
soon I shall be smaller.
In a little while I know
YOU will be the taller.

Little tree, I'll never stand
more than two feet higher,
but you'll stretch above the land
like a tall green spire!

MOTHER'S DAY

Mother's Day Off and On

Characters

JUDY, *about 11* ~~Haelee~~   Daile
ERIC, *about 10* Billy   Jake
PATSY, *about 6* Kara   Shane
FATHER Kenny   Justin
MOTHER Tonya

TIME: *Eight o'clock on the morning of Mother's Day.*
SETTING: *Two rooms of a house, the dining room and kitchen.*
AT RISE: JUDY *and* ERIC *are setting the breakfast table.* PATSY *is trying to help* FATHER *in the kitchen.*

~~JUDY~~: Haelee
  We've never been so nice and quiet.
~~ERIC~~: Billy
  We can do it, when we try it.
JUDY: Daile
  I bet Mom will think it's fun
  To find, for once, that breakfast's done.
ERIC: Jake
  If only Dad won't burn the toast . . .
  I saw him do it twice, almost.
  Kara ~~Judy~~, I'm afraid he'll botch it.
~~JUDY~~: KARA

321

I told Patsy she should watch it.

(*In the kitchen* FATHER *is puttering around.* PATSY *sniffs.*)

PATSY:

Daddy, look, the toast is burning.

FATHER:

Every time my back starts turning!   (*Shakes the toaster*)

What's the matter, anyway . . .

PATSY:

Ssh . . . don't shout on Mother's Day

Or we never will surprise her.

FATHER (*Putting down the toaster*):

She is sleepier than wiser.   (*He puffs out his chest.*)

I think I'm a magic-maker;

I got up . . . and didn't wake her.

(*In the dining room,* JUDY *and* ERIC *look over the Mother's Day gifts on the table.*)

JUDY (*Feeling a package*):

Pat's present feels all bumpy.

ERIC:

Wonder what can be so lumpy.

Patsy won't let on, you know.

JUDY:

She said one thing about it, though:

She said it was the *best* she had.

ERIC:

She likes secrets . . . just like Dad.   (*Picks up a package*)

His must be a box of candy.

JUDY:

Eric, wouldn't that be dandy!

ERIC:

Dad has something up his sleeve

In *addition*, I believe . . .

Something written in this letter.   (*Picks up a letter*)

JUDY (*Impatiently*): *Haelee*

If Mom won't wake up soon, I'll get her!
Do you think my poem's all right?

ERIC: *Billy*

Sure. And my invention?

JUDY: *Kara*   Quite.

Breakfast must be almost ready.

(*There is a terrific crash in the kitchen.* FATHER, *picking up
the teakettle to fill the dripolator, burns his hand. He drops
the kettle with a crash.*)

PATSY: *Daile*

Daddy, hold the kettle steady.

FATHER:

It's too late. It fell already.

(JUDY *and* ERIC *run to see what happened. They all scurry
around mopping up water and getting in each other's way.
Just then* MOTHER'S *voice is heard.*)

MOTHER (*Offstage*):

Goodness, what a frightful clatter.
Is there anything the matter?

JUDY: *Haelee*

Mother's coming. Hurry! Hurry!

FATHER (*Wiping furiously*):

We'll be through in time, don't worry.

PATSY: *Kara*

But we have to sing our song!

FATHER:

Go ahead . . . I'll tag along.

(JUDY, ERIC *and* PATSY *hurry to the dining room, awaiting*
MOTHER'S *appearance. When she comes in they begin to sing
lustily to the tune of* "Happy Birthday to You." *Midway in
the singing,* FATHER *appears, his apron rumpled and wet. He
joins in.*)

CHILDREN: *ALL*

Happy greetings to you,

Happy greetings to you,

Happy Mother's Day, Mother.

Happy greetings to you.

MOTHER (*Merrily*):

What a lovely reception, my darlings, my dears.

I haven't had so much attention in years.

And look at the table—all set to perfection.

~~PATSY~~ *Dale*:

And look at the presents.

~~ERIC~~ *Jake*:   Yes, make an inspection!

FATHER:

You *must* read the letter that's fresh from my pen.

~~PATSY~~ *Haelee* (*Sniffing*):

Oh, Daddy, the toast must be burning again.

(FATHER *hurries to the kitchen to rescue the toast.* MOTHER *beams at the children and at the table.*)

MOTHER:

I think I should take this occasion to mention

That Mother's Day is an *exciting* invention.

~~ERIC~~ *Billy*:

Invention! Just wait till you open up mine.

FATHER (*Returning breathlessly*):

I rescued the breakfast, so everything's fine.

Come, open your presents, and meanwhile we'll dine.

(FATHER *and* ~~JUDY~~ *bring in things from the kitchen, and all sit at the table while* MOTHER *begins on her presents.*)

MOTHER:

Now which shall I open up first? Let me see . . . (*Picks up gift*)

This says, "From your ~~Patsy~~ *Haelee*." Hmmm . . . what can it be? (*Opens it*)

Your ragdoll! Oh, ~~Patsy~~ *Haelee* . . .

ERIC (*Surprised*):

Well, buckle my shoe!

JUDY (*Amused*):

A ragdoll. Now, Mom, you'll have something to do!

PATSY:

The best doll I have . . . and the best is for *you*.

MOTHER:

Oh, thank you. But, darling, I give you fair warning
I *may* need your help with this child, night and morning.
(*That suits* PATSY. MOTHER *picks up another package, a large one.*)
This package is heavy. (*Reads card*) "From Eric, with love."
It's tied very tightly below and above.
(*She finally gets it open and takes out four triangular pieces of wood. She wonders what the blocks are for.*)
Oh, Eric . . . they're lovely!

ERIC: I cut them myself.

FATHER (*Bewildered*):

My boy, are they bookends . . . to set on a shelf?

MOTHER:

I hardly expect that was Eric's intention.

ERIC:

Why, Dad, don't you see? It's a special invention:
These blocks fit in corners. They're perfect for keeping
The dust out . . . they're super to help Mom in sweeping.
(ERIC *gets up and demonstrates.*)

MOTHER:

How really amazing. How thoughtful. How clever.

FATHER:

Corners for cutting off corners? I never!
(MOTHER *picks up a small flat parcel.*)

MOTHER:

Another nice present. I wonder what this is.
It says, "To my Mother, with love and with kisses,

From Judy.' (*Opens it*) You'd think it was *Christmas* today.
A beautiful hankie. (*Holds it up*) Look, isn't it gay?
And here are some verses . . . let's see what they say.

~~ERIC:~~ *Justin*

She made up that poem and it took her just ages.
It isn't so long, but she wasted whole pages!

FATHER:

I wasn't aware that this house held a poet.

MOTHER:

Just listen to this and, hereafter, you'll *know* it. (*Reads*)
For Mother on Mother's Day:
Half of your parents consists of a mother.
(Your father is also a half—he's the other.)
But though she is half, she is really three-quarters,
Because she stays home with her son and her daughters.

A mother, compared to a father, is smarter (FATHER *gives
   a start.*)
About getting dinner . . . that's only a starter.
She also knows more about sewing and mending
And cleaning and ironing—the list is unending. (FATHER
   gulps.)
She knows how to bake many things that are yummy
(Though carrots are better, she says, for your tummy.)
And oh, there are *so* many angles about her
We all would be lost in a minute without her!
(MOTHER *laughs*)

Mother I'm glad for those *angles*, or I'd be too fat—
If I were all curving, you couldn't say that!
But, seriously, Judy, your verses are splendid.
You don't know how much I enjoy being commended.
And now, one more package . . .

FATHER: My gifts, though, are *two*.
I thought of a dozen red roses for you,

And then I decided a *choice* would be better,
As you will observe when you open my letter.

PATSY (*Suddenly*):

Oh, Daddy—the kettle. I bet you forgot
To put on more water.

FATHER (*Jumping up*):

The kettle—great Scot!
(FATHER *rushes to the kitchen to put water in the kettle.* MOTHER, *amused, picks up the package and opens it. She calls out*)

MOTHER:

What wonderful candy. Oh, thank you, my dear.
(FATHER, *pleased, hurries back, and sits down.* MOTHER *opens the letter*)
And now for the letter. What choice have we here?
(*She begins to read aloud.*) "Dearest Wife and Mother. On this beautiful occasion of Mother's Day, my first thought was to buy you red roses as an expression of my deep love and appreciation. But, on second thought, it occurred to me I might give you a gift you would like even better. If you prefer the roses, though, just say the word, my dear. I have reserved some at the florist's until nine o'clock.

Here is my idea. Instead of roses, wouldn't you like to have a complete rest and change on this Mother's Day? Wouldn't you like to be *honorary* mother for the day, and let me take over all your duties and responsibilities? Perhaps there is a story you are eager to read or something . . ."
(MOTHER *looks up from the letter.*)
How *could* you have guessed it? Oh, that will be gay.
I'll read . . . and you handle my duties today.

ERIC (*To* FATHER):

It works out all right that today is a Sunday,
For, Dad, there's a *washing* to do every Monday.

. . .

MOTHER (*Finishing the letter*):

"And don't you worry one little bit. I am sure I will be
perfectly able to handle the duties of a modern mother."
(MOTHER *looks up with interest.*)
Modern mothers have it easy?
That's what you imply?

FATHER:

Oh, their lives are pretty breezy,
Matched with times gone by:
Take a good old-fashioned mother—
She was so immersed
In one labor or another . . .
Spinning, weaving, endless baking,
Quilting, making cheese,
Churning, soap and candle-making . . .
No more jobs like these.

MOTHER:

Yes, it's true that ceaseless toiling
Has a modern cure,
But . . .

JUDY: I hear the kettle boiling!

FATHER:

Kettle? (*Recollects himself*) To be sure.
(FATHER *rushes to the kitchen, fills dripolator, brings it in and
begins to pour a cup of coffee for* MOTHER. *Of course, the
water hasn't gone through yet, so some spills on the tablecloth.*)
You admit there's nothing to it—
Keeping house these days.
Just relax and watch me do it! (*Pats himself on the chest*)
Being efficient pays.

MOTHER:

Yes, of course, my dear. Take over!
I'm sure I shan't be missed.
All day long I'll be in clover . . . (*Looks mischievous*)

Better make a list
Of the things that must be finished
All in time for church.

FATHER (*Taking out pencil and paper*): Well? My zeal is undiminished.

MOTHER:

Don't leave me in the lurch!
First, the beds. And then the dishes.

FATHER (*Beginning to take notes, then turning to* PATSY *and* JUDY):

Daughters, make your plans
To carry out your mother's wishes!

~~JUDY~~ *Kara* (*Quickly*):

Mom always does the *pans*,
And cleans around the sink and table . . .

MOTHER:

Better put that down!
(FATHER *makes the note, and* ~~JUDY and PATSY~~ *Girls go out, with amused backward glances.*)
Make a pudding. Are you able?
Don't give such a frown.
Start the pot-roast early—very,
Braise it long enough . . .

FATHER (*Puzzled*):

Braise? (~~*To* ERIC~~) Go get the dictionary. (~~ERIC *exits.*~~)

MOTHER:

Or else it will be tough.
Shell the peas, and make the salad,
Sweep the kitchen floor . . .
Dear, you look a little pallid.

FATHER (*Weakly*):

Is there any more?
(ERIC *comes back with the dictionary which he hands to* FATHER. *He also hands* FATHER *a sock.*)

ERIC:

    Dad, you've got to do some mending.

    My Sunday sock—just look.

FATHER (*Looking*):

    The hole goes on without an ending!

    But, son, I've got to *cook*.

    (PATSY *comes running in with a dress. She goes to* FATHER.)

PATSY:

    My Sunday dress must have a pressing. (*She points*)

    Wrinkles here . . . and here.

FATHER (*With a sigh*):

    I'm finding this a bit distressing.

MOTHER (*Much amused*):

    Nothing to it, dear!

    (JUDY *runs in with a light-colored jacket, and hurries to* FATHER.)

JUDY:

    Daddy, find the spot remover.   (*Shows a spot*)

    Help me get this out.

FATHER (*Desperately*):

    Heavens, how can I maneuver

    My poor way about?

MOTHER:

    Modern mothers never worry—

    Nothing to be done!

FATHER (*Looking at his watch*):

    Almost nine! I'll have to hurry.

    Gosh, I'll have to *run*.

    (FATHER *dashes out, taking off his apron and banging into a chair as he goes.*)

MOTHER:

    What a dreadful rush and clatter.

ERIC (*Going to window*):

    You should see him sprint.

MOTHER (*Innocently*):
  I wonder what can be the matter.
  Can you give a hint?
JUDY:
  Perhaps he's gone to get the paper.
ERIC:
  Or maybe cigarettes.
MOTHER:
  It strikes me as a funny caper.   (*Then cheerfully*)
  But he'll be back, my pets.
ERIC (*Making a face*):
  I don't expect to like his dinner.
PATSY:
  He'll burn the meat, I fear.
JUDY:
  I guess by night we'll all be thinner.
MOTHER:
  Let's not shed a tear.
  I have a sort of inner feeling
  Things will turn out fine.
PATSY:
  Daddy's funny.
MOTHER: Most appealing!
JUDY:
  Daddy should resign—
  I mean, his trying to act for Mother.
ERIC:
  Yes, I think so, too;
  Each job is harder than the other,
  And what a lot to do—
  Cooking, darning, sweeping, pressing,
  Cleaning up the sink . . .
JUDY:
  Daddy said it was distressing.

MOTHER:

So easy, don't you think?

JUDY (*Thoughtfully*):

No. But, Mom, you're always cheerful.

PATSY:

You don't burn the toast,

Or drop the kettle. It was fearful.

ERIC:

Mom, you never boast,

But you handle things just dandy.

JUDY:

Yes, you always do.

MOTHER:

Thank you. Have a piece of candy?

(*She passes the candy box, then looks toward outer door.*)

Hmmm. I wish I knew . . . (*She turns to* ERIC.)

That sock . . . I'll darn it in a jiffy. (*Turns to* JUDY)

Nothing to that spot. (*Turns to* PATSY)

I'll make your dress look nice and spiffy

When the iron gets hot . . .

(*Just at that moment* FATHER *bursts into the room, panting, with a bouquet of red roses in his hand. Proudly he rushes to* MOTHER.)

FATHER:

Dear, a Mother's Day surprise!

Don't you think my choice is wise—

Much, much wiser than the other?

Roses . . . for the world's best mother!

THE END

That's the Way Mothers Are

GIRLS: What did she want for Mother's Day?,
        we asked when we were tiny.
          A pile of sand where it's fun to play,
          and a bucket new and shiny!

ALL: That's the way mothers are.

BOYS: What did she want for Mother's Day?,
        we asked when we were older.
          A camping kit and a water bag
          and a knapsack for her shoulder!

ALL: That's the way mothers are.

GIRLS: What did she want? Not anything
        as frail as flowers or candy!
          But a good strong rope (for a good strong swing),
          or a bobsled would be handy!

ALL: That's the way mothers are.

GIRLS: Now that we've found her out, at last,
        (after these years, who wouldn't?)
        we're making up for her "sandpile" past . . .
        though she always says we shouldn't!

ALL: That's the way mothers are.

Who?

1ST CHILD: Who's always there to help you out,
to soothe your doubt,
your tears, your pout,
to set your troubles right-about?
ALL: Mother!

2ND CHILD: Who's always quick to understand,
and lend a hand
to what you've planned,
who (most times!) thinks you're pretty grand?
ALL: Mother!

3RD CHILD: Who never wants to let you down,
who tries to drown
each fret and frown,
who's always doing things "up brown"?
ALL: Mother!

4TH CHILD: Who always has a smile to send,
a laugh to lend,
and love to spend?
Who's all in all, your chiefest friend?
ALL: Mother!

For Mother's Day

It isn't just on Mother's Day
that Mother likes a special smile.
Although we honor her in May,
it isn't just on Mother's Day
she likes the special things we say—
she likes them all the while!

Memorial Day

I

GROUP: It will be a day of flowers,
        honoring these graves of ours:
1ST GIRL: Lilacs heavy with the scent
        of countless Springs that came and went,
1ST BOY: Red geraniums in a pot
        on a green and hallowed spot,
2ND GIRL: Purple iris, deep-dyed blue . . .
        colors of the brave and true,
2ND BOY: Hawthorn, cherry, apple sprig—
        blossoms small and blossoms big,
GROUP: Flowers in bunches, wreaths, and bowers,
        honoring these graves of ours.

II

GROUP: It will be a day of flowers
        brightening the thoughtful hours:
GIRLS: All day long the flowers will glow
        near the crosses, row on row,
BOYS: All day long they will be bright.
        Then, upon the verge of night,
        lighting up the gathering gloom,
        there will be another bloom . . .

GIRLS: There will show, high up and far,
            the blossom of the Soldiers' Star!
GROUP: The Soldiers' Star—the first to pay
            its homage to the fading day,
            rounding out a day of flowers
            honoring these graves of ours.

NOTE: A good dramatic effect may be achieved by having the
  boys and girls in the first stanza carry the flowers mentioned
  in their lines as they enter.

Red, White, and Blue

RED for courage to do the right,
WHITE for faith with its guiding light,
BLUE for strength in carrying-through—
Hail to the red and white and blue!

The Soldiers Speak

"Place your flowers, but do not weep,"
the silent soldiers seem to say.
"We are peaceful where we sleep
on this bright Memorial Day.

"Think of us, but do not sigh,"
they seem to whisper on the breeze.
"We are peaceful where we lie
on this day of memories.

"Just to know that freedom thrives
and our banners proudly wave,
makes us know the best survives
of the gift of life we gave."

GRADUATION

Caves of the Earth

Characters

READER
CLERK
REGISTRAR
GAMECATCHER
YOUNG WOMAN
BOY
GIRL
BOYS AND GIRLS

TIME: *Not so far in the future.*
SETTING: *An outdoor scene, before the entrance of a deep cave.*
PRELUDE: *Before the curtain opens, a* READER *comes before the curtain and reads slowly from Isaiah 2:19.*

READER: "And they shall go into the holes of the rocks, and into the caves of the earth, for fear of the Lord, and for the glory of his majesty, when he ariseth to shake terribly the earth." (READER *exits and curtain opens on quiet stage. The* CLERK *and* REGISTRAR *are concentrating on papers at the table.* CLERK *takes up a long list and looks it through. After a moment . . .*)
CLERK: The list is almost finished now . . . as they ordered.

Two of every living thing, male and female. They will be
safe in the cave when the bombs begin to fall.

REGISTRAR: Almost finished, you say?

CLERK: Except for the last few. (*Turns over list, which is very
long indeed*) It is a long list.

REGISTRAR (*Looking at it*): And you and I at the very end.

CLERK: Yes, at the end. We go last and block the mouth
of the cave behind us. (*Scans the sky*) That is, if we are
not too late! Destruction can come in a moment now-
adays . . .

REGISTRAR: I shall write our registration cards now, to save
time. (*Looks at watch*) The Gamecatcher takes longer than
usual this trip.

CLERK: Yes. It is the rabbits! He has a hard time catching
the two rabbits, male and female, with their big ears to hear
him coming and their fast legs for running. (*Consults list*)
After the rabbits, the moles. They will be easier.

REGISTRAR: And they will be quite at home down in the cave,
in the darkness, almost a mile from the sun.

CLERK: *More* than a mile, they say. The deeper the safer,
you know, these days. Yes, you are right. The moles will
be quite at home.

REGISTRAR: And after the moles?

CLERK: After the moles, the Gamecatcher will be finished with
his work. He can enter, then, himself.

REGISTRAR: And after the Gamecatcher?

CLERK: The two children. The boy and girl, who have not
come. They are very late. Their names are near the front
of the list (*Points out place to* REGISTRAR), but they do not
arrive. In half an hour . . . it will be too late. (*Scans sky*)
We dare not wait longer than half an hour. If they are not
here then, they will have to stay outside!

REGISTRAR: I suppose there is some chance for safety outside
the cave. But who would choose to take it? Who can stand

against atom bombs? (*Looks toward wings left*) Ah, here comes the Gamecatcher now.

CLERK: With the rabbits, I hope. (GAMECATCHER, *with game bag slung over his shoulder, comes in wearily.*)

GAMECATCHER: At last, the rabbits. (*He goes to cave entrance and carefully puts his catch into the opening, then wipes his forehead*) They run faster now than when I was younger.

CLERK (*Amused*): Yes, I daresay they do. (*Gets businesslike*) Now, only the moles, and you are finished.

GAMECATCHER (*Going out left*): The moles will be easy. And they will need only the smallest corner of the sack.

CLERK (*Sighing*): Still the children do not come.

REGISTRAR (*Peering right*): Here comes someone now, over the hill. All in white. Perhaps it is the girl.

CLERK (*Peering*): No. The face is not a girl's face. It is a young woman. Who can she be, I wonder? (*Looks over list again*) There is no one else on the list.

REGISTRAR: She is carrying something in her hand. Now it flits to her shoulder, now to her hand again. It is a bird. A white bird.

CLERK: Perhaps she thinks we can make room for it in the cave, where it will be safe. (*Shrugs*) But our list is almost complete. We must not disobey orders. We must hold to the list. . . .

REGISTRAR (*Scanning list*): The young lady is not among those to be saved, sure enough. Nor the bird. What kind would you say it is, Clerk?

CLERK: A dove. A white dove.

REGISTRAR (*Checking "d's" on list*): Doe . . . dog . . . dolphin . . . donkey . . . duck. Why, the dove is not there! There is no dove on the list. What shall we do?

CLERK: Nothing. There must have been a reason. It is not for us to change the list. (YOUNG WOMAN *dressed in white comes in slowly, looking around. She holds the dove in her*

*hands gently. Note: Any soft white object will do for the dove.
The* CLERK *and* REGISTRAR *bend over their papers, pretending
not to see the newcomer.*)

YOUNG WOMAN (*As if thinking aloud*): Soon the Gamecatcher
will be back with the moles. They, at least, will not mind
the darkness of the cave. Then the children will come . . .

CLERK (*Startled*): Pardon me . . . but did you say the children
will come?

YOUNG WOMAN: They are on their way now, the boy and the
girl.

REGISTRAR (*Scanning sky*): I hope they hurry. There is no
time for slowness these days.

YOUNG WOMAN: There is time for what the children are doing.
Do not fear, they will be here before you seal the cave.

CLERK (*Looking at list, a little embarrassed*): You, Miss . . .
er . . . ah . . . I am sorry. I do not seem to find your
name on the list. Nor the bird's either.

YOUNG WOMAN: I am not surprised.

REGISTRAR: I . . . we . . . I mean, we have no authority for
even so much as a dove extra. It *is* a dove, is it not?

YOUNG WOMAN: Yes. A dove.

REGISTRAR: Strange, there is no dove on the list.

YOUNG WOMAN: Not so strange, my friends. But do not let
it worry you. Neither the dove nor I would survive in the
caves of the earth. Our victory is here in the sun, under
the broad sky, or not at all. (*Stares at cave entrance*) The
cave is the end, not the beginning. It houses fear, not faith.
It has no room for Peace. (CLERK *and* REGISTRAR *glance
at each other, puzzled. But before they can ask questions,
the* GAMECATCHER *arrives from wings left.*)

GAMECATCHER: The moles! I have them already. (*Carefully
he puts them in the cave.*) They needed only the smallest
corner of the sack.

CLERK: Well done, Gamecatcher. Now all the animals on the

list are accounted for. You will be needed, down there, to care for them. Are you ready to go?

REGISTRAR: Here is your card. As soon as the children come, we shall follow and block the cave. (*Slowly the* GAME-CATCHER *takes his card, looks at it, and starts for the cave. At the entrance he hesitates, then turns for a last look at the bright world. His eyes meet the eyes of the* YOUNG WOMAN, *and for a moment he does not move. Then, with a sudden motion, he pulls his cap down over his eyes and plunges into the cave.*)

YOUNG WOMAN: Poor fellow. He will miss the sun and the woods he knows, and the river, and the green field running up the hill.

CLERK: Of course he will. But he will be safe, he will survive! He will emerge with the rest of us . . . when the frightful danger is past.

YOUNG WOMAN: When the danger is past? It does not pass, my friend, unless it is met. It stands and waits. Or it follows. Yes, even into the holes of the rocks, and into the caves of the earth.

REGISTRAR (*Confidently*): Ah, but our greatest leaders have pronounced the cave entirely safe. Atom bombs cannot penetrate so far, and cosmic rays cannot reach us.

YOUNG WOMAN: But when you emerge, what then? Will the danger be past? Will the age of the rocket and the atom bomb be over? No. You will blink one hour at the sun and run back into the cave again. You cannot run and hide from danger. You must meet it face to face. Peace does not live underground.

CLERK (*Insistently*): Our only safety is in the cave, deep in the earth.

YOUNG WOMAN: If there is no safety here, in the sun, there is none under the ground . . . except for a passing moment, and that goes quickly. One must think of lifetimes, not moments. (*Suddenly holds up her hand and listens*) The children are coming!

CLERK (*Peering left and right*): Where?

YOUNG WOMAN: They will soon come over the hill, behind me. (*She moves backstage to be out of the way.*)

REGISTRAR (*Eagerly*): I have their cards all ready. Ah, they will come in time! (*In a low voice to the* CLERK) I wonder who the stranger is. She seems to know things . . . without looking.

CLERK (*Low tones to* REGISTRAR): Pay no attention. She is not on the list. She does not understand about the bombs.

YOUNG WOMAN (*Gently*): Oh, but I do, my friends. I understand completely. (CLERK *and* REGISTRAR *are more baffled than ever, but have no time to answer, for at that moment the* BOY *and* GIRL *come in from right. They look around.*)

CLERK (*Impatiently*): At last, children! You have kept us waiting for a long time.

REGISTRAR: Here are your cards. Come, you have dallied enough. You must hurry into the cave!

BOY (*Advancing for card*): Why?

CLERK: To survive, of course.

GIRL (*Advancing for card*): Where does the cave go?

REGISTRAR: Into the ground, child. A mile, more than a mile, down into the earth. (*Hands her card*) Here is your identification. You are fortunate to be on the list. Now, hurry. (*The children take their cards and look at them, but make no move toward the cave.*)

GIRL: More than a mile into the ground! How can we see the sun?

CLERK: You cannot, of course, until we emerge again.

BOY: When will that be?

CLERK: Who can say? A month . . . a year . . . ten years . . .

GIRL (*Shrinking away*): Oh! All that time under the ground in the darkness?

REGISTRAR: There will be lights on different levels. Our engineers have wires and switches. Our commissaries have stores of food. Water trickles out of cracks in the rocks. It will not be too bad. Why do you hesitate? It has all been prophesied! We are just fulfilling the prophecy. Read what it says on the back of your card.

BOY *and* GIRL (*Reading*): "And they shall go into the holes of the rocks, and into the caves of the earth, for fear of the Lord, and for the glory of his majesty, when he ariseth to shake terribly the earth."

BOY (*Slowly*): But . . . it is not true! We do not go into the cave for fear of the Lord . . . but for fear of man. For fear of the rockets and bombs and cosmic rays that man has made. For fear of atomic war.

YOUNG WOMAN: The boy is right. You do not hide for fear of the Lord, but because you have *forgotten* Him.

GIRL (*Looking at card*): The Lord does not arise to shake the earth. It is *men* . . . with their atom bombs.

CLERK (*To* REGISTRAR): What shall we do? Time passes. We cannot stand here and listen to the babble of children and be saved!

YOUNG WOMAN (*Gently*): And a little child shall lead them.

BOY (*Turning to* YOUNG WOMAN): Are *you* going into the cave? You and the white dove?

YOUNG WOMAN: No. If we cannot meet the danger here, we shall surely fail there.

BOY: I am not going either! (*He puts card back on table*) We met other children on our way here. That is what took so long. We talked to them.

GIRL (*Putting her card back*): We met all kinds of children, and they think the way we do. They think if we try to understand each other with kindness, there will be no more wars. There will be no need for caves in the earth.

YOUNG WOMAN: "Nation shall not lift up sword against nation, neither shall they learn war any more. They shall beat their swords into plowshares, and their spears into pruning hooks." *That* is your prophecy, my friends. These are the words to be fulfilled! Carve them in the rock.

REGISTRAR (*Impatiently to* BOY *and* GIRL): It is growing late. We cannot force safety upon you. But you have the chance —your names are on the list. Are you coming?

BOY *and* GIRL: No. We are not coming. (*They go to pet the dove.*) We shall help take care of the dove.

YOUNG WOMAN (*To* CLERK *and* REGISTRAR): The children choose to face the future here, my friends. Hurry into your cave. Seal the door. Search for your safety in the cracks of the rock. But do not be surprised if it is not there. The only peace is here, in the sun, in One World. You have but to make it. (*She holds up her hands and listens.*) I hear a great singing coming over the hill.

CLERK: I hear nothing but the ticking of time. And it ticks quickly! (CLERK *and* REGISTRAR *gather up papers, leaving table bare except for two rejected cards. They prepare to enter the cave, turning as they go in.*)

REGISTRAR: You are making a great mistake, children.

CLERK: Well, we are going. Goodbye.

YOUNG WOMAN: Farewell.

BOY *and* GIRL: Goodbye. (*For a moment there is silence, as the cave entrance closes tightly behind* CLERK *and* REGISTRAR. *The* YOUNG WOMAN *stands listening.*)

YOUNG WOMAN: They are coming.

BOY: Who?

YOUNG WOMAN: Your friends. The ones you talked to on the way. They are singing the song of One World.

GIRL (*Listening*): Where?

YOUNG WOMAN: You will hear them in a moment. They are just climbing the last hill. It will not be long. They are singing of One World . . . listen!

BOY: It is what we talked about! One world, without war.

GIRL (*Excited*): Here they come! (BOY *and* GIRL *step toward wings for American flags as numerous boys and girls, in national costumes if possible, come in from right carrying flags of different countries. They greet each other joyfully. Then all join in singing to tune of "Onward, Christian Soldiers."*)

ALL: Onward, every nation!
Fear and hate must cease.
Only when united
Can we live in peace.
Brotherhood will keep us
Safe from bombs and war.
Forward, to the Union
We are pleading for!

Onward, every nation!
Fear and hate must cease.
Only when united
Can we live in peace.

THE END

The Mountain Trail

1st Boy: The mountain trail is a steep trail
and rocky-rough and bare.

All: But most of the trails are steep trails
that get you anywhere.

1st Girl: The mountain trail is a hard trail
with pitfalls left and right.

All: But most of the trails are hard trails
that reach a beckoning height.

2nd Boy: So over the rocks we scramble!

2nd Girl: With never a mind to stop!

All: And few of us care it's a steep trail
for thought of the mountain top!

School Again!

BOY:
> Part of me's sad,
> and part of me's glad,
> and part of me's in-between:
> the weather is clear
> as crystal this year
> and maple trees still are green,
> but . . .

ALL:
> It's pencil and pen
> and counting by ten
> and reading and writing at—school again!

GIRL:
> Part of me's gay
> and part of me's gray
> and part of me's sort of blue:
> the summer was free
> as wind in a tree,
> but summer is mostly through,
> so . . .

ALL:
> It's paper and pen
> and spelling, and then
> arithmetic problems at—school again!

BOY *and* GIRL: Part of me blinks,
              and part of me winks
              as mischievous as an elf:
              for where'd be the fun
              now school has begun
              to stay at home *by myself!*
              So . . .

GIRLS: It's Nancy!
BOYS: And Glenn!
GIRLS: And Kathy!
BOYS: And Ken!

ALL: Hello there, hello there,—it's school again!

Autumn Leaves

1st Child: Leaves are falling,
            falling from the hedge,
2nd Child: falling from the ivy
            on the window ledge,
3rd Child: falling from the poplar,
4th Child: falling from the pear,
All: falling, falling, falling
            through the hazy air.

5th Child: Leaves are flashes
            of yellow and brown,
6th Child: orange and crimson
            fluttering down,
7th Child: big leaves,
8th Child: broad leaves,
9th Child: middlesized,
10th Child: small—
All: Showers of confetti
            in honor of fall!

A Gypsy Month

ALL: September is a gypsy month
        with gypsy things to do:
GIRLS: It dresses trees in red and gold
        with jewels of sun shot through.
BOYS: It makes the sleepy summer hills
        look brassy-bright and new.
GIRLS: It splashes color down each path
        and polishes each view.
BOYS: It decks the burnished countryside
        with scarfs of every hue.
GIRLS: It dangles leaves like butterflies
        against a sky of blue.
ALL: September is a gypsy month,
        a glowy, showy gypsy month,
        a dancing, prancing gypsy month . . .
        and we are gypsies too!

Leaf Boats

ALL: The pond was full of little boats
         floating up and down,
         with stems for masts, and colored sails—
         golden, red, and brown.

BOYS: Some went fast.
         Some went slow.
         Some had holes
         and couldn't go.

GIRLS: Some went east.
         Some went west.
         Some just sat
         and took a rest.

ALL: The pond was full of little boats
         (more than just a few),
         but where they sailed and where they went
         no one ever knew!

Polar-Bear Pines

ALL: Oh, every pine is a polar-bear zoo
when the fluffity, puffity storm is through,
for every branch holds a bear or two
when the fluffity storm is through.

GIRLS: Maybe-bears,
play-be-bears,
big and small and baby bears!

BOYS: Slumpy bears,
humpy bears,
never cross-and-grumpy bears!

ALL: Oh, every branch holds a bear or two
when the puffity storm is through.

GIRLS: They cling to the branches or lie down flat
out in the pine-tree zoo.

BOYS: Or balance themselves like an acrobat
(a *very* hard thing to do).

ALL: And they all are wonderfully white and fat,
such fluffity bears to marvel at,
when the puffity storm is through.

ALL: Oh, every pine is a polar-bear zoo
when the rollicky, frolicky storm is through,

for every branch holds a bear or two
when the frolicky storm is through.

GIRLS:　Droopy bears,
stoopy bears,
single ones and groupy bears!

BOYS:　Flimsy bears,
limbsy bears,
full-of-fun-and-whimsy bears!

ALL:　Oh, every branch holds a bear or two
when the rollicky storm is through.

GIRLS:　They cling to the boughs where they fell last night
out in the pine-tree zoo.

BOYS:　They sprawl on the branches or hold on tight
(a *very* hard thing to do).

ALL:　And they all are wonderfully soft and white
and make such a rollicky, frolicky sight
when the frolicky storm is through, is through,
when the rollicky storm is through.

Wee Little Feb.

1st Girl:

"Dear little
queer little
mere little Feb.—
just twenty-eight days!" said Jan.
"*Why*, now,
do I, now,
have three days more?
It sounds like a senseless plan."

1st Boy:

"Sweet little
neat little
fleet little Feb.—
just twenty-eight days!" March said.
"*See*, now,
take me, now,
I've three days more.
Why so?" And he shook his head.

2nd Girl:

"Trim little
slim little
prim little Feb.!"
said April and June and May.
"*Who*, now,

can view, now,
her short little life,
and not wipe a tear away?"

2ND BOY: "Fair little
spare little
rare little Feb.!"
said August, July, and Sept.
"*Where*, now,
is there, now,
a grain of sense
in the manner the months are kept?"

3RD GIRL: "Bright little
slight little
quite-little Feb.!"
December told Nov. and Oct.
"*Queer*, now,
that we're, now,
so big and strong,
and she is so little. I'm shocked!"

3RD BOY: Shy little
spry little
wry little Feb.
smiled up with her face alight:

ALL (*Soft chorus*): "Near ones,
and dear ones,
don't fret for me.
I don't mind my size a mite!"

"Strength isn't,
length isn't
everything!

I'm noted in other ways:
Who, now,
of you, now,
is quite so full
of wonderful holidays?

"Lincoln,
I'm thinkin',
belongs to me.
And Washington's mine! Ahem,
who, now,
has two, now,
such famous dates?
I'm something because of *them*.

"Also
recall, so
you'll fret no more—
St. Valentine lives with me!
Come, now,
who's glum, now?
Not wee little Feb.!
I'm gay as a month can be."

To a Groundhog on February 2

ALL: Wake up, sleepyhead!
Put your dreams away.
Everyone is waiting
for what you have to say:

GIRL: Will your shadow make a blot
on the snow today or not?

BOY: Will the sun start turning hot?
Will the month be cold, or what?
Hurry, sir, and tell us on this Groundhog Day.

ALL: Wake up, sleepyhead!
What's a little snow?
If your shadow follows you,
back inside you'll go.

BOY: Will the coming six weeks be
wintry, cold, and shivery?

GIRL: Balmy, warm, and summery?

ALL: Groundhog, what's your prophecy?
Better put your *glasses* on, so you'll really know!

Rain on the Roof

(Starts very slowly, gets faster and faster)

1st CHILD: With a peck
              a raindrop comes,
              like a bird to peck at crumbs.
2nd CHILD: Then another.
3rd CHILD: Then some more,
              sharper, louder than before.
4th CHILD: Faster, faster,
              rain-birds flit
              to the roof to peck on it.
5th CHILD: Dozens,
6th CHILD: hundreds,
              neck to neck:
7th CHILD: Peck, peck,
8th CHILD: Peck, peck,
ALL: Peck-peck-peck.

Early Crocus

BOY: A chubby little crocus,
GIRL: A nubby little crocus,
BOY: A fubby little crocus
      peeked up to see the sun.
GIRL: Before the cold was over,
BOY: Beside a sleepy clover,
ALL: It looked the garden over—
      before the snow was done.

GIRL: A little snowbird spied it,
BOY: And for a moment eyed it,
GIRL: Then settled down beside it
      and said to it:
ALL: "Oh, dear,
      I hope you brought your mittens
      and furs, like willow-kittens . . .
      or you'll get chilled to bittens
      so early in the year."

Who Is It?

GIRLS: We know someone—
               try to guess!
1ST CHILD: She wears a gold hat.
2ND CHILD: She wears a green dress.
3RD CHILD: She wears glass slippers
               the color of rain.
4TH CHILD: And around her neck
               is a dandelion chain.
5TH CHILD: She scatters flowers
               over the hills,
               some of them plain
               and some with frills.
6TH CHILD: She listens when robins
               and blackbirds sing.
7TH CHILD: And she laughs at winter,
               because she's . . .
BOYS: SPRING!

May Day

BOY: You heard the screen door open?
GIRL: You heard the hinges squeak?
BOY: You heard the doorknob rattle—
    before you got a peek?

GIRL: You heard the porch boards creaking
    beneath some hurrying feet?
BOY: You saw a little shadow
    go flitting down the street?

GIRL: And then you found a basket
    with flowers inside, you say?
ALL: To think you had forgotten
    it was the first of **May!**

PRODUCTION NOTES

THE WEAVER'S SON

Characters: 3 male; 2 female.
Playing Time: 20 minutes.
Costumes: The women wear long full skirts, aprons, dark bodices and long-sleeved blouses. Domenico and the two boys wear hose and long-sleeved doublets.
Properties: Basket of tangled yarn.
Setting: A combination work-room-living room. If possible, a loom or spinning wheel should be in one corner of the room. A plain work table is at center, and near it are several stools. Other furnishings—chairs, piles of wool, etc.—may also be included.
Lighting: No special effects.

DAY OF DESTINY

Characters: 10 male.
Playing Time: 20 minutes.
Costumes: All the characters wear hose and long-sleeved doublets. The sailors wear faded blue, the page, green, and Columbus, dark blue. Columbus may wear a cape and hat.
Properties: Book, cup, bird, lantern.
Setting: All that is needed is a backdrop showing a ship's rail, some masts, and some ocean. If desired, ropes, kegs, masts, etc., may be placed around the stage.
Lighting: No special effects.

THREE AND THE DRAGON

Characters: 5 male; 5 female; two male voices.
Playing Time: 30 minutes.
Costumes: Modern dress for the three families. The Stranger may be dressed in a white robe.
Properties: Account books for

Mr. Grabberoff, book for Bonnie, newspaper for Mr. Stickler, letter for Mrs. Stickler, mechanical gadget for Tucker, socks and darning equipment for Mrs. Doolittle, magazine for Sally, pillowcase for Mr. Doolittle, and three papers for the Stranger.

Setting: A street in Anytown. Three signs, Grabberoff, Stickler, and Doolittle, are placed upstage. Around each sign should be placed three chairs and a small table on which there is a box painted to look like a radio. Doors and windows of each house are imaginary.

Lighting: No special effects.

A PLAY WITHOUT A NAME

Characters: 16 male; 5 female.
Playing Time: 25 minutes.
Costumes: No special costumes are required.
Setting: The only furnishings required are four chairs which the Stage Manager places on the stage, two on each side of the chalk line; and signs reading "Now,"
"1787," "Any Town," "Boston," "London," "Washington, D. C.," and "Philadelphia."

Properties: Chalk, knitting, sewing, pencils, pad, paper, newspapers.

Lighting: No special effects required. If desired, spotlights may be trained on the two sides of the stage as action takes place on them.

GHOSTS ON GUARD

Characters: 4 male; 3 female.
Playing Time: 15 minutes.
Costumes: Mrs. Briggs wears a housedress. Mr. Briggs is dressed in a white shirt and sheets. Harry wears a shirt and short trousers until Mr. Briggs dresses him as a ghost. The rest of the children wear masquerade costumes and masks.

Properties: Scene 1: Pins, rope. Scene 2: Paper bags, laundry soap, tick-tack, noise-maker, rope.

Setting: Scene 1: The living room of the Briggs' home. The room may be furnished with a few chairs and a table. Scene 2: In front of the Briggs' home. A few "bushes" or "trees" are all that is necessary. Note: If desired, this play may be produced without any scenery at all.

Lighting: Scene 1: Bright lights. Scene 2: Dimmed lights or a dark stage with a spotlight.

THE VOICE OF LIBERTY

Characters: 6 male; 4 female.

Playing Time: 30 minutes.

Costumes: The Dawson family and Gram wear everyday modern dress. Isaac, William and Stephen wear costumes suggesting the colonial period.

Properties: Instruments that will make the proper sound effects offstage: an abrupt clang, a discordant crash, and the clear sound of a bell.

Setting: The living room of the Dawson home. Chairs, tables and lamps are placed around the room to make it look attractive and comfortable. In one corner of the room, downstage, a

gauze curtain is hung; the flashbacks take place behind this curtain.

Lighting: If possible, the lighting behind the gauze curtain should be a little dimmer than the lighting on the rest of the stage.

Note: This play could be used as a radio play with very little change.

ONCE UPON A TIME

Characters: 11 male; 5 female; Reader may be either male or female; as many male and female characters as desired may take the parts of the Old Woman's children, although 4 male and 4 female actors are all that is necessary.

Playing Time: 20 minutes.

Costumes: The Reader wears everyday dress. The Old Woman wears a long full skirt, white blouse, and tight bodice. Her children can wear everyday clothes or peasant costumes. The Baker's Man is dressed in white and has a tall white chef's hat. Whizzer wears a long full black cape and a tall black hat. A book on a string is tied around his neck. Although costumes for the book characters are desirable, they are not necessary, since each character is identified in the text. If costumes are worn, they can be copied from illustrations in the various books.

Properties: Book for Reader, platter with pie for Baker's Man, wand for Whizzer, white gloves and fan for White Rabbit, small cake for Alice, umbrella and carpet bag for Mary Poppins, bow and arrow for Robin Hood.

Setting: All that is needed is an easy chair for the Reader, a stool, a table, and a few chairs. A telephone is on the table. There are exits at left and right. (The Children can sit on the floor.)

Lighting: No special effects.

TREASURE HUNT

Characters: 13 male; 11 female; more if desired.

Playing Time: 20 minutes.

Costumes: Miss Brooks and the children are dressed in modern clothing. The characters from books are dressed in appropriate costumes. For suggestions, consult the books mentioned in the play.

Properties: Thimble, stuffed cat, slippers, compass, rolls, bow and arrow, "tail," flowers, box of candies.

Setting: Scene 1: A sidewalk in front of the school, or a corridor. This scene may be played in front of the curtain. Scene 2: A classroom. Miss Brooks' desk is downstage right. Chairs or desks for the children are placed in rows facing Miss Brooks.

Lighting: No special effects.

UNEXPECTED GUESTS

Characters: 6 male; 6 female.

Playing Time: 10 minutes.

Costumes: All the characters wear typical Pilgrim costumes.

Properties: Cooking equipment, food, buckets, nuts, wood, peas.

Setting: A kitchen-living room in a Pilgrim home. At the

end of the room is a large fireplace. The simple furniture has been moved against the walls to make room for work tables holding cooking equipment and food. On the upstage wall is a window, and near the window a long sheet of paper which Mistress Winslow consults.

Lighting: No special effects.

ANGEL IN THE LOOKING-GLASS

Characters: 3 male; 5 female.
Playing Time: 20 minutes.
Costumes: Modern dress. Lucy wears a white flowing robe typical of the angel's costume in a Christmas pageant.
Properties: Pins, tape measure, halo.
Setting: Before the curtain there is a large full-length mirror placed on one side of the stage. The stage itself is divided into three "apartments." In the Youngs' apartment are two chairs and a table. In Aunt Martha's apartment are an overstuffed chair and two hassocks. In Zorlova's apartment are a chair and a modernistic dressing table. On the dressing table is a telephone. Note: This play may be produced without any scenery at all; the apartments may be indicated by signs.

Lighting: No special effects.

THE MERRY CHRISTMAS ELF

Characters: 6 male; 5 female; Elf may be male or female; male and female extras.
Playing Time: 20 minutes.
Costumes: All the characters should wear everyday winter clothing except the Elf, who is dressed in red and green and has a pointed cap with a bell on the tip.
Properties: Purse, pencil and pad for Mrs. Fuddy, pad and pencil for Writer, box for Elf, greens, wreaths, bells, sled for small boy, newspapers.
Setting: Outdoors on Pine Street. No furnishings are necessary but if furnishings are desired, a street sign, some bushes, a fence, etc., may be placed on the stage.

Lighting: No special effects.

TIME OUT FOR CHRISTMAS

Characters: 3 male; 1 female; 24 male or female.

Playing Time: 20 minutes.

Costumes: Rag Doll wears a long dress with white apron and black shoes. Teddy Bear is dressed in a costume to suggest what he is. Tick and Tock are dressed in the same costumes—small pointed hats, shirts with matching shorts. The Days wear very simple costumes and each one wears a large cardboard letter with its numeral printed on it.

Properties: Handkerchiefs for Rag Doll and Teddy Bear, half-finished present.

Setting: On one side of the stage there is a large clock whose hands point to almost 12 o'clock. The face of the clock may be painted on a large sheet of wrapping paper and pinned to a screen. It should be large enough so Tick and Tock can come from behind it. On the other side of the stage there is a large calendar. This may also be painted on wrapping paper (a winter scene at the top and December printed in large letters beneath) and pinned to a screen. A few small chairs complete the setting.

Lighting: No special effects.

A CHRISTMAS TREE FOR KITTY

Characters: 2 male; 4 female; male and female extras.

Playing Time: 10 minutes.

Costumes: Everyday dress. Willa, Martha, Mike and the Carolers wear outdoor clothing.

Properties: Small Christmas tree with ornaments, catnip ball, tissue paper, ribbons, wrapping, bow of red and green ribbon, plate of cookies, tag.

Setting: The living room may have a couch, chairs, lamps, etc. The only essential furnishing is a table at center which holds the little tree.

Lighting: No special effects.

THE SPIRIT OF CHRISTMAS

Characters: 2 male; 4 female; Reader and Spirit may be either male or female.

Playing Time: 10 minutes.

Costumes: The Spirit of Christmas is dressed in a red and green jester's costume. He wears a long, pointed cap with a little bell on his head, and bells are attached to the tips of his shoes with silver ribbon. The rest of the characters wear appropriate modern dress.

Properties: Trays of cookies, coffeepot, milk bottles.

Setting: No setting is necessary, although the stage may be decorated with Christmas greens.

Lighting: No special effects.

THE CHRISTMAS CAKE

Characters: 2 male; 1 female; Narrator may be either male or female.

Playing Time: 10 minutes.

Costumes: Everyday dress. Mrs. McGilly could wear a long full skirt; she puts on an apron when she enters, and when she goes out she takes off the apron and puts on a cloak.

Properties: Mixing bowl, spoon, paper with "recipe" on it, whittling knife, paper, kindling, pan for cake batter, half-finished carving for Boy, cherries.

Setting: The McGilly kitchen. A table and two chairs are at center. Cooking equipment is on the table and on one of the chairs are Mrs. McGilly's apron and cloak. At right is a stove, and near the stove a box of kindling. Upstage center is a window.

Lighting: No special effects.

ABE'S WINKIN' EYE

Characters: 4 male; 4 female.

Playing Time: 25 minutes.

Costumes: All the characters wear plain working clothes of the period. Mrs. Lincoln and the girls wear long skirts. The boys and Mr. Lincoln can wear overalls and work shirts.

Properties: Jacket, knives, vegetables, corn bread,

honey, eggs, iron skillet, bowl, spoon, water pail, cans containing "shortening" and "sugar," stone.

Setting: The interior of the Lincoln cabin. There is one door and one window. The cabin is simply furnished, but clean and neat. Cooking is done at a rude fireplace, upstage center. Pots and pans hang near the fireplace. A four-poster bed stands in one corner, a home-made bed cleated to the wall in another corner. There are several chairs and benches, a table, and a cupboard in the room. A rag rug is on the floor. A ladder at one end of the room leads to the loft.

Lighting: No special effects.

NEW HEARTS FOR OLD

Characters: 3 male; 3 female.
Playing Time: 20 minutes.
Costumes: Modern dress.
Properties: Valentines, newspaper, cardboard box containing old-fashioned valentine, heart-shaped box, perfume bottle and satchet bag, red paper, scissors,

plate of tarts, large red heart-shaped candy box, small package containing perfume bottle.

Setting: A comfortably furnished living room. At one end of the room (the living room part) is a small table with valentines on it. Near the table are some chairs. At center are two large armchairs. At the other end of the room is a large dining table with six chairs around it. One door leads to the kitchen, another to an outer hall.

Lighting: No special effects.

HEARTS, TARTS AND VALENTINES

Characters: 6 male; 3 female; male and female extras.
Playing Time: 20 minutes.
Costumes: The Reader wears everyday clothing. All the rest of the characters are dressed in appropriate fairy tale costumes with hearts on them.
Properties: Book of fairy tales, megaphone, platter covered with napkin, piece of lace,

envelopes, valentines, plate of tarts.

Setting: The kingdom of the King and Queen of Hearts. No furnishings are necessary except a throne upstage center for the King.

Lighting: No special effects.

WASHINGTON MARCHES ON

Characters: 26 male; 7 female; male and female extras. (This is a maximum cast; many of the parts may be doubled up.)

Playing Time: 25 minutes.

Costumes: If costumes are used, all the characters should wear costumes appropriate for the time and place of their particular scenes.

Properties: Paper, ink, quill pen, packet of mail, map, magnifying glass, tripod, sewing, newspapers, knitting, letters, Bible, books, flags.

Setting: On stage are two chairs and a table holding paper, ink and quill pen. If a blackboard is used, it should be placed at a downstage corner of the stage.

Lighting: No special effects.

ON STRIKE

Characters: 8, either male or female.

Playing Time: 15 minutes.

Costumes: The characters may be dressed completely to look like the animals, or may have only marks of identification like a red breastplate for the Robin. Or they may simply have signs pinned on them with the names of the animals. Owl wears glasses.

Properties: Book and watch for Owl, handkerchief for Robin, notes for Squirrel.

Setting: A clearing in the woods. Several trees, stumps and bushes should be placed around stage.

Lighting: No special effects.

MOTHER'S DAY OFF AND ON

Characters: 2 male; 3 female.

Playing Time: 20 minutes.

Costumes: Modern dress.

Properties: Dishes, silverware, toaster, kettle, dripolator, doll, triangular pieces of wood, hankie, candy (the four gifts are wrapped with paper), letter, pencil, papers, dictionary, sock, dress, jacket, bouquet of red roses.

Setting: Two rooms of a home, the dining room and the kitchen. In the dining room there is a table with five chairs. There is also a table in the kitchen. The rest of the equipment may be imaginary, and the division between the two rooms may be indicated by placing the furniture in them near the right and left walls of the stage.

Lighting: No special effects.

CAVES OF THE EARTH

Characters: 5 male; 2 female; male and female extras.

Playing time: 25 minutes.

Costumes: Everyday modern clothes. The Young Woman is dressed in a long white dress.

Properties: A Bible, papers, game bag for Gamecatcher, a soft white object representing a dove, two small cards, American flags, flags of different countries.

Setting: If desired, a backdrop of an outdoor scene may be used. The cave may be a simple arrangement of dark curtains draped over screens or chairs. At the right of the cave is a long table or desk with two chairs.

Lighting: No special effects.